IMPOSSIBLE CITIZENS

IMPOSSIBLE CITIZENS

DUBAI'S INDIAN DIASPORA   **NEHA VORA**

Duke University Press · Durham and London · 2013

Printed in the United States of America on acid-free paper ∞
Text design by Courtney Leigh Baker
Cover design by Amy Ruth Buchanan
Typeset in Whitman and Lato by Keystone Typesetting, Inc.
Library of Congress Cataloging-in-Publication Data
appear on the last printed page of this book.

This book is dedicated to **EDMOND CHO** and **CAROLINE MELLY**, who have been at my side for every step of this journey, and without whom none of this would be possible.

CONTENTS

ACKNOWLEDGMENTS

This book began as a dissertation project at the University of California, Irvine, for which, in 2004, I traveled to Dubai for the very first time. As a graduate student who had never before conducted fieldwork outside of the United States and who had never been to the Gulf region, I found arriving in Dubai without an established network of friends, family, or even academic contacts to be daunting, to say the least. At that time, too, existing scholarship on the Gulf region, which has since grown almost as fast as the cities themselves, was sparse, particularly in my areas of interest. So I was in many ways landing without a parachute. I discovered quite early on that urban ethnography can be a lonely and alienating process, but I also encountered in Dubai incredibly supportive people, from all walks of life, who fostered my research, were generous with their time, invited me into their lives, and enriched me in ways that words can never fully express. I count many of them as friends and colleagues to this day. In addition to my interlocutors, whose stories form the core of this book and whose amazing personalities I hope I have done justice to here, I would like to thank Liz Faier, Nitin Gogia, Paresh Dholakia, Chitra Dholakia, N. Janardhan, Susan Strickland, Christopher Davidson, Sulayman Khalaf, Anar Amlani, and James Onley for their academic and personal support while I was in Dubai. I would also like to thank the large online community of Dubaiites with whom I regularly interacted on blogs and forums for easing my life as a new resident of a city that I have since grown to think of as home.

This research was funded by several generous grants from the Department of Anthropology, the Women's and Gender Studies Program, and the School of Social Sciences at the University of California, Irvine. I am also grateful to Bill Maurer for his personal support of various portions of my fieldwork, and to the American University of Sharjah for sponsoring my residency while I was in the United Arab Emirates. Funding from the Texas A&M Glasscock Humanities Center allowed me to make follow-up research visits to Dubai and provided me with time to turn the dissertation into a book manuscript.

Throughout the many stages and iterations of this manuscript, my mentors and colleagues have been extremely generous, providing feedback and critiques that have challenged me to become a better thinker and writer. At the University of California, Irvine, my dissertation chair, Bill Maurer, and my committee members, Inderpal Grewal and Karen Leonard, were invaluable to the completion of this project and unwavering in their faith in my abilities. I also want to thank Michael Montoya and Tom Boellstorff, along with the wonderful faculty, staff, and graduate students in both Anthropology and Women's and Gender Studies, for their support through the process of graduate school and dissertation writing. In particular, my dissertation writing group—Sylvia Martin, Jennifer Chase, and Judith Pajo—helped me learn how to get over the hurdles of writing, and I would not have finished my dissertation without them.

In addition to the amazing community of scholars whose feedback I have received at various conferences and presentations over the years, I am incredibly grateful to the colleagues who read portions of the book-in-progress and provided excellent suggestions. They include Vanita Reddy, Ahmed Kanna, Andrew Gardner, Attiya Ahmad, Pardis Mahdavi, Kris Olds, Edmond Cho, Liz Faier, Zulema Valdez, Jayson Beaster-Jones, Fahad Bishara, Dan Humphrey, James Rosenheim, David McWhirter, Nancy Plankey-Videla, Rebecca Hartkopf Schloss, Nitin Gogia, and Priya Shah. Above all, Caroline Melly, who at this point probably knows this book better than I do, has been a constant interlocutor and writing partner whose wisdom I could not do without.

I thank Ken Wissoker for his vision in seeing the potential of this project, as well as the anonymous readers at Duke University Press, whose input helped me polish my arguments. Parts of chapter 3 appeared as "Unofficial Citizens: Indian Businessmen and the State-Effect in Dubai, UAE," *International Labor and Working Class History* 79 (2011): 122–39, and as "From Golden Frontier to Global City: The Shifting Forms of Belonging among Indian Businessmen in Dubai," *American Anthropologist* 113, no. 2 (2011): 306–18. Portions of chapter 4 were published as "Producing Diasporas and Globalization: Indian Middle-Class Migrants in Dubai," *Anthropological Quarterly* 81, no. 2 (2008): 377–406. A section of the conclusion appeared as "The Precarious Existence of Dubai's Indian Middle-Class," *Middle East Report* 252 (fall 2009): 18–21. Some of the arguments presented in chapter 5 were first published online as a short blog post, "Globalized Higher Education in the United Arab Emirates: Unexpected Outcomes," *GlobalHigherEd* (blog), 25 June 2008, http://globalhighered.wordpress.com. All are reprinted with permission.

Finally, I would like to thank my parents—Shobhana Vora, Bhupendra Vora, Laxmi Soni, Yi Sook Cho, and Young Kap Cho—and my partner, Edmond Cho. Not only have they nurtured me and my career in countless ways; their stories of migration, identity, family, labor, loss, and gain have inspired my academic interests and deeply informed the stakes of my scholarship. I love you dearly.

EXCEPTIONS & EXCEPTIONALITY IN DUBAI

In this book I argue that although Indians cannot become legal citizens of Dubai, an Arab city-state on the Persian/Arabian Gulf, they are in many ways its quintessential citizens.[1] Indian foreign residents' everyday practices, performances, and narratives of existing within the city are integral to understanding larger questions about the nature of governance, citizenship, neoliberalism, and cultural identity in this small but globally important place. In Dubai, as in all contemporary urban spaces, human elements, geographies, and institutions are co-constitutive, and forms of belonging and citizenship take place at several scales beyond the juridico-legal definition of "nationality."

At the beginning of the twenty-first century, a mythology began to develop around Dubai, driven by the emirate's many exceptionalities: it was a conservative monarchy with one of the most open markets in the world; although located within the United Arab Emirates (UAE), one of the largest oil-producing countries, it had successfully diversified its economy away from oil reliance into tourism, real estate, and finance; and it managed to balance seemingly divergent temporalities of traditional Bedouin pasts and postmodern, futuristic cityscapes.[2] Newspaper articles, television shows, and travel guides chronicled the meteoric rise of Dubai, the rapidly shifting geography of the city, and the armies of exploited workers—mostly from South Asia—that were constructing it. The ethnographic entry point for an academic interested in entanglements between South Asia and the Gulf seemed almost obvious at the beginning of the century, as the South Asian presence in the Gulf was defined almost entirely through accounts of human-rights violations and economic exploitation of the poorest strata of laboring classes, usually construction workers or maids. However, my mythology of Dubai was not of this century, nor was it rooted primarily in a story of capitalism and development.

My knowledge of Dubai had been established in suburban New Jersey, among the large diasporic Indian community who lived in the New York metropolitan area. When I was a child, my middle-class relatives and their friends spoke so often of trips to Dubai and of family members who lived there that I grew up thinking Dubai was a city in India. I knew it must be a special place, however, since it was regularly referenced in Bollywood movies, since my relatives often brought us gifts from Dubai or showed off the latest jewelry styles they had purchased there, and since everyone seemed to have a relative or a friend living in the city.[3] Dubai, for the middle-class Indians who defined my community, was both a site of material possibility and a place that held a certain affective, historical, and cultural position within a transnational understanding of Indianness. As my personal story intermingled with my academic career and I started to focus on Indian diasporas and their forms of identification and belonging, this history of engagement with the Gulf region, and especially with Dubai, remained of interest. Yet where was the Indian diaspora, which I knew had been in existence since at least the 1970s, in the media's fascination with Dubai's boom and, more recently, with its bust? I arrived in the city for the first time in 2004 in order to answer this question—to understand why the lengthy history of Indian settlement and influence in Dubai was largely absent in the knowledge that was circulating about the emirate at the time. I found that Dubai's exceptionality relied precisely on the exception of long-standing Indian communities and their everyday lived experiences from internal and external ideas about the emirate's development, social structure, and forms of governance.

In this book, I examine citizenship and belonging in Dubai among those I argue are its most typical residents—the middle-class, working-class, and, to some extent, elite Indians who populate the downtown neighborhoods of the city but are mostly erased in contemporary accounts of the emirate's rise and fall. Over the last few decades, as Dubai's economic focus shifted toward mega-development projects and away from maritime trade, the older downtown neighborhoods surrounding the Dubai Creek became increasingly geographically segregated from newer parts of the city, and also increasingly forgotten in representations of the city, which tended to focus on extremely polarized populations of wealthy Arab citizens on the one hand and temporary migrant laborers on the other. Dubai, and particularly the downtown neighborhoods on which I focus in this book, is predominantly South Asian, as is indexed by the linguistic, religious, sartorial, and commercial forms visible in the city, as well as by its demography—the majority of Dubai residents hail from South Asia, and of this population Indians form the largest national group. Additionally, South Asians comprise the main workforce of the private and public sectors of the city, at every level of skillset, salary, and education. The entanglements between the Gulf and South Asia mean that in many ways Dubai is experienced as an extension of the subcontinent for *all* residents of the city. In recent years, a small but important body of scholarship has assessed the Gulf region from a transnational perspective, paying particular attention to the historical and contemporary role of migration and cosmopolitanism.[4] This work challenges the idea that migration from South Asia is solely due to post-oil development and highlights the multiple stakeholders and historical traces involved in the making of the modern Gulf States. This emerging conversation within anthropology, history, Indian Ocean studies, and South Asian diaspora studies suggests that current conceptions of "area" elide these cosmopolitan histories by considering the Gulf States as exclusively Middle Eastern, not as part of Indian Ocean networks. Similarly, this book gestures to the need to rethink the distinctions between "South Asia" and "Middle East" in scholarly work across disciplines by highlighting the ways in which Dubai—past and present—is in many ways more oriented toward South Asia than toward the Arab world. While the Emirati government considers foreign residents temporary guest workers, the South Asian–dominated neighborhoods of Dubai's city center have been flourishing for over a century and many foreigners are into their second, third, or even fourth generation in the emirate. However, these residents remain reliant on short-term renewable work visas to enter and reside in the United Arab Emirates and have no formal access to citizenship. The central paradox that drives this study is how Indians experience, narrate, and perform belonging to Dubai within a state of permanent temporariness.

While their legal status places them squarely outside of the Emirati nation, Indians in Dubai are integral to the operation of governance, to national identity and citizenship, and to the functioning of Dubai's liberalized and globalized market forms—they are, therefore, *impossible citizens.* While they disavow belonging to Dubai, they nevertheless stake certain historical, cultural, and geographic claims to the city. This book explores the conflicting and multiple narratives and practices of belonging and citizenship by Indians in Dubai's downtown neighborhoods. This involves understanding the multiple logics of citizenship and governance that circulate within Dubai among its various residents, institutions, and spaces, and, by extension, the multiple logics of governance that frame the relationships between contemporary subjects in nation-states, citizen and noncitizen. Until recently, the UAE has been studied primarily as a nonliberal "rentier" state, wherein the rental of oil prospects or the export of oil to foreign clients provides the country's main income, and in which citizenship is structured in a patrimonial corporatist fashion whereby nationals receive heavy welfare benefits from the government but have little political participation. Noncitizens in a rentier state exist solely to furnish the managerial and service labor for the country's day-to-day functioning, and thus they are not usually considered beyond their role in the economy— the social and cultural aspects of migrant life are understood to lie outside of Emirati society because migrants are temporary. However, if we shift our gaze to consider how governmentality also produces particular *expatriate* subjects, who also circulate classed, religious, and ethnic understandings of membership from their transnational and national backgrounds, we can see that the Emirati state actually relies on several discourses of citizenship that seem contradictory but serve to produce its legitimacy. Certain expatriates are welcomed into the UAE and governed through technologies and rhetorics of a free and open market that purportedly allows anyone to succeed if they perform neoliberal self-enterprising subjectivities, while others are deemed insignificant and invisible to the fabric of the city-state. The middle-class Indians who formed the majority of my interlocutors overwhelmingly espoused discourses of neoliberal entrepreneurship that made Dubai a favorable location for immigration. They were supposedly able to belong to Dubai's market without any challenges to their national identity. While they disavowed Emirati social and political membership, however, Dubai Indians also staked claims to Dubai through historical memory, racialized identifications, urban belonging, and cultural proximity between India and the UAE. Therefore, the division between an "open" market that hails foreigners and a nativist nation that strongly polices membership is actually quite porous—the lived experiences of Indians in downtown Dubai contained within them not only neoliberal market-based narratives but also scales and forms of citizenship that extended beyond these accounts of voluntary, temporary economic migration.

Those who constitute exceptions to citizenship, like Indians in Dubai, are, by virtue of their exclusion, necessary to defining the parameters of citizenship and the legitimacy of the state. That is to say, their every-day practices, performances, and rhetorics actually prop up the citizen-noncitizen divide and the authoritarian patrimonial governance system through which they are regulated as outsiders. By disavowing legal belonging and claiming economic belonging, middle-class Indians recuperate the division between market and nation through which the nonliberal Emirati state and its forms of national identity and citizenship derive their legitimacy. The centrality of those who are supposedly outsiders in a nation-state to its functioning is not exceptional to the Dubai, Gulf, or Middle Eastern context, but rather can inform us more broadly about the nature of contemporary citizenship, transnational identities, and modes of belonging. This study is therefore concerned with "provincializing"—to borrow a term from Dipesh Chakrabarty—Western-dominated understandings of migration, diasporic identities, governance, citizenship, and subjectivity.[5] By centering Dubai and its supposed exceptions, we can see the various logics that inform belonging in other places as well.

I am interested in multiple, sometimes contradictory, ways of thinking about what it means to be a citizen of a place, how these ways of thinking have been approached in anthropological and other literatures, and how they articulate with the daily lived experiences of Indians in Dubai. Many urban anthropologists have explored how citizenship is produced through the process of moving around within the city, through everyday interactions with and within urban space—not only through a legally prescribed relationship with the state. Citizenship at the scale of urban belonging, however, is not legitimized either by the Emirati state or by most scholarly accounts of belonging within Gulf cities.[6] In this project, I aim to loosen and multiply definitions of "citizenship" within the urban spaces of Gulf cities. Citizenship is not simply a matter of having or not having legal membership; one does not exist solely within this binary formulation. Rather, the excluded and the impossible need to be brought into the same frame in order to study citizenship as a shifting and dynamic form of legality, membership, state-making, and governance. I am interested in exploring how Emirati citizenship and national identity are made meaningful in many ways *because of* the South Asian presence in the Gulf. Scholars working on the Gulf States, for example, have argued that citizenship and national identity are defined precisely against foreign bod-

ies.[7] However, if Indians are not just excluded, as my research indicates —
if they also rehearse citizenship-like affects and actions—then the division between Emirati and non-Emirati is actually quite porous, and the
disavowal of belonging *by Indians themselves* becomes all the more necessary for the production of a bounded citizenry.

I explore how meanings about belonging and exclusion are produced
within encounters between differently raced, classed, and gendered members of the Indian diaspora; between Indians and other groups in the UAE;
and between foreign residents and governmental institutions. In addition,
I am interested in the encounters between anthropologists and "informants," how our own logics of citizenship and belonging produce ethnographic "truths" through the fieldwork encounter, and how the interiors
and exteriors of epistemological categories shift within the conversations
between researcher and "researched." As a South Asian American woman,
my encounters with Indians in Dubai contained moments of contradiction as well as commonality that challenged my own American diasporic
parochialisms of belonging and exclusion, and I engaged my various "field
sites" in Dubai in ways that impacted my choices and actions while there.
A less overt but equally important stake of this project is therefore to
recognize how knowledge is produced in encounters that include the
anthropologist as both inside and outside of her field site.

Capitalism Run Amok? Why the Dubai Story Is Incomplete

At the beginning of the twenty-first century, Dubai erupted onto the world
stage as a media and tourism spectacle. A small emirate that had transformed from an ancient mercantile port into a "global city" in a matter of
decades, it was breaking world records and luring tourists and investors
with man-made islands in the shape of palm trees and over-the-top luxury
hotels and shopping malls. At the beginning of the millennium, Dubai
seemed to many to exemplify what Jean and John Comaroff have described as "millennial capital"—a neoliberal fantasy-world of consumerism and real-estate speculation built on the backs of a transnational, transient, majority proletariat population.[8] The plethora of metaphors that
have been used in the last few years to define Dubai mark it as an exceptional place of capitalist excess with little room for the ordinary and
mundane.[9] Dubai has been described as a Disneyworld, Las Vegas in the
Arabian desert, plastic Arabia, sinister paradise, Singapore of the Middle

East, gilded cage, dreamscape, and kingdom of bling, to name but a few.[10] All of these descriptions intimate a place of fantasy not of reality, one that lacks enduring character and that has emerged from a mixture of hope and greed. Based on these representations, one could argue that Dubai is the quintessential example of the highs and lows of neoliberal capitalism in today's world. The human elements of the city seem to exist at extremes, with wealthy—and exploitative—Gulf Arabs and international business tycoons on one end, and downtrodden construction workers and maids, mostly from South Asia, on the other. In fact, the majority of attention to South Asians and other migrant groups in the Gulf, both popular and academic, echoes the Comaroffs' arguments about capitalism and class at the turn of the millennium by focusing either on the lack of human rights afforded to migrant workers, or on the absence of forms of civil society in the authoritarian Gulf States that disenfranchises both foreigners and citizens alike, albeit in different ways. The millennial story about Dubai emphasizes a new form—or "second coming"—of rampant neoliberal capitalism, with both its spectacles and its abuses. In fact, when Dubai's bubble supposedly burst in 2008, the overwhelming media reaction was one of "I told you so" satisfaction.[11]

Given the fast pace of change in the emirate over the last decade, the vast amounts of oil wealth Gulf countries have accumulated in a short period of time, and the levels of migrant labor flows required to sustain the daily functioning of the UAE, it makes sense that much writing about Dubai is underpinned by economic analysis. This is particularly the case for political economic writing on the region and for commentaries on Gulf cities that come from within a Marxist or "millennial" tradition of suspicion toward capitalism, globalization, and authoritarian rule. Economically driven narratives of the city, however, by attributing migration almost completely to oil discovery and "post-oil" development, also make it difficult to see the multiple forms of governance and citizenship that actually exist on the ground, and they therefore reify the idea that Gulf migrants are temporary and thus do not belong. In addition, by relying heavily on abstractable models of economy, migration, and state, this scholarship undermines the role of human agency, strategizing within constraints, and ambiguous or contradictory choices that various residents of the Gulf deploy in their day-to-day lives. Many of these millennial stories inadvertently subsume into a narrative of temporary economic migration the complex affects and experiences of the people to whom they are attempting to draw political attention. This risks colluding with rather than critically analyzing Gulf State projects of nation-building and governance, which are interested in maintaining rigid parameters of citizenship and the exclusion of noncitizens from national imaginaries.[12] In contrast, an anthropological approach to the region that begins with the narratives, affects, claims, and experiences of foreign residents themselves allows for building theories that center how noncitizen belongings and exclusions are dynamic and constantly negotiated by various actors, and how local, national, and extranational institutions do not precede and produce subjects but rather are co-constituted with them.

THE "RENTIER" STATE: OIL, DEVELOPMENT, AND MIGRATION

Political-economic scholarship on the Arabian Peninsula, and specifically on the member states of the Gulf Cooperative Council (Oman, Saudi Arabia, Bahrain, Qatar, the United Arab Emirates, and Kuwait), draws heavily on "rentier" or "petro-state" models to discuss economics, state formation, and migration in the Gulf, and these models also inform discussions of diversification projects away from oil, like many of those implemented by the Dubai government in recent years.[13] Rentier states are defined as countries that derive the majority of their revenue from external (foreign) sources through rent (in this case, of land to oil companies) instead of through taxation and domestically generated revenue.[14] Recent economic diversification projects in Gulf countries are generally seen as extensions of this rentier system, where "rent" is derived from service economies, real estate, and tourism, rather than through oil extraction. While it allows for ways to think about relationships between oil wealth and other processes, the analytic of the rentier state also relies on certain top-down ontological divisions, such as those between market and nation, pre- and post-oil, citizen and noncitizen, liberal and illiberal, which are seen to structure the experiences of all residents in the Gulf; in so doing, the rentier state analytic does not allow for critical attention to the ways in which these categories are messy, overlapping, porous, and produced on the ground. Scholars often use rentier state and other models comparatively in order to discuss rates of development and forms of governance and citizenship, and to predict future trajectories for different countries in terms of democratization and economic growth.[15] This comparative approach privileges top-down, "ideal-type" models in favor of empirical field data that might contradict the typology within which they are placed. In addition, a typological approach to political economy often relies on centering, sometimes inadvertently, Western capitalist and liberal-democratic historical narratives as the yardsticks against which the Gulf States are measured and defined.[16] Gulf State histories, for example, are usually divided into pre- and post-oil, and, as such, oil becomes the primary catalyst for economic, social, and governmental development in the region. As an abrupt rupture from what came before, oil discovery and the subsequent fast pace of development in these countries produced what some scholars consider unnatural and often chaotic change. For example, D. S. Massey and colleagues posit that economic growth and political systems in the Middle East are due to the "historical accident" of oil discovery, instead of to a natural evolution of economy and state as supposedly occurred in Europe and the United States during industrialization.[17]

Scholars have also explored how citizenship in these states, unlike in the West, is based on generous welfare benefits, such as housing, healthcare, and guaranteed income, rather than on political participation by the citizenry. In fact, some argue that rentier-based societies freeze the power of wealthy monarchs and remove any possibility for real democratization or even for civil society.[18] Others have maintained that rentier states are weak or "quasi" states because they were created by and remain economically dependent on foreign countries.[19] Gulf States emerged from unequal treaties with imperial powers in the region, particularly the British Raj government, and were thus known as "Trucial States" at the time. They continue to be embedded within uneven international relations of power, a situation that has been described as "neo-imperialism" by several scholars.[20] While recognizing the imperial history of the Gulf region is fundamental to understanding much about contemporary Gulf countries and the people who reside in them, the analytical categories we use to examine the Gulf need to also be considered for their own imperial genealogies. This is an alternative to approaching Gulf States either as failures of state formation or primarily as products of foreign manipulation.[21] Questions about the legitimacy of such states and the possibilities of rights or civil society in the region actually recuperate certain teleological ideas about progress and success, those which privilege Western forms of development and thus risk defining Middle Eastern states, especially oil economies, as illiberal nonmodern outgrowths of primordial tribalism due mostly to the "accident" of oil discovery and its finite future.[22] The idea that oil discovery has accidentally produced the Gulf States gestures to an illegitimacy and immaturity endemic to these countries, and therefore to futures that are, by definition, less certain and less stable than those in the rest of the world.

Not only is oil often seen as the determinant of social, political, and economic formations in the region, but it is also considered the primary catalyst for migration.[23] While oil companies and the infrastructural growth following oil discovery created a large spike in migration to the Gulf, the idea that oil precedes migration makes it difficult to understand the multiplicity of economic and political activities occurring in Gulf port cities like Dubai, which have rich cosmopolitan pre-oil mercantile pasts and entrenched diasporic communities that pre-date European colonialism in the region.[24] A narrative of unnatural or excessive economic development persists in recent attention to Dubai's rate of growth, particularly within representations of migrant labor exploitation as somehow derivative of and exceptional to Dubai's over-the-top development projects. While true of other Gulf cities as well, Dubai in particular emerged in popular media sources such as *Vanity Fair*, *Slate*, the *New York Times*, and the *New Yorker* at the beginning of this century as an anomaly of modernity, in which a postmodern city—as evidenced by mega-shopping malls, themed hotels, and excessive consumption—with a neoliberal economy was run as an almost-totalitarian illiberal monarchy. In particular, these articles aimed to expose the dark underbelly of migrant exploitation that lay under the shiny veneer of Dubai's skyscrapers and hotels, focusing their attention on the contrast between expensive luxury-development projects and the large numbers of exploited and underpaid laborers, mostly from South Asia, who were building the city.[25] Such "exposé" pieces implied that migrant-labor exploitation problems were not those of modern nation-states in global capitalism, but rather a result of Dubai's unique nonmodernity and lack of legitimacy in the face of unnatural economic growth.

Parallel to discussions of rentier states as weak or illegitimate, academic and media assertions that the high levels of labor exploitation in the Gulf are somehow symbolic of the backwardness of Gulf governments and their lack of "modern" rights such as freedom of speech, freedom of organization, and gender equality run the risk of exceptionalizing these spaces as thoroughly distinct from other destinations of migration. While the *kafala* system of migrant sponsorship in the Gulf, which I explore in the following chapters, presents foreigners with several unique legal and economic obstacles, the implicit message that migrants are treated worse in the Gulf reproduces a civilizational narrative about the Middle East while erasing the hardships many migrants face in Western countries, often as a direct result of state-sponsored policies that explicitly disadvantage noncitizens over citizens or perpetuate tolerance of racism, profiling, and violence against immigrant groups.[26] While several studies of lower-wage migration to the Gulf do not exceptionalize the region, these accounts focus mainly on rational-actor models of push-and-pull factors or on Marxist accounts of structural exploitation to understand decision-making processes and experiences of migration. Studies from both sending and receiving countries therefore tend to characterize migration, particularly of working-class people from poorer nations, as motivated almost exclusively by economic concerns.[27] Within Indian sociology, for example, a substantial body of work looks specifically at South Asian migration to the Gulf.[28] These studies focus mostly on remittances and return migration and the changes they produce in household structure, employment, and village wealth. In these studies, migration to the Gulf is also approached primarily as a post-oil phenomenon, as well as a form distinct from other outmigration, such as when entire families emigrate to Canada or Great Britain.[29] Since these studies are focused mainly on men who migrate without their families to the Gulf, there is a built-in assumption that the primary attachments for migrants remain in India with heteronormative family structures, and thus that migration is merely a temporary, economically driven choice that would not be made if enough well-paying jobs were available in home villages or neighboring cities.[30] When these studies focus on the daily lives of migrants in the Gulf, they are interested in saving and remittance strategies, labor exploitation, and other aspects of migration as driven by economic globalization, rather than in social networks and forms of belonging within host countries. These models, like the rentier-state literature, privilege the economic dimensions of migration without adequately attending to people's affects, definitions of betterment, and contradictory experiences of power.[31]

Studying migration in the Gulf through the lens of labor—focusing on human rights, coping strategies, remittances, or "modern-day slavery," for example—effectively collapses migrant lives into economic terms and removes possibilities of community formation, political agency, cultural hybridity, emotional attachment, consumption, leisure activity, and other forms of belonging from South Asian experiences in the Gulf.[32] Thus, migrants are often written out of the possibility of belonging to Gulf cities before we can even ethnographically explore their own understandings, claims, narratives, and affects of the places where they sometimes spend the majority of their lives. To avoid these pitfalls and to highlight the ways that migrants in Dubai are members of society who contribute to the formation of urban space, Sharon Nagy uses the term *foreign residents* to describe noncitizens in the Gulf.[33] This naming does not recuperate autochthonous notions of belonging, and it allows us to interrogate how multiple sets of residents experience and produce the city. In addition, a focus on daily lives of foreign residents that moves beyond labor and economic determinism challenges top-down categorizations of Gulf countries as "rentier" states, categorizations that presume certain historical trajectories, economic structures, and forms of governance, in favor of studies that attend to the specificities and contradictions of transnational migration in the Gulf and the potential overlaps they may have with urban spaces that are deemed dissimilar in contemporary scholarship.

MULTIPLE LOGICS OF GOVERNANCE

I propose an approach to studying citizenship and belonging that attends to the circulation and practice of multiple forms of governance in contemporary nation-states. This approach avoids exceptionalizing particular parts of the world and instead acknowledges that globally and locally circulating vocabularies of economy, belonging, and rights are assembled, disassembled, and reassembled *everywhere*. This approach does not disavow the specificities of different contexts, but rather resists thinking of them as anomalous, spectacular, or pathological—as is often the case within representations of Dubai and the Gulf.[34] While rentier states are by definition nonliberal, this is not as much a function of on the ground practices, scales, and rhetorics of governance and belonging as it is a definition that is solidified through a convergence of academic literature about Gulf States and official Gulf State discourses themselves. Gulf States tend to narrate themselves as antiliberal, even as they adopt and proliferate certain practices that could be regarded as neoliberal or even liberal, as well as invest in forms of self-described Westernization.[35] The production of differentiated subjects in Dubai relies on these multiple logics of governance. Neoliberal market models combine with illiberal forms of patronage and welfare and with liberal contract-style relationships to produce the *effect* of an "open" global economy and a "closed" autochthonous nation. This division allows for complementary and contradictory techniques of governmentality that produce citizens as well as noncitizens, belonging as well as exclusion.

National identity in Dubai and the UAE is dependent on the production of a division between the nation and the economy, a division that appears obvious but is in fact a purification of a multiplicity of entanglements between the state and its many residents. To produce an imagined community for a relatively new nation (the UAE became independent in 1971), the state narrates Emirati identity through autochthony, projects of heritage, and the erasure of precolonial and colonial cosmopolitanisms, as I explore in greater detail in chapter 1.[36] State discourses represent economic diversity and migrant labor as necessary evils of oil wealth that constantly threaten the long-standing cultural history of Gulf natives.[37] Migrants therefore are placed into a timeline in which their existence is solely derivative of oil development. In fact, national identity as timeless has been naturalized through the presence of foreigners, as there was no cohesive identity even at the formation of the Gulf nations in the second half of the twentieth century.[38] The migrant, through this move, is relegated to the sphere of the economic and cannot enter the discourse on Gulf national identity. The result of these processes is the production of certain "global" or foreign spaces in Dubai and certain "local" or indigenous ones.[39] The nation, and those who are seen to embody it, is defined precisely against a global economy that is driving Dubai's diversification away from oil, producing its image as a center for megadevelopment and tourism, and threatening Emirati culture through its continued need for foreign workers. The large proportion of foreigners in the Gulf combined with high levels of wealth due to oil and other resources means that the category of "citizen" holds a great deal of importance—it is the identity through which most official forms of social status, belonging, and access to rights are defined.[40] While many scholarly works and media accounts stress the lack of rights afforded to Gulf citizens due to authoritarian rule, particularly in relation to Western liberal democracies, it is important to consider how political communities and relations of production operate and are legitimized through the nexus of citizen-noncitizen.[41] Christopher Davidson, for example, argues that there is a "ruling bargain" between the Emirati rulers and the citizenry that is reminiscent of a "social contract" and that ensures citizen acquiescence for welfare benefits.[42] These liberal forms of governance constitute citizen identities alongside the illiberal forms of patronage and heavy welfare benefits that seem to define the Gulf States.[43] According to Nazih Ayubi, the Gulf States are marked by several modes of production that "articulate" differently with structural power than they do in the West, and by a corporatism that produces not individual subjects or classes, but rather different collectivities in relation to the state.[44] Corporatism, Ayubi argues, produces state legitimacy through clientelist networks, but also increases privatization. He contends that some practices, like patronage, are precapitalist forms that survive today in part as the kafala system of individual citizen sponsorship of foreigners. Many scholars and nongovernmental organizations (NGOS) have criticized the kafala system as the primary source of migrant exploitation in the Gulf, for it affords very little centralized oversight of working conditions or transparency within the processes of migration and employment. But is this a "precapitalist" survival from a tribal past, as Ayubi and others assert? Instead of being "precapitalist," I argue, kafala is actually synchronous with the privatization of migration regulation that theorists of neoliberalism have connected with the rise of global cities.[45]

Aihwa Ong, for example, has written about how neoliberal practices are reconfiguring relationships between governments and populations in Asian countries, including Malaysia, Singapore, and China.[46] Her work tracks "a new relationship between government and knowledge through which governing activities are recast as nonpolitical and nonideological problems that need technical solutions."[47] She argues that neoliberal calculation as a governing technology is spreading to places where neoliberalism is not the norm. Not only do governments create spaces of exception in which they deploy neoliberal logics, but certain groups become exceptions to neoliberalism and are excluded from neoliberal calculation and self-managing subjectivities. My approach to the illiberal UAE state, which appears as an exception to modern or liberal state formations, builds on Ong's work in addressing how state institutions and public-private cooperative ventures deploy certain neoliberal logics, create zones and forms of exception (and "freedom") for different groups, and incorporate a multitude of relationships between market, state, and society in their narratives and practices of governance. While on the ground there is not full privatization or liberalization of the economy, the appearance of open markets and the domination of the "private" sector by foreigners produce, on the one hand, entrepreneurial subjects that reify globalized markets, and on the other, parochial citizen rentiers.[48]

Rather than consider differences between groups of residents as stemming primarily from institutions of economy and governance, I argue that different groups in the UAE also circulate different logics of citizenship and belonging that intermingle with and shift the forms of governmentality within which they are inculcated. There are multiple forms of belonging and exclusion at work in Gulf societies, including juridico-legal, religious, raced, classed, consumerist, ethnic, and settled versus nomadic.[49] While the welfare-state structure has fostered among nationals forms of consumer and performative citizenship (especially when it comes to dress), for example, nationals also participate in global market forms and entrepreneurship.[50] Middle-class and elite South Asians, in contrast, espouse certain neoliberal market values and liberal ideas about citizenship while participating in nonliberal forms of patronage and exploitation that reproduce social stratification and forms of hierarchical citizenship among the Indian diaspora in Dubai. This is particularly true in the case of longstanding Indian merchant communities, which I explore in chapter 3. Foreign residents, consistently referred to as temporary outsiders—the exceptions to citizenship—are actually integral to the production of national identity, not only as passive foils to the nation-state, but also in their active practices and narratives of belonging. Thus, they are politically integrated to some extent in the UAE.[51] It is therefore important to investigate the UAE not primarily as an oil or rentier state that is markedly different in its structure than other countries in the West or even the Global South, but rather as a modern state deploying multiple logics of governance and forms of belonging as a means to interpellate several groups of differently positioned subjects.[52] The *effect* of these processes of governmentality, belonging, citizenship, and exclusion in the Gulf is that of the exception to modernity and its teleologic—a hypermodern globalized economy of millennial capital, an authoritarian state, authentic indigenous Arab citizens, and temporary, newly arrived foreigners. However, as many scholars of modernity have argued, the epistemological assumptions of ontological domains produce their very effects.[53] In this book, I argue that the exceptionality of Dubai turned inside-out—made ordinary—reveals the epistemological assumptions embedded in scholarly inquiry about migration and citizenship in other parts of the world as well.[54] This project of provincializing citizenship and viewing the inside from the site of exception reveals the disjunctures between social categories, legal statuses, and the on-the-ground experiences and effects of belonging and exclusion in the contemporary world.

Citizenship and Its Exceptions

The exception is what cannot be included in the whole of which it is a member and cannot be a member of the whole in which it is always already included.—GIORGIO AGAMBEN, *Homo Sacer*

The Gulf Cooperation Council (GCC) countries have some of the largest noncitizen populations in the world, with noncitizens often outnumbering citizens many times over. The governments of these countries, due partly to the sense of threat their migration demographics represent and partly to the large welfare benefits that come with citizenship, define foreign residents as social, legal, and cultural outsiders to the nation-state. Various residents, as well as scholars, consider this insider-outsider dichotomy to be the structural cause for most inequality in the region and for the legal exclusion of noncitizens from almost all aspects of Gulf society. Why, then, is the concept of citizenship—an impossibility for almost all migrants—so important to this ethnography about Indians in Dubai? I argue that citizenship is defined and solidified *precisely through those who mark citizenship's limits*—temporary, transient, transnational, yet entrenched subjects. These subjects participate in the production of shifting legal categories of inclusion and exclusion in modern nation-states, and they rehearse several forms and scales of citizenship and belonging. Indians, as the primary exceptions to citizenship in Dubai and the UAE, are not only crucial to the maintenance of an imagined community of Arab and Muslim indigencity, but they actively participate in processes of citizenship and governance while simultaneously producing themselves as outsiders to the nation. Thus, their citizenship practices exist *within and through* conditions of legal impossibility. In fact, the ability for certain Indians to belong as substantive citizens in Dubai and perform governance over other migrants not only works to maintain the appearance of a rigid citizen-noncitizen boundary, but also reifies the effect of a neoliberal economy and a nonliberal state.

As the primary logic of contemporary membership, citizenship frames —both positively and negatively—the social positioning and experiences of all people, including those denied juridico-legal inclusion in illiberal states like the UAE. The experiences of Indians in Dubai highlight some of the assumptions embedded within citizenship as a category of modern belonging as it is approached through anthropological and other scholarship. While Benedict Anderson and others have argued, for example, that nations as "imagined communities" rely on the production of the other to national identity—the exteriority of the nation—citizenship studies remain for the most part about the various technologies, discourses, and practices that produce differentiation within the *interiority* of the nation-state.[55] It is equally necessary, however, to address how citizenship also occurs in the encounters between that which constitutes the inside and the outside of belonging in modern nation-states. Citizenship is not determined primarily from within individual states, but, more importantly, outsiders to the state also define both sovereignty and the parameters of citizenship as a contemporary logic of membership and as what Hindess calls a "regime of government."[56] This is particularly true in the case of non-Western and postcolonial states, which are increasingly subject to external definition by unequal systems of global capital and "development," direct intervention by stronger nations, and NGO-ization. Because the fissures, unevenness, and multiplicity of sovereign power are often more evident and openly contested in these contexts, they are especially vital sites for exploring the contemporary workings of citizenship, sovereignty, and the state. Thus, the UAE, as seemingly exceptional in its state formation and citizenship, is actually rich ground for exploring citizenship and sovereignty and for challenging the normative analytical frameworks through which scholars have thus far approached these concepts.

EXCEPTION AND ITS EXCEPTIONS:
CENTERING AGAMBEN AND DUBAI IN CITIZENSHIP STUDIES

Giorgio Agamben's formulation of exception to describe the founding of the modern nation-state and democratic citizenship focuses on the forms of violence and exclusion at the center of Western liberalism, and his work, though seemingly not directly relevant to non-Western spaces, is actually incredibly salient for a study of Indian diasporic belonging in Dubai. Agamben's work points to how Western sovereignty was founded on violent exclusions, both of individuals supposedly within the body politic, and of those entities and subjects that supposedly lay outside of it. It is precisely from the site of exception that we can learn most about the workings of citizenship and develop more nuanced and critical theories of politics and belonging. As such, it is not only Indians as exceptions to citizenship in the UAE that allow scholars to question governmentality, nationalism, and identity in the Gulf, but the Gulf itself—as exception to Western liberal democracy—that provides a lens through which to reflect on the taken-for-granted ways in which anthropological and other scholarship approaches state-making, civil society, and the political.

Agamben argues against Foucault's historiography of biopolitics as a form of governance that breaks with previous juridico-institutional forms.[57] Rather, he suggests, governance over "bare life," the biopolitical body, is the *originary act of sovereign power* in Western states; it is through the exclusion of bare life (what Aristotle refers to as *zoe*) that political life can exist at all. While the focus on Agamben's use of "bare life" in recent scholarship has mostly relied on his later arguments about how contemporary states reduce certain populations or individuals to that which can be killed, my arguments derive primarily from Agamben's first use of bare life as that which is excluded in the originary formation of the state.[58] For example, the Roman *polis* was not derived from a social contract among equals—a supposed core feature of democratic politics—but rather from the giving over of the capacity to be killed by men in order to enter into political society. As such, one could argue that it is not biopolitics (the governance over life itself) but necropolitics (the governance over death) that is at the center of Western statehood.[59] As Agamben argues, "In Western politics, bare life has the peculiar privilege of being that whose exclusion founds the city of men."[60] The paradox of modern democracy, therefore, is that freedom is generally believed to be located in the realm of zoe, or bare life, which is supposedly outside sovereign power—the "private"—when in fact it is the very giving over of zoe that produces man's subjugation to the sovereign. Thus, the root of citizenship and, by extension, of political identity in what we presently delimit as democratic societies is not necessarily very different from that of authoritarian regimes for both forms of governance rely upon similar exclusions in the formation of sovereign power, and therefore the day-to-day experiences of people living in these states should not be approached in our scholarship as always already incommensurable.

Agamben's formulation of exception as a constitutive feature of citizenship and the state challenges the abstract promise of liberal-democratic citizenship—which is in essence based in violence rather than in egalitarianism—in favor of a focus on its on-the-ground incompleteness and failures. His arguments about the foundational exclusion of the liberal state point to similarities in form between modern democracies and totalitarian regimes, or between seemingly liberal and illiberal states, urging an approach to places like the UAE that does not render them or their forms of citizenship and governmentality exceptional.[61] Agamben's formulation of exception, however, does not attend to how *multiple* violent exclusions underpin the sovereignty of the Western state, not only the governance over "bare life" within the polis. As Achille Mbembe and others have pointed out, even the state of exception in Europe was reliant on other (and *othered*) exceptions.[62] These specters and states of exception and terror—namely, slavery, racial violence, apartheid, and colonialism— were integral to the production of Western state sovereignty and citizenship. Sovereign states that were outside of imperial purview, for example, were treated as illegal entities; one could say that they were in a "relation of exception" that both legitimized Western sovereignty and produced the justification for conquest.[63] In the case of the Gulf, discourses of piracy played an important role in justifying British encroachment and the establishment of forced Trucial contracts with tribal leaders in Arabia.[64] Contemporary liberal citizenship and sovereignty, therefore, are not only produced against excepted individuals and groups from within the metropole that can be reduced to "bare life," but also through non-Western and postcolonial states, which have developed through histories of colonialism, imperialism, development, and global capitalism, and continue today as other(ed) exceptions to the sovereignty of contemporary Western states.[65] The field of postcolonial studies, from which this book draws heavily, has centered the relational development of national identity, the modern state, and liberal citizenship within systems of power, beginning with colonialism and imperialism and extending today to globalization and neoliberal market expansion. Countries have to be legible within the international community of nation-states, for example, while their sovereignty is simultaneously challenged by the presence and intervention of other, more powerful nations and supranational organizations like the World Bank. This is particularly true in the case of the Gulf States, which have recently emerged from a long history of British imperial intervention, currently host large American military bases, and are often rendered illegitimate or "not yet" in scholarly discourse about them. Nonliberal, nondemocratic, and postcolonial contexts therefore provide rich sites for interrogating the processes of citizenship and state-making from within and without, while also informing us about how multiple logics, rhetorics, and technologies circulate in the production of supposedly distinct state forms and their accompanying categories of membership and exclusion.

Many of the assumptions about belonging and nonbelonging embedded in liberal-democratic understandings of citizenship and its exceptions—those highlighted by Agamben and Mbembe—contribute to the elision of Indian urban, diasporic, and substantive citizenship from Dubai, for the labeling of the rentier state as an exception to modern state formation does not acknowledge that the polis itself also emanated illiberal and authoritarian modes of sovereignty and exception, and was therefore *just as necropolitical as it was biopolitical*. Focusing on the narratives and practices of those who are excepted from nonliberal citizenship—like Indians in Dubai—highlights the relevance of this group to the legitimacy of the Emirati state: these subjects exist outside of territorial, legal, and imagined forms of the nation, outside of official citizenship—the exceptions to sovereignty that produce sovereign power. More important, however, such a focus also questions the dominant ways that academic scholarship thinks about states, sovereignty, and citizenship in the contemporary world.

SUBSTANTIVE AND LATITUDINAL CITIZENSHIP
WITHIN DUBAI'S INDIAN DIASPORA

Citizenship occurs in the nexus of multiple—often contradictory—rhetorics, actions, and technologies deployed by those who are produced as insiders and outsiders of the nation-state by institutions of governance, and by those who produce themselves as such through their own narratives and claims to belonging and exclusion. Exception is not a singular category, however, but rather one that is occupied by several groups, full of multiple meanings, and continually generating its own exceptions. Thus, the boundary between sovereign and exception is tenuous and constantly emergent. The state, as well as the multiple institutions and groups of residents in Dubai and the UAE, mobilizes categories of foreignness in different ways to produce the parameters of its power and the distinctions among different groups of residents. Indians in Dubai mark the limits of citizenship in the United Arab Emirates but also move in and out of legibility, and their narratives and practices produce both sovereignty and its exception. It is important, therefore, to investigate the logics of belonging and exclusion Indian foreign residents deploy, and how these logics support or challenge state definitions of the national community.

In Dubai, as in other parts of the Arab Gulf, inclusion and exclusion are defined primarily through a dichotomy of citizen-noncitizen, in which all access to state resources, social capital, mobility, and belonging seems tied to the juridico-legal category of "Emirati." While scholars of migration and urban space in Western contexts have extensively explored substantive citizenship, urban citizenship, and social citizenship—that is, citizenship that occurs at scales and spaces beyond the level of the formal legal category proffered by the state—any form of belonging for foreigners in the Gulf seems impossible because of the rigid structures of citizenship and migration in these countries: the category of "citizen" is patrilineal, and there is little room for naturalization; citizens receive heavy welfare benefits that noncitizens cannot claim; and there is a perceived lack of civil society or politicization, which would allow for greater interactions between citizens and foreigners.[66] In addition, the kafala system of migration sponsorship, through which individual citizens sponsor migrants on temporary, renewable work contracts, makes any real integration of noncitizens into the fabric of social and cultural life in the UAE seem impossible. However, if the state deploys multiple forms of governance to regulate its citizenry—not just a patrimonial nonliberal welfare system—it actually proliferates several types of citizenship as well. This includes liberal contract-style relationships, neoliberal and consumer citizenship models, and opportunities for civil society through online and offline organizations. These are forms of governance and subjectification that apply not only to citizens, but also—and even more important—to the majority noncitizen population of the country. My research indicates that the production of a neoliberal economy in which certain—middle- and upper-class—expatriates are kept satisfied and given increasing "rights" is integral to the maintenance of "closed" citizenship and the purity of national identity. These expatriate "clients" play a very significant role in the liberalizing reforms of the state, particularly in the Dubai context. For example, as I explore in chapter 4, middle-class Indians were invested in liberal and neoliberal understandings of success and citizenship and they reified the distinction between foreign and national in Dubai through their insistence that they were "good" self-enterprising foreign residents of the city and not "bad" welfare-reliant citizens. The Emirati state thus produces neoliberal subjects while promoting a patrimonial approach to citizenship through illiberal and welfare models. By relegating neoliberal reforms to certain areas that operate under different juridico-legal structures, such as Dubai's many "free zones," the state goes even further toward maintaining the distinction between citizen and foreigner while allowing for the development of certain forms of migrant belonging.

These practices by the Emirati state also rely on preexisting uneven relationships among South Asians both in "home" countries and transnationally. Aihwa Ong's work on Asian transnational migration investigates the differences in status and experience between wealthy elite "astronauts" who hold multiple passports and can easily move between spaces, and low-wage migrants and refugees who are unable to navigate the exclusions and laws of a nation-state to their benefit.[67] This creates opportunities for what she calls "latitudinal citizenship" among diasporic populations, where some entrepreneurs are able to be flexible citizens by exploiting their compatriots in ethnicized power hierarchies. The Emirati state similarly provides opportunities for wealthy expatriates to own businesses and govern over their compatriots, in effect behaving like citizens of the country and participating in some of the substantive benefits of the supposed rentier state. While technically it is citizens who are *kafeels* (sponsors), in practice it is more often their foreign business partners who manage the day-to-day governance of migrants, usually from their own home countries, as I explore in chapter 3. The disavowal of formal belonging by Indians despite these practices of governance recuperates sovereignty from the site of exception and is a necessary performative practice for the constant legitimization of state power in the Gulf in the face of large demographic imbalances, Orientalist representations, media spectacles about human-rights concerns, and, more recently, an economic downturn and growing discontent among the citizenry. Since 2010, for example, citizens have held protests across the Gulf region about the lack of jobs, about women's rights, and about censorship and democratization.[68] Without the appearance of a rigid citizen-noncitizen divide and what Sulayman Khalaf calls the "image of unlimited good" for the citizenry, there are strong possibilities for further civil unrest in the Gulf States.[69] The legitimacy and sovereignty of the Gulf Arab States, therefore, are reliant on the practices of latitudinal citizenship and citizenship as exception by their large foreign resident populations, particularly South Asians who have long-standing ties to the region and participate in acts of governance while simultaneously narrating themselves as outsiders to national identity.

Are Indians in Dubai Diasporic?

While anthropologists and other scholars have produced a significant body of knowledge about racialization, community formation, and identity among South Asian and other diasporic communities in Western countries, scholarship focused on South-South migration, and particularly on transnational groups that do not fall into Western legal, scholarly, or popular definitions of minority or migrant populations, has been scant. In particular, the UAE's 1.5 million South Asians, who constitute the majority of the population, are surprisingly absent from anthropological literature on migration, transnationalism, and diasporas.[70] In my research with Indians in the downtown neighborhoods of Dubai, I found that my interlocutors' narratives actually resonated in several ways with characteristics associated with South Asian diasporas in other parts of the world: Dubai Indians articulated forms of belonging both to the Gulf and to India, and they rehearsed dynamics of gender, class, ethnicity, generation, and religion that were both specific to the context of Dubai and shared within a transnational network of imagined "Indianness." These identifications did not emerge despite their state of permanent temporariness and their difficulties in negotiating the kafala system of migration, but rather were enabled through the specificities of the Dubai context and through the relationship between the Indian state and its citizens in the Gulf. Their narratives, however, also revealed several disconnects from the South Asian diaspora literature, namely their sense that Western South Asian experiences were very different than theirs, their lack of nostalgia for homeland or sense of cultural "loss," and their ambivalent positions vis-à-vis the Indian state. In fact, exclusions built into their relationship with the Indian state were integral for understanding Dubai Indians' affects, claims to belonging, and forms of identification.

Thus far, I have argued that in order to examine citizenship among Dubai's Indian diaspora—from the site of exception and impossibility—we need to rethink taken-for-granted assumptions about rentier states and their attendant forms of citizenship and migration. This project also requires a critical investigation of the concept of diaspora in order to highlight how Dubai and India are both locations of impossible citizenship for Dubai Indians, and how forms of citizenship, belonging, and exclusion that circulate within and between both places impact my interlocutors' communities, daily lived experiences, and ideas about homeland and hostland. As a concept that describes conditions of mobility and community formation, "diaspora" does particular work in projects of statehood and in scholarship on migration, transnationalism, and globalization—work that contributes to the elision of Dubai's Indian diaspora from both. Thus, exploring in conjunction the ways that the Indian state and diaspora scholarship utilize "diaspora" to delineate particular groups and exclude others is important for understanding the positionality of Dubai Indians and their various modes of belonging and exclusion. Studies of diaspora often rely on liberal juridico-legal citizenship and permanent settlement not only to explain the migration process but also to operationalize diaspora as an epistemic category. Within this framework, supposed "temporary" migrants become illegible as diasporic. Additionally, the Indian state, which actively attempts to fold its diaspora into the nation, relies on ideological and classed definitions of diaspora that erase the histories and contributions of certain Indian emigrants, including many in the Gulf. While the post-oil narrative of Gulf migration that accompanies political-economic writing about the region tends to erase pre-oil cosmopolitanisms and forms of substantive citizenship among Dubai's Indian communities, it is ironically the pre-oil and pre-independence *presence* of Indians in the Gulf region that produces them as not diasporic enough for the Indian state and its projects of nationalism and economic development. Indian state projects to reach out to its diaspora and academic approaches to diasporas, taken together, suggest through the exclusions built into each that Indians in Dubai are somehow exceptional within the context of South Asian transnational movement, when in fact their narratives, practices, affects, and identities resonate in many ways with other South Asian immigrant stories, and with migration experiences more generally, both historical and contemporary. Reading contemporary and historical migrant circumstances and experiences through Dubai's Indian communities therefore enriches as well as challenges diaspora as a critical lens for reflecting on cultural formations within transnationalism.

WAVES OF INDIANNESS:
TAKING AND MAKING THE NATION OVERSEAS

Over the last few decades, the government of India has been quite active in projects that expand the nation-state beyond territorial India in order to hail members of the diaspora as central actors in the country's economic growth. Since the 1970s, the Indian government has been implementing changes that make remitting and investing in India easier for nonresident Indians (NRIS), meaning those with Indian citizenship who reside primarily outside India.[71] In 1999 the Indian government introduced the Person of Indian Origin (PIO) card for Indians living abroad with foreign passports.[72] These cards not only provide certain benefits for cardholders while they are in India (visa-free entry, the ability to open bank accounts, investment opportunities), but can also be obtained by second- and even third-generation émigrés, implying not only that Indianness is in one's heart wherever one is, but that the Indian nation recognizes certain *jus sanguis* definitions of membership. More recently, in 2003, India hosted the first annual Overseas India Conference (Pravasi Bharatiya Divas), in which it was announced that India was exploring a dual-citizenship model with certain countries (called Overseas Citizenship of India, or OCI).[73] It would appear that the Indian nation, as well as the state through these new citizenship models, is expanding to the places where its emigrants have either settled or gone for seasonal work, is hailing them as part of the nation, and is providing incentives to visit, invest in, and remit money "home." However, the application of these categories is uneven.[74] Dubai Indians, hailed by the state on some levels and disregarded on others, have a particularly complicated relationship with the homeland that continually affects their understandings of belonging and exclusion in both Dubai and India, as I explore in chapter 2.

The definition of diaspora deployed by the Indian state contains ideological assumptions of what constitutes a good Indian subject. However, this definition is also connected in large part to divergent histories of emigration from the subcontinent during colonialism and postcolonialism, and to discourses surrounding overseas Indians at different periods in the country's history. The unevenness of India's relationship with its emigrants—and vice versa—leads us to question whether everyone who can claim some heritage back to India is also diasporic, as Indian state and scholarly discourses would suggest.[75] Embedded in the supposed inclusiveness of the way diaspora is deployed by Indian state discourses are large exclusions that impact the day-to-day lives of differently situated overseas Indian communities. In particular, communities that fall "in-between" historical cleavages or that are tangentially hailed by the state's economic and ideological projects, like Indians in the Gulf States, occupy an interesting position from which to explore the Indian state's relationship with its overseas populations, past and present. Because of the continuous connectivity with South Asia, Dubai Indians straddle the colonial-postcolonial dichotomy that defines the relationship (or nonrelationship) of many Indian emigrant communities with the Indian state. It was with the birth of the postcolonial state, in 1947, that India's relationship with its overseas population changed drastically. Under Nehruvian politics of non-alignment, previous emigrants were abandoned by the Indian state, which was interested primarily in what occurred within its territorial boundaries and not with intervening on the behalf of Indians who remained overseas.[76] In addition, the formation of two states at independence—one Muslim, one "secular"—made defining the boundaries of Indianness imperative, and "Indian" started becoming even more aligned with discourses about "traditional" Hindu culture. As Constantino Xavier argues, "Nehru shifted from an inclusive *jus sanguinis* policy to an exclusive *jus soli* definition of the nation."[77] Thus, only Indians in postcolonial territorial India were considered true Indians.

The recent moves by the Indian government to bring the diaspora back "in" represent a break from the Nehruvian model, extending certain forms of citizenship extraterritorially and defining the diaspora as both marked by affect for the homeland and as having a neoliberal subjectivity that will aid in India's growth.[78] Within cultural studies, scholars have noted how Indian film and television are now produced and marketed primarily for the diaspora, and how representations of Indians abroad have hailed them as members of the nation.[79] The diaspora, however, does not in actuality include all Indians overseas. In particular, the PIO card, which grants citizen-like economic benefits, is available only to Indians who migrated after 1950, thus excluding communities formed by colonial indentured labor as well as those displaced by Partition. Indians living in Dubai during Partition, who found themselves with either Indian or Pakistani passports based on their religion or where they traced their family roots, are therefore ineligible for PIO status. Overseas Citizenship of India, the newest model proposed by the Indian state, goes even further in delimiting the diaspora by location; there are only certain countries from which Indians can obtain OCI status, none of which are in the Middle East (excepting Israel), Africa, or the Caribbean (the three regions containing the largest overseas Indian communities).[80]

Because they cannot get citizenship in the Gulf but reside outside of India, Dubai Indians are classified as NRIs. In fact, the NRI classification, developed in 1973 by the Foreign Exchange Regulation Act, was in large part created to ease and increase the flow of remittance money from the Gulf to India.[81] Today, India's economy relies even more on remittances than in the 1970s, and workers in the Gulf in particular are responsible for major parts of the Gross Domestic Product in places like Kerala and Andhra Pradesh.[82] However, NRIS are in a much more liminal space than are their PIO counterparts. They enjoy certain economic benefits in India, but not political ones. For example, NRIS were not allowed to vote until very recently (a bill put forward in 2006 only made it out of committee in 2011), and there continues to be a heated debate within India about whether NRIS deserve a say in the running of the country. Since PIOS and OCIS hold passports from elsewhere, and this elsewhere is usually the West, they are enfranchised in ways that Gulf Indians can never be.[83] Ironically, then— and interestingly absent from the literature on migration in the Gulf—it is the Indian state *in the first place*, and not the kafala system, that removes political rights from Indians in the Gulf. Thus, it is evident that the Indian state has a very narrow description of diaspora, one that privileges professional classes, newer migrants to the West, and non-Muslims.[84] Diasporic subjects, in turn, have political and economic clout in India, and they impact state policy, popular culture, development, and communal tensions.[85] Indians in Dubai, in relation to these various modalities of inclusion and exclusion, fall neither completely outside nor completely inside the state's hail. The Indian state's approach to diaspora aligns with the way diaspora is deployed within scholarship on Indian and South Asian immigrant communities to produce similar elisions, particularly of supposedly temporary or transient subjects, like Indian in Dubai.

LOGICS OF BELONGING AND CITIZENSHIP IN DIASPORA STUDIES

The concept of diaspora, used in reference to voluntary and involuntary movements of people and their interconnectivities, has allowed for more nuanced understandings of migration, particularly because diaspora studies have tended to focus on social, cultural, and affective aspects of belonging for migrant communities in ways that are not economically reductive. Diaspora theories have moved beyond traditional sociological analyses of push-pull factors and economic need to account for other dynamics that shape the migration process, including colonial and imperial linkages between "home" countries and locations of migration.[86] They have accounted for the movement of more than just human bodies, paying attention to how commodities and information also travel and affect community formation.[87] Diaspora theory has provided a nuanced approach to identity that challenges the discourse on assimilation by introducing concepts like nostalgia, hybridity, and diaspora space.[88] Diaspora scholarship has also provided ways to delink nation from territorial state through investigations of long-distance nationalism and emerging categories of belonging, like, in the case of the Indian diaspora, the OCI, NRI, and PIO classifications.[89] All of these approaches to diaspora in the literature encourage us to consider migration in and through other processes and to attend to multiple scales and forms of identity, community, and racial formation.

Many newer concepts of diaspora as migration from any homeland (those that move beyond earlier Jewish or Black Atlantic examples of forced dispersal), however, also suggest that diaspora comes into existence temporally after the nation-state. In the Indian context diaspora studies often relies on Western case studies of migration that took place after the birth of independent India; the majority of writing on the South Asian diaspora, for example, is interested in migration to Western countries enabled by postcolonial policies and "globalization."[90] This reliance includes assumptions of homeland nostalgia, privileged forms of migration, and liberal-democratic notions of citizenship and belonging, effectively producing a teleology of naturalization or permanent settlement that makes nonliberal forms of belonging and temporary migrants less legible as diasporic.[91] Historians, however, have noted many instances in which dispersed, networked groups were central to the production of national identity, indicating that nation and diaspora do not exist in a linear relationship, but rather are co-constitutive. For example, the British were a diaspora long before they became a nation, and British national identity was actually consolidated through imperialist processes.[92] Indian national identity was also scripted within the diaspora. Under British colonial rule, Indians overseas were treated legally as Indian subjects of the British Raj, to the point that the British government kept census records about Indians living outside of South Asia.[93] These subjects may have had fuzzy and overlapping loyalties—to region, language, caste, and religion—but they were considered to be racially and legally Indian, and thus were treated as such under imperial law. In fact, Gandhi, often referred to as the father of the nation (*bapu*), developed his Indian nationalist politics through experiences of and activism against racist anti-Indian policies in South Africa.[94] These experiences formed the core of his anticolonial politics in South Asia, and were hugely significant to the eventual formation of not only independent India, but also, by virtue of the implicit and explicit exclusions within mainstream Indian anticolonial nationalism, Pakistan as well.

While the foundation of an independent India can therefore be considered a *diasporic* undertaking as much as it was an anticolonial one, diaspora literature tends to underemphasize the experiences of colonial migration in favor of more privileged middle-class journeys to the West while also claiming all people who once migrated from a place as diasporic. This double move ends up implying that we can extend the findings of certain case studies to other parts of the world or other waves of migration, for diasporas as objects of study share certain characteristics.[95] For example, in a recent special issue of the *Journal of Intercultural Studies*, titled "Indian Diaspora in Transnational Contexts," four out of six research articles are case studies from the United States.[96] In explaining this, the editors for the special issue write, "Several of the papers are based on personal interviews in selected American cities. They explore problems encountered in attempts at negotiating an identity that is a balance of 'Americanness' and 'Indianness.' In so doing, the papers address themselves to questions frequently posed in connection with diasporas worldwide."[97] However, an article on Indo-Fijians in Australia in the same issue directly challenges this model of diaspora and the idea that experience in the United States can be transplanted onto all Indian migrant communities, by pointing out that this twice-migrated group not only does not have nostalgia for India but is also rather uninteresting to the Indian state.[98] In fact, scholarship that addresses the experience of NRIS and PIOS in the United States does not usually account for the historical presence of indentured Indian labor in the United States and the community formations that arose out of conditions of servitude, racism, and poverty.[99] And, even among so-called American NRIS, there are some who disclaim belonging to the Indian nation because of its exclusionary (and violent) policies and practices, such as those in the Khalistan movement.[100]

Because of the unexplored ways in which ideas about citizenship, identity, and belonging get reassembled in *other* diaspora spaces and time periods, postcolonial Indian diasporic citizenship in the West becomes the form through which South Asian migration is understood. This is usually through a narrative of naturalization or desired permanence based on liberal forms of citizenship and middle-class achievement. In fact, assertions of nostalgia and homeland orientation or of cultural "in-between-ness" would not be as salient without the idea that diaspora groups have settled elsewhere. Diaspora scholarship that claims diasporic subjects as challenges to the nation-state, or as dialectically produced in webs of power and governmentality within nation-states, relies heavily in both instances on defining citizenship or the lack thereof through and against juridico-legal rights and liberal-democratic forms of belonging.[101] This does not necessarily have to be the case. For example, as Lok Siu has explored, Chinese in Panama, although they did not have access to many legal rights of citizenship, expressed belonging to Panama, to a broader Chinese diaspora, and to China's shifting definitions of national iden-tity.[102] In much of the scholarship on South Asian diasporas, even that which considers the complicity of certain South Asian diasporic subjects in projects of exclusion by the Indian state, there is a relatively unques-tioned assumption of a shared understanding of citizenship between South Asia and the West; both rely on a particular notion of individual social contract with the state and universal rights (even as this universality is always-already understood to be based on a set of gendered, racialized, classed, religious, and sexual exclusions), and both are proliferating newer forms of neoliberal and consumer citizenship. This understanding runs the risk of naturalizing liberal citizenship as a constitutive feature of being diasporic, which can lead to the erasure of subjects who are permanently temporary and practice forms of citizenship that fall outside of juridico-legal rights—like Indians in Dubai—from diaspora scholarship. However, these groups, as they are often leveraged as the foil to national identity, are inculcated into their host nations through acts of racism and discrimina-tion. Thus, rather than being invisible and evacuated of meaning, the illegitimate or temporary migrant's position is full of meanings about what belonging looks like and what is at stake in claims to rights and citizenship by various groups.[103] This book addresses the multiple forms of citizenship and belonging among Dubai's Indian diaspora. I have maintained the term *diaspora* in order both to intervene in and to expand the normative narra-tives and assumptions that frame the majority of current accounts of India in a transnational context. I therefore highlight in this project how the narratives of Indians in Dubai can be read both as claims for including their experiences within state and scholarly deployments of diaspora *and* as disavowals of the policies, projects, subjectivities, and theories that these deployments proliferate.

Everyday Citizenship in Exceptional Spaces

Citizenship is both a regime of governance and a logic, an idea that is leveraged differently for and by different populations in various contexts and at several scales.[104] Indians in Dubai are important to understanding citizenship because as diasporic subjects they impact the forms of citizenship in both countries, India and the UAE; as exceptions to legal citizenship they validate the UAE nation-state and its ethnoracial and religious foundations; and as latitudinal subjects they recuperate as well as transform classed, gendered, ethnic, caste, and religious divisions within transnationalism. The site of exception is a useful starting place for a study of citizenship. However, this book is also about doing ethnography within "exceptional" places—ones that are not easily categorized or do not conform to epistemological types like "liberal democracies" or "petro-states." Dubai is in several ways the ultimate contemporary site of exception and exceptionality, as is evident in the media representations that abound about the city-state. Many scholars and journalists have lamented rapid large-scale development in the Gulf as an indicator of cultural loss, a McDonaldization or Disneyfication that is eroding "traditional" Arab cultural values and practices, as if those values and practices existed in the past and are not iterations of the present. I have been told, for example, by numerous friends, family members, colleagues, and even scholars of the Middle East that Dubai is a place without soul, without culture—a mirage. In chapter 1, I explore some of the reasons for this perception of Dubai by focusing on how Dubai's center was shifting during the time of my fieldwork in 2006, when Dubai's boom was at its height. At that time, the downtown neighborhoods near the Dubai Creek—the historical center of maritime trade in the emirate—were becoming increasingly distanced (economically, geographically, demographically, and historically) from "New Dubai"—the rapidly developing southern part of town marked by over-the-top development projects such as the Madinat Jumeirah, a five-star resort complex that re-creates an air-conditioned luxury version of the Dubai Creek for wealthy Western tourists and expatriates. The discourses and projects of the Dubai government and of mixed public-private corporations contributed to the production of a triptych of identifications in Dubai at the time—"local," "expatriate," and "migrant"—and luring wealthier cosmopolitan expatriates was necessary both for Dubai's neoliberal development projects and for the production of a bounded and purified national identity. The downtown neighborhoods of the Dubai Creek and the South Asians who inhabited them did not fit neatly into these new categories of belonging and exclusion, and the production of Dubai as a cosmopolitan "global city" relied on the erasure of older forms of cosmopolitanism represented by the mercantile communities of the Creek area. By thinking about Dubai not as one bounded space but as a city full of many potential "field sites," I hope to bring daily life for Indian residents in these neighborhoods into relief. In fact, their narratives and practices reveal forms of urban citizenship that push against this triptych of identities and against popular imaginings of Emirati pasts and futures.

Dubai's fleeting and exceptional qualities seem to preclude an inquiry into urban and substantive citizenship forms, particularly in the case of foreign residents, who are tied to temporary work visas and defined by the government as guests. However, for my interlocutors in the field, ephemerality was a constant, enduring, and even expected part of their daily lives. As I explore in chapter 2, the neighborhoods of the Dubai Creek area were experienced by many of the people residing there as quite entrenched Indian spaces that were distinct from the rest of the city, even as they were marked by transience and insecurity. The history of these neighborhoods and my interlocutors' perceptions of them made them at once "extensions of India" and "diaspora spaces" distinct from the subcontinent. This duality within daily life in Dubai's downtown neighborhoods challenges understandings of the Gulf and South Asia as distinct areas of anthropological research, and it also provides different narratives of emigrant life from those found in other scholarship on South Asian diaspora, particularly Western case studies. The historical and contemporary connections between the Gulf and South Asia meant that most Indians in downtown Dubai experienced their surroundings as an extension of India and thus in some ways as not diasporic, particularly because they did not exhibit the nostalgia for homeland or the sense of cultural loss scholars often associate with diasporic populations. However, my interlocutors' ambivalences about living in the Gulf were increasing with the growth in both Dubai's and India's economies, heightening their awareness of how their lives differed from those of Indians in mainland India, as well as of how the Indian state treated them differently than it did other emigrants.

In chapter 3, I examine how Indian businessmen, particularly gold merchants, were responding to the shifts that Dubai's government had made in the preceding two decades away from small family-trade firms to large multinational corporations. Indian merchants experienced nostalgia for a past in which they held privileged positions due to colonial and postcolonial relationships between Great Britain, India, and the Gulf region, and through a largely illegal gold smuggling industry. At the same time, Indian merchants were attempting to maintain their ethnic monopolies in the face of neoliberalization in Dubai through political engagement with the state and through governance over other migrants from India. While the kafala system technically privatized governance into the hands of citizens, it was actually more often foreign elites who were handling the day-to-day regulation of their compatriots, and this role constituted a primary form of unofficial citizenship for Indian merchants in Dubai. In addition, practices of migrant governance and ethnic monopoly by Indian merchants in Dubai's Creek neighborhoods produced latitudinal citizenship among Dubai's Indian communities and contributed to the exploitative conditions under which many foreign residents from South Asia lived and worked. The forms of citizenship that circulate in the places that migrants live mingle with values about belonging and exclusion that have developed historically in the context of colonialism and postcolonialism in their home countries.[105] Indians in Dubai circulated particular ways of thinking about citizenship from the colonial and postcolonial Indian context, which included liberal, neoliberal, and nonliberal values and expectations. Indian citizenship in Dubai therefore included the interaction of multiple logics of belonging in the formation of subjectivity and forms of self-governance. Indian communities in Dubai, as in other parts of the diaspora, reproduced patriarchies, class exploitation, and communal ideas about religion.[106]

Along with latitudinal relationships between Indians in Dubai, however, were shared values of what it means to be South Asian. Dubai Indians narrated allegiances that cut across national, ethnic, and religious lines, which were informed by their experiences of migrating to the Gulf. In chapter 4, I explore two modes of subjectivity that I observed among my middle-class interlocutors: racial consciousness and consumer citizenship. Both were emergent from the experience of living in Dubai and were forms of identification and belonging that resembled diasporic subjectivities noted by scholars of South Asian diasporas in Western liberal contexts. My interlocutors consistently disavowed belonging to the UAE, and in so doing, reified the dichotomy between an "open" globalized economy and a "closed" nation-state. The middle-class Dubai Indians that

I spoke to and interacted with on a regular basis defined themselves and their class and ethnic identities precisely against the trope of the migrant "slave" laborer. The logics of citizenship that they deployed asserted economic choice and freedom in the decision to migrate and a voluntarism of staying, despite, in many cases, conditions of suffering and distress. However, while they narrated their migration in economic terms, their subjectivities—racial consciousness and consumer citizenship—constituted new forms of diasporic belonging that exceeded the economic determinism through which most scholarship, most state discourses, and most foreign residents themselves discuss Gulf migration patterns and experiences. Through their expressions of identities enabled by migration and daily life within Dubai, my interlocutors asserted claims to the city that challenged the very divisions between citizen-noncitizen and nation-economy that they themselves articulated.

In chapter 5, I address a group that knows no other home and yet is most impossibly *of* Dubai—young Indian citizens born and raised in the emirate who, at the cusp of graduating from university and losing their parents' visa sponsorship, were faced with questions of how they would stay in the country. Recent shifts in education in the Gulf, particularly the introduction of globalized higher education, were making diasporic youth both more entrenched and also more politicized. The primary and secondary education system in Dubai—where citizens attend free Arabic public schools and foreign residents pay for private schooling based mostly on national origin—is designed to produce parochial identities in which foreigners expect to be temporary. However, the introduction of private higher education options in the last decade has allowed for ethnically and nationally integrated classrooms and has extended the amount of time diasporic youth can stay in the UAE. Their experiences in these institutions led to shifts in the claims they staked to Dubai, claims that were increasingly divergent from those of other Dubai Indians I discuss in this book. South Asian diasporic youth narratives were beginning to resemble liberal calls for rights and equality, and were pushing against their sense of being "second-class" citizens in the only place they knew as home. The futures that these young people expected, therefore, were potentially changing the landscape of Indian citizenship and belonging in Dubai.

Indians in Dubai, as temporary but settled, transnational but parochial, voluntary but structurally disadvantaged, occupied multiple truths and multiple positionalities. It is imperative to explore this multiplicity to understand how contemporary migration produces categories of belonging and exclusion, and how both nations—home and host—become defined through systems of migration and return. In the conclusion, I revisit the forms of citizenship—urban, diasporic, latitudinal, substantive, consumer, racial, and "second-class"—that Indians in Dubai's downtown Creek neighborhoods articulated, practiced, and claimed, and how these can better inform our understandings of the contemporary Gulf and Middle East, particularly given the tremendous changes in the region following the economic downturn in 2008 and the Arab Spring uprisings of 2010–11. The absence of foreign resident experiences and the role of migration in analyses of these processes is quite glaring, especially given that foreign residents constitute large proportions of the population around the region, particularly in the United Arab Emirates. I thus reiterate in the conclusion my theoretical and ethnographic interventions into Gulf and South Asian diaspora studies, but through the lens of these momentous events, exploring how a focus on migration and multiple forms of belonging is necessary to better understand what constitutes democracy, citizenship, and the political, not only for scholarship on the Arab world, but for anthropology more generally.

The experiences of Indians in Dubai are built on decades of living both day-to-day and within firmly rooted communities. Yasser Elsheshtawy writes that the Indian-dominated neighborhoods of downtown Dubai—those that are ignored in the literature and considered "exotic" by Western expatriates—are highly important "places where everyday life is taking place" even as they are marked by a lack of permanence.[107] While the guests at the Burj al-Arab—Dubai's "7-star" hotel—and the guestworkers of Sonapur—Dubai's largest labor camp—have captured our attention thus far, they are not indicative of an entire city, nor are they markers of a two-dimensional form of globalization. Dubai is not a nonplace without culture or a city of smoke and mirrors. The anthropologist's project, put as simply as possible, is one of narrating the ordinariness of a place. This project addresses the ephemerality of Dubai not as fantasy or obscenity, but rather as a quite mundane—and therefore anthropologically very important—aspect of life for Indian foreign residents, the exceptions to citizenship that are the most representative—yet impossible—citizens of this not-so-exceptional urban space.

1 · A TALE OF TWO CREEKS

COSMOPOLITAN PRODUCTIONS AND COSMOPOLITAN

ERASURES IN CONTEMPORARY DUBAI

On my first visit to Dubai, in 2004, Gautam, a family friend who would come to be one of my primary interlocutors, picked me up from my hotel on Al Rolla Street in the downtown Bur Dubai neighborhood and drove me out to a newly constructed hotel complex named Madinat Jumeirah on the edge of town, in an area that was beginning to be called "New Dubai." It was the beginning of September—the hottest time of the year—and the resort had only recently opened. A megacomplex consisting of two hotels, an indoor mall, a theater, and several restaurants and nightclubs, Madinat Jumeirah was styled as a "traditional" Emirati village surrounding a reproduction of the Dubai Creek, the main body of water that divides the emirate of Dubai and that has until recently been the historical center of the city's maritime trade. Madinat Jumeirah's creek reproduction was complete with *abras* (water ferries) to shuttle hotel guests to private villas, and it boasted a stunning view of the sail shaped ultramodern Burj al-Arab hotel in the background (see figure 1.1). Even with many of the storefronts empty and the restaurants not yet open, the place was breathtaking. Gautam and I spent hours walking around the complex, ducking into narrow alleys in the indoor *souk* (market) to see what we would find, having a drink "creekside," and convincing an Indian security guard to grant us access to the even more posh area reserved for hotel guests. I was enthralled by the perfect beauty of the architecture and by the air-conditioned luxury that surrounded me, a stark contrast to Bur Dubai and the other neighborhoods surrounding the actual Dubai Creek, where I was living and conducting research.

For that short first visit, I stayed in a "business" hotel, rather upscale for the mostly working-class neighborhood and also newly constructed. Every

FIGURE 1.1 · Madinat Jumeirah with the Burj al-Arab in background.
Photograph by Neha Vora.

day I walked the seemingly endless blocks to the nearest Internet café, or
even farther to the souks surrounding the Dubai Creek, soaked with sweat
by the time I got to my destination from the searing 45° C sun, which not
only bore down from above, but also reflected up from the empty sand lots
separating buildings. I was jetlagged and having trouble adjusting to the
different paces of life in Dubai: corporate and government offices were
open from 8 AM to 4 PM, while small businesses in my neighborhood
closed for hours in the middle of the day and stayed open late into the
night. Therefore, I was often out and about during the hottest hours of the
day, when others were resting, and asleep by 9 PM, when the neighborhood came alive. The temporal differences between corporate and government office hours and the street-time of the retail venues within souks
coincided with a growing geographic distance between the neighborhoods in downtown Dubai where I spent the majority of my field visits and
the newer parts of town that I visited as a tourist and occasionally as a
researcher, like the offices and malls near Madinat Jumeirah.[1] Despite
concerns about drugs and commercial sex-work on Al Rolla Street, I decided that the business hotel was worth the money for me to stay in when I

came back for long-term research, in 2006. Unlike the high-rise buildings and commercial complexes in newer parts of town, downtown Dubai was mostly walkable, and the predominantly South Asian population (though mostly male) allowed me to blend in more easily than I did elsewhere. My hotel was close to Indian, Arab, and European grocery stores, surrounded by South Asian beauty salons, shops, and restaurants, and easily accessible to most of the Indian-dominated areas of the city where I planned to focus my research.

The Bur Dubai I found when I arrived in January 2006, however, was very different. The hotel that had cost $50 a night just eighteen months before—and even less if one paid monthly—was now over $200 a night, and thus out of my budget. I had been unable to secure an apartment from overseas, so Gautam suggested I stay with him and his family until I got on my feet, but he warned me that space would be limited: his family had been evicted from the three-bedroom apartment they had been renting in a prime area of Meena Bazaar, because the building was being turned into studio apartments for executives, and they had recently relocated to a more expensive but much smaller one-bedroom apartment behind the Khaleej Center shopping mall, very close in fact to the hotel where I had been hoping to stay.[2] Gautam's apartment was even smaller than I had expected, less than five hundred square feet. Gautam, his wife, Reshma, and their young son shared the bedroom. The living room had a small mattress where they sat to watch television and eat meals and where I was to sleep during the few weeks I stayed with them. Looking out over the buildings that surrounded Gautam's from the one small window of the living room, I could see laundry strung outside windows, men in *lungi* lounging on rooftops, and several children running in building parking lots while women clad in *saris* and *salwar kameez* supervised them and chatted among themselves.[3] The streets were cleaner than I remembered, and more businesses had opened in the area. There were also fewer empty spaces between buildings and little sign of the commercial sex-work and nightclub scene that had previously flourished around Al Rolla Street. This was now a solidly middle-class South Asian neighborhood, one that left me wondering what had happened to the lower-income people who had occupied it just eighteen months before, and how middle-class people like Gautam and his family were coping with the rising costs of living in this boomtown city.

While foreign-resident Indians in downtown Dubai were in many ways substantive citizens of the city-state, their existences were becoming increasingly tenuous with Dubai's boom at the beginning of the twenty-first century. Two distinct Dubais were being produced at that time, the two "Creek worlds" I moved between during my research: one was the new "global city" of cosmopolitanism and heritage-for-consumption marked by Dubai's boomtown development projects, like the Madinat Jumeirah and its reproduction of traditional Dubai; the other was the increasingly segregated downtown core of what I call "old Dubai" and the forms of mercantilism and Indian Ocean cosmopolitanism it represented. In this chapter, I explore the physical reorganization of the city into these distinct spaces and delineate my particular "field" and the interlocutors that occupied that field in relation to this shifting geography. The particular elisions built into governmental rhetorics and technologies of Dubai's boom illuminate the lived experiences of belonging and exclusion among the Indian communities of downtown Dubai.

The process of circumscribing and producing an anthropological field through daily activity and movement within space highlights how spaces themselves are products of social invention and interaction, and how "cities," as seemingly bounded entities, in fact contain within them a multitude of sites that are experienced differently by differently situated actors, and that in turn interpellate different citizens.[4] At the time of my research, the signifiers *migrant*, *expatriate*, and *local* circulated widely in Dubai and other Gulf cities to mark particular spaces and who could occupy them, who was visible and who was invisible, who was new and who was old, who was permanent and who was temporary, and which bodies contributed to national development and which ones threatened it.[5] While most residents of the city were considered to fall into the triptych of local, expatriate, or migrant—and most of the city's emerging geography delineated distinct locations for these populations—my interlocutors, the spaces they inhabited, and their everyday practices of belonging were not easily contained by this division.[6] The result of the shift away from oil and maritime trade and the focus by the global media on Dubai's "newness" meant that the communities of the Dubai Creek area and the forms of cosmopolitanism they represented were increasingly becoming what Yasser Elsheshtawy has called "forgotten places," and that the everyday lives of the primarily middle- and working-class Indians and other foreign residents who occupied these spaces were mostly elided in state and media representations of the city.[7]

The specific spaces that make up my field site—the neighborhoods of "old" Dubai—are not meant to be revelations of an authentic city that countersupposed postmodern "nonplaces" of shopping malls and hotels, but neither are they more fractured or partial than representations of the city that privilege more hegemonic national, religious, gendered, economic, or ethnic narratives.[8] My argument is therefore informed by anthropological and cultural geographical work on cities as spaces of belonging and exclusion. In particular, following scholars like de Certeau, I consider both how citizenship is a technique of spatial organization and how legal categories of citizenship may not map onto forms of lived urban citizenship that take place at the scale of everyday life.[9] Thus, the shifting geographic aspects of the city and its demographic mappings have to be explored in conjunction with projects of governmentality in order to understand how citizenship in Dubai takes place at several scales and in different forms, particularly among its long-standing Indian majority population.

New Dubai and the Production of Global Futures

The two photos below, taken nearly twenty years apart, chronicle the fast pace of development at the previous outskirts of Dubai on Sheikh Zayed Road (see figures 1.2 and 1.3). From the top of the World Trade Center building, the photos look south, away from the downtown core of the city, toward Abu Dhabi. Additionally, the computer-generated "satellite map" below, produced in 2005 by the Dubai Municipality, projected what Dubai's development would look like moving into the twenty-first century, most of which was focused on building up the spaces of New Dubai, seen to the left of the Dubai Creek, along the south shore of the emirate (see figure 1.4).[10]

These images, taken together, detail how Dubai's downtown was shifting in the mid-2000s, away from the Creek area that was historically its mercantile center (seen on the right side of the map just to the left of the not-yet-existing Deira Palm project) to what used to be the outskirts of the city and is now called New Dubai.[11] This shift, which occurred despite the failure of many of the proposed projects, represented the Dubai government's focus on producing a "global city" through large-scale development projects, tourism, free zones, and multinational corporate investment. The spectacular and exceptional spaces meant to increase Dubai's international recognition—Palm Tree islands, the sail-shaped Burj al-Arab

FIGURE 1.2 · Sheikh Zayed Road from the World Trade Center,
early 1990s. ©Gulf News, Dubai.

FIGURE 1.3 · Sheikh Zayed Road from the World Trade Center, November 2012.
Photograph by Nitin Gogia.

FIGURE 1.4 · Computer-generated "satellite map" of Dubai's projected development, produced in 2005. Source: burjdubaiskyscraper.com.

(which was once on all Dubai license plates), the Burj Khalifa (the tallest building in the world), an indoor ski slope, the free zones of Dubai Knowledge Village, the Dubai International Financial Centre (DIFC), Dubai Media City, and the World islands—are located for the most part between Jebel Ali, the industrial free zone on the road to Abu Dhabi, and the World Trade Center, the vantage point of figure 1.2, and effectively the previous external limit of the city.[12] While the newly opened (but not fully completed) Dubai Metro and the recently instituted Salik toll-road system have made significant improvements for connecting "new" and "old" Dubai, at the height of my fieldwork, in 2006, these spaces were becoming increasingly distanced by wealth, nationality, temporality, forms of capital, and traffic congestion. While these are not distinct spaces by any means, the shifting urban center of the city—from the neighborhoods around the Dubai Creek to the business, tourism, and residential areas of New Dubai —signified the emergence of new forms of cosmopolitanism, governance, and subjectivity in the city, and also served to marginalize certain groups while centralizing others, both national and foreign resident.

While large-scale development and tourism projects did not focus much on the neighborhoods of Bur Dubai, Deira, and Karama, where I conducted most of my research, the people who lived there were substantially affected by inflation, rising rents, longer commute times, and shifts in their positions along geographic, social, and work hierarchies in the city. While many of my informants moved between these spaces in their daily lives, as did I as a researcher and foreign resident of the city, these spaces signaled different forms of belonging and exclusion for the Indian diaspora, which located its cultural and social centers of daily life primarily in the neighborhoods of downtown Dubai. These neighborhoods and the people who populated them were becoming increasingly isolated from both the "global city" models of neoliberal development undertaken by public-private conglomerations in Dubai and by projects of heritage and nationalism through which Emirati pasts and futures were narrated and performed. In particular, the kinds of cosmopolitanism signaled by Dubai's boom hailed as "expatriates" certain foreign subjects who contributed to the city's growth even as they produced anxieties about the erosion or Westernization of Emirati national identity.

The Dubai government website explains that the emirate has established e-government services to "ease the lives of people and businesses interacting with the government and [to] contribute in establishing Dubai as a leading economic hub."[13] This statement summarizes the Dubai government's primary interest in economic development as well as its attitude toward the foreign investors participating in economic-development projects. The government is therefore focused on facilitating certain types of expatriate economic belonging, and this is done through a range of neoliberal strategies. In fact, Sheikh Mohammed has often said that he is not the ruler of Dubai as much as its CEO, highlighting how he uses business models to shape his governing decisions. Many of Dubai's residents share this sentiment as well—that Dubai is what Kanna has called a "city-corporation," and what government and corporate interests have labeled "Brand Dubai."[14] The Madinat Jumeirah complex is one of many large development projects within the city-corporation of Brand Dubai, and it represents the Dubai government's goal to establish itself as a regional trade and tourism hub as well as a "global city."[15] However, creating a global city requires not only increased foreign investment but also large numbers of foreign workers to build and manage the city, adding to a demographic imbalance that has worried the Gulf States since the discovery of oil and the fast pace of development that ensued. At the time of my research, it was estimated that anywhere from 80 to 90 percent of the UAE population was noncitizen, and these numbers were growing due to the increasing need for construction work, hotel and restaurant staff, managers, IT experts, and others to create, manage, and run the boomtown projects that were being undertaken so rapidly, especially in the emirate of Dubai.[16]

Given the government's stance on the importance of luring foreign business, it might seem contradictory that Sheikh Mohammed's Dubai Strategic Plan for 2015, introduced early in 2007 in a speech entitled "Dubai . . . Where the Future Begins," lists as its first objective "Preserve National Identity." In his plan, Sheikh Mohammed stresses the need to maintain a balance between national identity and international business, arguing that Dubai as a "global city" is not a threat to national identity, but rather that "adopting best global standards and practices is the only way to preserve national and cultural identity."[17] The Sheikh's balancing act between satisfying the needs of global business and assuaging the insecurities of nationals is clear in this speech, and he leverages the language of minimal government interference in market processes to do this. These two seemingly contradictory goals—the development of a future-oriented international and cosmopolitan city, and the preservation of a pure, "traditional" national identity—are compatible in Sheikh Mohammed's view because Dubai's economy can be open to noncitizens while Emirati national identity remains impervious to foreign influence. Thus, the government actively promotes heritage projects and protonatalist policies, closes off possibilities for foreign residents to naturalize or reside permanently in the country, and produces versions of Emirati identity and culture that are purified of foreign elements but also attractive to tourists and investors. For example, all migrants in the United Arab Emirates, as in other Gulf countries, are governed through an individual-sponsorship (kafala) system, whereby citizens sponsor foreign residents for renewable temporary visas of up to three years, either as employers or as 51 percent partners in businesses.[18] This means that foreigners, even those born in the UAE, are under temporary or dependent status and are not legally able to naturalize or reside permanently in the country.

While the majority of foreign residents were from South Asia, newer immigration patterns from East and Southeast Asia and from Europe, South Africa, North America, and Australia were contributing to a racial and ethnonational hierarchy in which whites and Gulf Arabs generally made the most amount of money in well-placed managerial positions, while Asians, Africans, and non-Gulf Arabs tended to make up most of the middle and working classes in the city.[19] The wealthier "expatriates"—the foreigners hailed by Sheikh Mohammed and by business and tourism ventures—played a significant role in the liberalizing reforms of the state, particularly in the Dubai context. In fact, my research indicates that the production of a neoliberal economy in which expatriates were kept satisfied and given increasing "rights" was integral to the maintenance of the legitimacy of the state's welfare-based citizenship system and the purity of national identity. Both state and private enterprises praise Dubai's "multicultural" and "international" environment and leverage the number of nationalities and cultures present in the emirate in order to lure foreign businesses, tourists, and workers, marketing Dubai as a global city that is in fact more "global" than its competition. However, multiculturalism as it works in the production of Dubai as global is both posited as part of Dubai's post-oil present *and* relegated to the realm of the economic, distinctly outside of national identity. In addition, by producing certain areas, such as Dubai's many "free zones," which operate under different juridico-legal structures than the kafala system and other regulatory regimes that govern foreign residents in the UAE, the state goes even further toward maintaining this balance while allowing for certain forms of noncitizen belonging.

The UAE government has been implementing neoliberal policies since its inception, in 1971, and has in the last two decades taken several steps toward increasing opportunities for foreigners to benefit from and contribute to Dubai's economic boom. The UAE is free of sales and income tax, and the government has produced new investment opportunities, mainly for foreigners, through free zones. Dubai opened its first industrial free zone in Jebel Ali port in 1980, formalizing the emirate's history as a "re-export" center for the Indian Ocean and the Middle East and North

Africa (MENA) region through a legally and spatially distinct area outside of the city center that offers 100 percent business ownership, minimal duties, and relaxed rules governing work visas and business set-up. Jebel Ali has been an incredible success, and in recent years the emirate has initiated several themed free-zone projects centering less on industrial sectors and more on investment, service industries, and new media. During my fieldwork, Dubai Internet City, Dubai Media City, DIFC, and the Dubai Multi-Commodities Center were operational, and other projects, such as Healthcare City, Knowledge Village, University City, Business Bay, and International City, were well under way. These free zones were attracting major multinational companies because of their relaxed structures. Not only did they provide fully furnished, turnkey offices for their clients, but free zones also operated to some degree outside of the parameters of the "Islamic principles" discourse that the UAE government deploys to justify censorship of media and other restrictions on personal liberties. For example, there was no Internet censorship inside free zones.[20] Additionally, newer free zones and developments were providing commercial and residential spaces for employees. In many of the newer zones, wealthy foreigners can own "freehold" property, which comes with a residence permit and a ninety-nine-year lease, meaning the owner would potentially not need to be tied to a citizen-sponsored work visa.[21] Thus, many expatriates in these spaces never had to leave the sanctuary of their immediate environs and be subject to the more restrictive laws of Dubai, a privilege that further contributed to the mapping of "expatriate" subjects onto particular geographies of the city.[22]

The boundaries of newer free zones and mini-cities, however, were not distinct. There were no checkpoints as there were in Jebel Ali, and when one was in a restaurant or hotel, it was not always obvious whether one was within a free zone. Often I learned that friends lived within the boundaries of a free zone only because they could access websites that I could not. I found it unusual, for example, that while record stores across Dubai black out the image of the Buddha on CDs put out by the popular Buddha Bar lounge (idolatry goes against Islamic principles), a two-story Buddha was built within the restaurant itself—until someone pointed out to me that the Buddha Bar and the hotel that houses it are actually located within the Dubai Marina, one of the newest and most mixed (in terms of commercial, residential, and business offerings) development projects in New Dubai. The exact investment "theme" of the Marina is unclear. It seems therefore to simply replicate what is outside of it in greater Dubai while engaging neoliberal forms of what Aihwa Ong calls "graduated sovereignty" for the benefit of expatriate residents and clients.[23] In this formation, the welfare state and the benefits enjoyed by UAE citizens are perfectly compatible with the ways in which foreign entrepreneurs are encouraged to settle in Dubai through "open" markets. The government, therefore, invests differently in different populations, providing welfare for its citizenry, while offering neoliberal economic belonging to expatriates.[24]

Selling Arabia: Producing Differentiated Foreign Subjects

Among foreign residents, certain populations get to be citizen-like stakeholders who are kept satisfied through neoliberal economic policies, while other populations are governed by disciplinary practices in which they know that their nationality determines the extent to which they have to police their behavior and speech. There are many ways in which Dubai's supposedly open economy differentiates between populations, and the UAE government has encoded differential governance of various residents and citizens even as it has made moves toward presenting itself as a liberalizing state. For wealthier expatriates, Dubai is alluring because it maintains positions of privilege, whether racial, national, or class, which they may find to be threatened at "home." For example, salary and benefit levels in the Gulf Arab States are often set by race and nationality, with white Europeans usually making much more for the same job than do other immigrants.[25] Additionally, geographic spaces in Dubai are often segregated by class and national background.[26] Brand Dubai is therefore marketed to a particular kind of foreigner: the upper-class—usually Western or white—tourist or expatriate who does not experience the negative effects of racial and class stratification in the UAE, but rather benefits from them. Though *expat* implies the foreign population of the country, it carries classed and raced meanings that privilege Western-educated, upper- or middle-class, English- and Arabic-speaking people who represent unmarked cosmopolitan or "global nomad" identities.[27] Thus, the scores of South Asian "migrants" who are the subjects of Human Rights Watch reports and government and private-sector efforts to "clean up" neighborhoods and malls in Dubai are not included in the definition of *expat* that circulates widely within the UAE.[28] These understandings of cosmopolitanism derive both from transnationally circulating discourses and forms of global capital and from local negotiations of various national and cultural identities. Projects and discourses of Dubai as a cosmopolitan global city combine with the production of a purified Emirati national identity to allow belonging for elite expatriates while continually erasing and denying belonging to migrant laborers, who are rendered both discursively and geographically invisible: they are relegated to work camps far removed from the social and commercial spaces of the city, and they are understood primarily through the lens of labor. The future of Dubai, therefore, is open to "expats," for they not only choose economic forms of belonging that are separated out from official Emirati identity, but they also participate in discourses and practices that preserve it. The "migrant," on the other hand, remains solely a temporary worker, and one whose perceived lack of hygiene, morality, and decorum threatens instead of contributes to the future of the nation.

Not only is the state invested in national identity and in policing the division between citizen and noncitizen, but national identity also serves as a way to increase revenue in the tourism and hospitality industries, growing Dubai as a global destination for foreign investment and travel, and producing forms of consumer belonging among citizens as well as expatriates. Corporate reconstructions of the UAE's past in the form of shopping malls, hotels, restaurants, souks, and desert safaris also participate in the production of national identity, engendering belonging among middle- and upper-class expatriate populations by providing access to "tradition" in the form of difference. Practices of foreign consumption of this heritage and identity, in turn, reinforce the notion of a narrowly defined Emirati nation. Traditional Dubai is sold to foreign consumers in the form of megadevelopment projects and tourist adventures that allow access to a supposedly pure Arab and Muslim "culture" without the inconveniences of stepping outside of a luxury lifestyle. These reconstructions of tradition for the purposes of consumption provide commodities for expatriate residents and tourists of Dubai that allow them to maintain a certain comfort level while also interpellating them into the production of nationalist discourses as privileged *outsiders* to the nation.

The Dubai Creek area in old Dubai is congested, contains many lower-middle-class Asian families and "bachelors" (the term for men who have migrated without their families, usually living in groups), and is full of small South Asian restaurants that are not allowed to serve alcohol. The

Madinat Jumeirah complex, on the other hand, located well outside of the congested parts of the city, in an area with many five-star hotels, shopping malls, and luxury residential complexes, offers a reproduction of the Dubai Creek within an environment sterilized of lower-class—often subcontinental—patrons. Restaurants lining the Madinat Jumeirah's Creek reproduction serve alcohol and pork products and provide other amenities that cater to the tastes of wealthy Western expatriates and tourists. The complex contains a reproduction of a traditional souk; however, instead of being a crowded market where customers feel harassed by pushy merchants selling low-end merchandise, this souk is air-conditioned and full of shops with attendants who speak English and sell designer clothing, art, and antiques at fixed prices. Madinat Jumeirah was one of the top destinations for middle- and upper-class consumers in Dubai at the time of my fieldwork, and it remains full of tourists and visitors even today, after the economic downturn of 2008. The complex—which has two high-end hotels that charge upward of $500 a night, several nightclubs that host world-renowned DJs (and are often accused of denying access to South Asian men), a plethora of bars, valet parking, and free *abra* (water taxi) and golf-cart service between venues—is owned by the Jumeirah Group, one of the city's major developers of luxury resorts. The Jumeirah Group owns several five-star hotels, as well as the world's only self-proclaimed "7-star" hotel, the Burj al-Arab. The Jumeirah Group is one of the public-private collaborations with connections to the royal family that exemplifies Brand Dubai and the model of "city as corporation" that Sheikh Mohammed has been pursuing for the emirate.[29]

The website for the Madinat Jumeirah resort features pictures of white women in sleeveless dresses shopping for ornaments, a white couple dining by the creek, and an abra shuttling yet another white couple around the resort (see figure 1.5). The text on the website, which is similar to the text on many other web pages for resorts in Dubai and the UAE, reads, "Madinat Jumeirah, The Arabian Resort of Dubai, is a magnificent tribute to Dubai's heritage and is styled to resemble an ancient Arabian citadel. Luxurious and ornate, combining the height of opulence with an overwhelming sense of tradition." The imagined consumer of this resort and others like it, as indexed by Madinat Jumeirah's websites and promotional material, is a wealthy white European or American.

The Madinat Jumeirah is by no means unique in its marketing or aesthetic; there are scores of activities and sites in Dubai and in other

FIGURE 1.5 · A photograph the Madinat Jumeirah uses on its website to advertise its souk. Source: The Jumeirah Group.

parts of the Gulf that use traditional culture, Arab hospitality, and Western amenities to sell national identity as a commodity. The Emirates Group (another hybrid state and private corporation), for example, runs Arabian Adventures, a wildly popular desert-safari expedition that features belly dancing, Arabic food, *shisha* (flavored tobacco smoked from a water pipe), henna "tattoos," dune bashing, and camel rides. Many high-end restaurants and hotels, unlike other restaurants and hotels in Dubai, feature employees wearing traditional Gulf clothing, and other luxury hotels recuperate colonial nostalgia for consumers through valets and attendants dressed in outfits resembling those worn by "natives" during the time of the British Raj.[30] In Al Qasr, one of the Madinat Jumeirah hotels, the valets and doormen are seven-foot-tall African men dressed in turbans and carrying swords. Thus, "Arabian" hospitality is also a hospitality through which certain tourists and expatriates can experience white privilege and revisit a fantastic colonial past.

Products and experiences marketing traditional "Arabian culture" often focus on the Dubai Creek as a major symbol of Dubai, and on souks, hospitality, Arabic food, and shisha as symbols of the Gulf region. The Burj Khalifa complex also has a Creek reproduction called "Old Town" which includes a constructed souk, Souk Bahar. A mixed residential, commercial, and business free zone called "Culture Village," which is being planned by Dubai Holdings, features wind towers, a souk, and an educational mosque. And Ibn Battuta Mall reproduces the famous explorer's travels through pavilions featuring architecture and art from different countries mentioned in his journals.[31] In all of these cases, the tradition offered by development groups and corporations is a cosmopolitan commodity for (predominantly white) consumers who expect luxury surroundings, excellent service, and Western amenities. This is cosmopolitanism because it invites the consumer into difference, but a difference that is bridgeable. This is modernization, but interwoven with "tradition." And the tradition being offered is one that mirrors the representations of Emirati history and national identity produced by state projects, one in which cultural hybridity and non-Western cosmopolitanisms are erased in favor of Arab and Muslim purifications for the benefit of privileged foreign consumption.[32] Expatriates who frequent places like Madinat Jumeirah can participate in forms of consumer belonging that do not challenge but instead replicate state-sponsored versions of national identity—versions that allow for a past and future for Emirati "culture" and "tradition" that remain separate from the foreign presence required to build Dubai.

Within this formation, cosmopolitan discourses and practices enter Dubai through elite Western subjects following oil and the growth of Dubai's tourism sector. Cosmopolitan subjects therefore do not challenge but rather prop up the divisions between citizen and noncitizen that frame nationalist discourses in the UAE. The global city that Sheikh Mohammed has billed as "Where the Future Begins," therefore, relies on these models of traditional pasts and the people who populated pre-national and pre-imperial Arabia even as it recuperates a modernized colonial nostalgia to market a luxury experience for expatriate consumers of Brand Dubai.

❦

Making Purified Pasts:
Heritage, Citizenship, and National Identity

The strong demographic imbalance between citizen and noncitizen, as well as the many forms of "Westernization" in terms of architecture, tourism, and economic growth around the UAE, has led to active measures by the government to police the boundaries of citizenship more closely, and to define Emirati national identity as homogenous, timeless, and implacable in the face of perceived foreign threat. Many Gulf Cooperative Council (GCC) states have actively undertaken projects to Arabize culture, producing narratives of tradition that are purified of foreign influence and encouraging citizens to distinguish themselves from the West and from migrant workers through markers of traditional identity.[33] The triptych of residency in contemporary Dubai—expat, migrant, local—relies on certain productions of the past that erase earlier cosmopolitanisms in order both to produce a strong imagined community of Emiratis and to place cosmopolitanism and the presence of foreigners into a timeline that coincides with oil and post-oil development. The UAE government, along with public and private corporations, attempts to produce national identity and the image of a homogenous citizenry not only in relation to foreign residents but also from within the heterogeneous history of Indian Ocean cosmopolitanism that underpins the contemporary UAE and its supposedly autochthonous population. There has been, for example, a strong push over the past few decades to "renew" traditional activities such as falconry, camel racing, and forms of dance; to build and promote heritage projects; and to discourage foreign marriage and promote higher native birth rates.[34] These productions of national identity hinge on the elision of the Gulf's long-standing engagement in networks of trade and more intimate connectivities across the Indian Ocean, both before and during European imperialism in the region. Emirati identity, therefore, is solidified through a double move—the production of cosmopolitan futures and the erasure of cosmopolitan pasts.

In contrast to the narratives about homogenous autochthonous pasts favored by Emirati and corporate revivals of tradition, Indian Ocean historiographers have traced vast networks of communication, travel, and exchange between Asia, the Middle East, Africa, and the Mediterranean back to before the arrival of oil or European presence.[35] These works highlight kinship networks, religions, and languages that stretch across continents, indicating that the pre-oil cultures of the Gulf and coastal South Asia were anything but homogenous and providing openings for academic approaches to cosmopolitanism and diaspora that provincialize Western mobilities. This body of literature draws on administrative, trade, and travel documents to directly challenge the idea that empire and oil were the catalysts for Indian Ocean trade and cosmopolitanism. Additionally, these texts show that trade and travel were not limited to professional traders; instead, many people dabbled in these activities to meet expenses, while others were forced to participate in them as slaves. In the context of the Indian Ocean, Europeans were actually seen as interlopers trying to penetrate an already active market, and it has been argued that the British discourse on "piracy" in the Indian Ocean and Arabian Gulf was actually a political excuse to cement control over this trade.[36] The Gulf, therefore, was cosmopolitan long before the discovery of oil and also long before European "world travelers" appeared in the region. Instead of considering Middle Eastern and Asian cosmopolitanisms as derivative of Europe and the West, these histories directly challenge anthropologists of the Gulf to reframe our thinking—what happens to our "field" and to our modes of inquiry if we consider the Gulf and the Indian Ocean as *originally* global, prior to state formation, colonial contact, and "globalization"? In particular, a study on contemporary South Asians in a trade port like Dubai is reconfigured through understanding the long-standing connections between the two regions.[37] This challenges researchers to question the possibility of exploring distinct racial and ethnic identities in places like the Gulf seaports. Who was a South Asian and who was an Arab during the long period of pre-European maritime trade in the Indian Ocean region? These texts seriously dispute the idea that Europe's (and anthropology's) "other" was ever bounded by culture or territory.[38] In addition, they allow us to question the newness of the subjects and objects of globalization, and how these subjects are represented as "new" within media and state discourses about Dubai.

Prior to the arrival of the Portuguese and then the British, pearling was the major industry in the Gulf. Many families spent months apart during the pearl-diving season, and divers lived in a cycle of constant debt, diving to pay off money owed from the prior season. The Gulf was not as wealthy or as developed as its neighbors across the sea, India and Iran. Indian and Iranian merchants (who traded pearls, dates, and other Gulf items from Bombay and other coastal cities around the Indian Ocean) had branches in the Gulf and often lent money to divers and pearling ship owners. Thus, Indians in the Gulf were sometimes seen as exploitative. However, India was also considered a cultural center for the Gulf—people who had money traveled to India when they could, Indian goods were coveted items, and Hindi and Urdu were widely spoken. These long-standing networks of trade and communication in the Indian Ocean region became formalized and entrenched through the Trucial Agreements imposed by the British government on Gulf sheikhs. Under Trucial Agreement with the British empire, trade activities were limited to British colonial holdings, which further intensified connections between South Asia and the Gulf. With the arrival of the British and the establishment of treaties that restricted trade, the Indian presence in Arabian port cities grew, as did the Gulf's dependence on the subcontinent. Treaty agreements between the British Raj and Arabian Gulf sheikhs were in place as early as the 1820s, and an exclusive treaty agreement was in place by 1892. The imperial relations between Gulf leaders and the British reveals quite a bit about the heterogeneity of identities in the pre-oil Gulf. First of all, "locals" were by no means united: some tribal leaders were anticolonial and resisted the British government; others were forced to comply with Indian and British demands; and others were supportive of and friendly with Indian merchants and colonial officials. Those who were settled along the coast distinguished themselves from nomadic peoples from the interior. Bedouins were often in tension with merchants, who symbolized debt and poverty for them; merchants often grew wealthy at the expense of poorer groups, including Bedouins. And sheikhs were beholden to several sets of rival interests, as well as to pressures from various outside tribes and governments. Foreigners already made up a large proportion of Dubai's population—25 percent of the 20,000 in 1939—before the discovery of oil.[39] Trade and oil, which was first struck in Bahrain in 1932 and led to full-scale oil prospecting among British and American interests, further increased this proportion. The stratification of different communities in Dubai today is derived from these prior tensions and forms of exchange. However, these historical and contemporary connections and tensions are mostly omitted from common discourses surrounding national identity.

THE MAKING OF TRADITION

The framing of culture and tradition in government discourses and markers of tradition produces a picture of pre-oil Gulf society as homogenous and tribal, despite the historical transnational connections between the Gulf and other parts of Asia, Africa, and Europe, and it explains the contemporary citizen-noncitizen imbalance in terms of post-oil development.[40] Major sites for the production of tradition in the UAE are heritage areas and museums that have been funded by the Ministry of Culture and by private corporate enterprises, which are often themselves partially owned or funded by the state, and that produce a version of Gulf heritage for consumption both by citizens and foreigners. Heritage sites in the UAE include the Dubai Heritage Village, the Dubai Museum, the Sharjah Heritage area, and the Bastakiya neighborhood of Dubai, among others. Museums and forts in every emirate display historical artifacts, many coffee-table books on Gulf history and customs are available for sale throughout the UAE, and in the past few decades "traditional" activities such as falconry, camel racing, and sword dancing have experienced a revival.[41] Also, both government and private interests are invested in archaeology of the region, and archaeological documents and items are used as evidence of an Emirati culture that predates history. The prehistory of the UAE is now written as far back as five thousand years, documenting a society called Dilmun, which, like the Emirates of a few decades past, was known for exporting pearls and dates.[42] Through architecture, language, objects, and performances of cultural identity, heritage sites participate in the production of an Arab and Islamic picture of both Dubai's history and the UAE's national identity, creating what Benedict Anderson calls an "unbound seriality" of nationalism, to which all citizens can theoretically have access, out of the heterogeneous reality of "bound" identities, which have uneven relationships to the state.[43] These performances, sites, and productions pay little attention to the cosmopolitan history of settlement and trade in Dubai, which underpins the history of the Indian commu-

FIGURE 1.6 · Dubai Heritage and Diving Village. Photograph by Nitin Gogia.

nities that are the focus of this book, and which accounts for the differences between citizens themselves in the contemporary UAE.

In the Shindaga region of Dubai, at the mouth of the Dubai Creek, is the Dubai Heritage and Diving Village, a government-funded tourist attraction that includes reproductions of old homes, restaurants, and shops, attempting to re-create the feeling of life in Dubai before modernization (see figure 1.6). The building in figure 1.6 is meant to be a traditional Emirati home, with wind towers to circulate air and, though not visible, a central open courtyard in which the family and servants can congregate and perform housework. The Dubai Heritage and Diving Village reproduces historic Dubai for visitors through these buildings and through live craftspeople, who prepare traditional bread, weave baskets, offer camel rides, and sell Bedouin jewelry and clothing.[44] Similarly, the newly refurbished Bastakiya area of Dubai, much of which was gifted to Iranian merchant families by Sheikh Rashid, houses several museums on Arabic calligraphy, architecture, and history, as well as cafés, restaurants, art galleries, and a hotel for tourists (see figure 1.7).[45] As in the Heritage and Diving Village, in Bastakiya visitors can experience buildings with wind towers, smoke shisha in outdoor courtyards, and learn about old Dubai by

FIGURE 1.7 · Lane in Bastakiya. Photograph by Nitin Gogia.

FIGURE 1.8 · Al Fahidi Fort. Photograph by Neha Vora.

visiting various cultural centers. Bastakiya, however, is not old as tourist guides might imply, but rather is a project undertaken by the Dubai government to produce a reproduction of tradition with amenities designed to lure foreign consumers.[46]

Just up the road from Bastakiya is the Al Fahidi Fort, now the site of the Dubai Museum, which offers a re-creation of an old Emirati house and *majlis* (council chamber), archaeological findings from around the Gulf, and an interactive area with scenes of life in "traditional" Dubai, complete with merchants' shops, pearling boats, and women in Bedouin dress (see figure 1.8). The fort as a symbol of Gulf tradition is particularly interesting, for it places buildings that were at the edges of the coastal towns and meant to defend against the interior at the center of Gulf history, thus asking tourists and nationals to look at culture and heritage as more connected to the Arabian Peninsula than to the Indian Ocean.[47]

The influence of South Asian, European, African, and Persian items such as rugs, clothing, jewelry styles, and food, along with the presence of British and other imperial officials during this period in Dubai's history, is mostly missing from state-sponsored heritage projects like the ones I have introduced. Visitors are not informed that the teak wood used for doors and window frames came from India, that pottery clay came from Iran, that there is a strong African influence in "Arabian" music, that falcons for the national sport of falconry were caught in Pakistan, or that "traditional" henna designs originated in the subcontinent. While the Dubai Museum acknowledges that foreigners play a role in the UAE by displaying a striking contrast of images from pre- and post-oil Dubai (similar to the images of Sheikh Zayed Road), this representation again produces a causal narrative that links the presence of foreigners in the Gulf to oil discovery. Their presence is thus an inconvenience to be tolerated for the moment and not the result of a longer history of trade, colonial influence, intermarriage, slavery, and migration across the Indian Ocean.[48]

Possibly the most strongly deployed marker of national identity, however, is the national dress that has become common for all Emiratis and is encouraged by state leaders and also sold as a commodity in high-end shopping malls across the country. Emirati men wear *dishdashas* (long, white robes) with *kandouras* (white headscarves secured by a black rope), and Emirati women wear *abayas* (long, black cloaks) with *chelas* (black headscarves). In fact, national dress distinguishes an Emirati from a non-Emirati (and a Gulf Arab from a non-Gulf Arab) more reliably than do skin color, language, facial features, or mannerisms, which range widely. But national dress, like national identity, is a modern formation; not until the 1970s did it become common for citizens to mark themselves off from noncitizens in this fashion.[49] As James Onley has explored, many different forms of clothing existed in the Gulf prior to the formation of the GCC states.[50] It is through the purification of cultural hybridity in the form of dress and other visible signs of "foreign" influence that national identity was produced and continues to be reinforced in the Gulf. In addition, the current version of Emirati national dress would not have been worn by all Emiratis in the past, as certain jobs were physically impossible to perform in the white dishdasha that men wear today. The dishdasha is therefore a symbol of class status that, while defining the distinction between Emirati and non-Emirati, also erases prior distinctions between Emiratis themselves.

These historical, sartorial, and performative markers of citizenship imply a homogenous and timeless quality to Emirati national identity. While the "imagined community" is one of unbound seriality, however, in practice citizenship benefits are uneven and the category of "local" contains within it several stratifications and hierarchies.[51] First, citizenship is patrilineal and operates through laws of *jus sanguis* rather than *jus solis*, so in order for one to be a citizen of the UAE, one's father has to be a citizen. In some instances, however, Emirati men marry women from other parts of the world, usually India, Pakistan, Bangladesh, Indonesia, or the Philippines. These marriages are not uncommon, especially among less wealthy Emiratis or those taking a second wife, because the *mehr*, or bride gift, is much cheaper in the currencies of the women's countries than it is in UAE dirhams.[52] Divorce in these cases, however, poses significant problems for wives and children. On divorce, foreign women can be subject to deportation; thus, marriage in these situations is not necessarily a path to citizenship. And children from these unions can be easily denied by their fathers and therefore denied access to the benefits of citizenship, or they can be kept by their fathers while their mothers can no longer legally reside in the country. In contrast, when Emirati women marry non-Emiratis, their children are usually unable to claim UAE citizenship at all, and if they do receive citizenship, they may still be denied access to the welfare benefits of Emirati nationality. In order to curb foreign marriage, the UAE has set up a "marriage fund" that grants nationals access to a lump sum of cash if they marry other citizens.[53] In some Gulf countries, like Bahrain, foreign marriages must be approved by the state and are much less likely to be allowed for women than for men; and in Kuwait, citizen women married to foreign men are at risk of not being able to sponsor their husbands and children. Gender is therefore extremely important to the process of citizenship in the GCC countries, and citizens are governed differently based on gender. Even though the discourse surrounding national identity suggests a homogenous national "family," foreign marriages continue, and they remain a source of anxiety for the state.

Citizens also face other processes of differentiation based on ethnicity and family history. In the UAE, this is most apparent in the distinction made between "nationality" and citizenship. Having UAE citizenship—holding a passport, for example—does not guarantee the generous welfare benefits that the state promises. Instead, one must also have a nationality card, which requires a family book proving Emirati lineage. Without a nationality card, one can hold UAE citizenship (as do many naturalized Palestinians and Yemenis, for example), but cannot obtain free health-care, free schooling for their children, housing allowances, and other state benefits. This works toward creating a hierarchy among citizens in which certain populations are privileged as more pure than others.[54] The sup-posed "Arab" racial purity of the Emirati national family is easily chal-lenged, of course, just by looking at the variety of people who claim UAE citizenship. Race, ethnicity, tradition, history, and kinship as modes of identity production therefore fall short and are difficult for the state to fully leverage in nationalist discourses.

Not only is there a historic trade connection between the Arabian Gulf and South Asia, but there are many more intimate connections that be-come invisible through a focus on the public sphere of economy and politics.[55] Within the home, South Asian nannies, maids, and other house-hold workers were (and are) ubiquitous, and they are often the primary source of nurturing and education for Emirati children.[56] Many Emiratis grew up with Indian or Pakistani teachers, doctors, advisors, and em-ployees surrounding them. Until recently, too, India was a favored site for higher education and a primary source for popular culture; many Emirati boys, for example, were sent to India to spend four years at university in Indian classrooms with Indian peers. Thus, the labor of Indians and the influence of India was present at every level in the production of Emirati citizens themselves. The very acts of nursing, nurturing, cleaning, teach-ing, and healing Emirati children, and thus reproducing the next genera-tion of citizens, has for generations fallen to South Asians as well as to others from around the Indian Ocean area. These intimate connections, and not simply "trade," account for the fluency Emiratis exhibit in South Asian languages, their knowledge of Indian pop culture, their taste for Indian food, and their familiarity with the subcontinent. Until very re-cently, when Filipinas and other Asians have begun taking over domestic work, and universities have opened in the Emirates, Indians and India played a primary role in the formation of what we call the "Emirati." It is this hybridity that has been so difficult for the state and other institutions to erase, and it is this hybridity and not the threat of "Western influence," which is another dominant discourse in the UAE, that is an unnamed yet forever present challenge to current constructions of national identity in the Gulf States.

The hybridity that comes out of Indian Ocean cosmopolitanism can be seen most strongly not in the purified reproductions of tradition in New Dubai and the heritage sites around the city, but rather in the hustle and bustle of daily life in the older neighborhoods surrounding the Dubai Creek, where the ways in which India has always been a part of Dubai are showcased in merchants' historical memory, in the languages and mannerisms of the people, in the products and services offered in this area, and in the very physicality of architecture and unplanned constructions.[57] Deira, for example, on the Dubai Creek, is a thriving souk area with small shops that sell electronics, spices, gold, and dry goods. As one of the oldest and most congested parts of Dubai, Deira is also one of the few places in the city where rents are not quite as inflated, and where working-class "bachelors" can still afford cafeteria-style meals and chai served in small plastic cups.[58] In Deira the discovery of oil has not had much impact on the day-to-day trade practices of independent merchants and small family businesses. The shiny Chamber of Commerce building, five-star hotels, and many international banks are located in Deira, and there is a glaring and growing disparity between street life (which consists of bartering, small businesses, groups of unskilled South Asian residents, and commercial sex-work) and high-rise life (where well-to-do expatriates move from air-conditioned homes to air-conditioned cars to air-conditioned offices and restaurants). However, old wooden dhows still offload goods from around the Gulf, businesses that date back to the early 1900s are still in operation, Arab merchants still refer to money in terms of rupees and paisa, and Indian families live in apartments they have inhabited for several decades. Everywhere one looks, if one looks closely enough, there are traces of the thriving, cosmopolitan, pre-oil trade port and particularly of the intense levels of connection between the Indian subcontinent, Iran, and the Arabian Penninsula. It was within places like Deira that my Indian interlocutors were living urban citizenship. The older, more entrenched communities of Dubai—historically South Asian, but marked by a sense of permanent temporariness—were mostly left out of government and media accounts of Dubai's boom, and they were largely ignored by corporate and state discourses and practices designed to both hail certain "expatriates" into the emirate, while also demarcating them from "locals" and from the "migrant laborers" who were building the spaces of New Dubai. The everyday practices, affects, and concerns of Indians in old Dubai, however, pushed against the triptych of resident categories that seemed to define Dubai during its boom and that continue to circulate today as primary forms of identification and categorization in the emirate.

Conclusion

"Expats," "locals," and "migrants" are produced as distinct populations in Dubai through deployments and erasures of cosmopolitanism. While identities are indeed fluid and difficult to pin down, these three categories are generally used by government discourses, commercial enterprises, individual residents, and media sources to identify and self-identify different people who live in the Gulf Arab States and the geographic spaces they occupy within Gulf cities. In the case of Dubai, the "other" to national identity is not the cosmopolitan wealthy expatriate, because this subject is offered belonging through consumption of Brand Dubai and through opportunities for business investment in the emirate. "Expatriates" are the subject of multicultural discourses by the state and in fact reinforce state and corporate nationalisms. The others to national identity are instead "migrant" laborers, who are necessary evils of development, demographically larger in number, yet socially and culturally insignificant. Therefore, the working class is not the target of Brand Dubai's message of internationalism and multiculturalism, but rather is considered the dark underbelly of the glistening city; media representations of Dubai, state discourses, and, more recently, blog postings lament this supposed contradiction between a luxurious city and the exploited workers who are building it. This is not a contradiction, however, but a fundamental necessity in the production and maintenance of narrow definitions of belonging in the UAE. The "migrant," particularly from South Asia, must be produced as invisible and as outside of society in order to maintain the illusion of a purified national identity—and he (or she in the case of domestic workers) must be placed historically into a timeline where the presence of the foreign coincides with oil. To acknowledge the long history of South Asians in the Gulf is to allow space for both past and present forms of hybridity and cultural exchange, which may create a crisis in what Ahn Nga Longva has termed an "ethnocratic" system, where political participation and belonging is determined primarily by ethnicity and nationality.[59]

The South Asian diasporic communities that populate the neighborhoods around the Dubai Creek, which have a historical engagement with the Gulf that precedes both oil and colonialism, do not overlap neatly with the subject position of the migrant laborer, who is necessary for the development of Brand Dubai but rendered physically and socially invisible through labor camps, uniforms, and regulations around which spaces he can occupy. Nor are Indians in old Dubai easily defined as expatriates, for this category privileges the experiences, skin color, and supposed cosmopolitanism of newer Western arrivals lured by the business incentives and tourist experiences of Brand Dubai. The South Asian diaspora of the previous downtown center of Dubai is both transient and historically entrenched within spaces that are becoming increasingly forgotten by this triptych classification of Dubai's residents and the temporalities of belonging and exclusion that they have come to represent. The Dubai Creek area and its residents, if discussed at all in media or travel-guide representations, become "exotic" spaces and peoples that tourists and other Dubai residents can visit.[60] The people who reside in these neighborhoods are both disadvantaged and able to move between Dubai's many worlds, as with Gautam and his family, who spend most of their lives within the radius of a few blocks but are able to save enough to "travel" to luxury development sites on special occasions to consume the spectacles of Brand Dubai. I now turn in greater detail to the Indian diasporic neighborhoods of the Dubai Creek, focusing on the hybridities and forms of belonging and exclusion that permeate the daily, lived experiences of citizenship among the residents of these communities and on the ways that Dubai Indians experience old Dubai both as an Indian city and as diaspora space with community and identity formations that are distinct from those found within the Indian nation-state.

2 · AN INDIAN CITY?

DIASPORIC SUBJECTIVITY AND URBAN
CITIZENSHIP IN OLD DUBAI

Indians in Dubai, both in relation to the Indian state and to the scholarly literature on transnational migration, do not fit easily into the category of diaspora. As Avtar Brah and others have argued, the concept of diaspora is not applicable to every journey, every group that travels, every movement across or within borders. What is notable about diaspora, she says, is that "diasporic journeys are essentially about settling down, about putting roots 'elsewhere.'"[1]

Since that "elsewhere" is usually achieved in the diaspora scholarship through voluntary migration and naturalization in Western countries, liberal forms of citizenship become the ends through which diasporic subjectivity is operationalized. Indians in Dubai challenge this normative understanding of diaspora in many ways. First, they both have and have not "settled." They have formed specific communities that are and are not distinct from India. They are and are not hailed by the Indian state's recent efforts to include its diaspora in the nation. They are not a minority population, yet they exist in a racialized and economic power hierarchy with those who are considered native. And, perhaps constitutive of all of these conditions, Dubai is in several ways not "elsewhere" due to the histories of power, migration, and cultural exchange across the Indian Ocean. In addition, two of the hallmarks of diasporic identity in the academic literature—nostalgia and hybridity—are largely missing from the narratives of Dubai Indians. Thus, the scholarly approach to migration as a rupture that leads both to nostalgia for "homeland" and enculturation into "hostland" is not adequate for understanding Indians in Dubai and their experiences.

Indian communities in Dubai are entrenched as well as transitory, maintaining constant connections to India while also thinking of Dubai as home. Indians experience Dubai not as a hybrid elsewhere, but as a space infused with Indianness and not fully distinct from the subcontinent, and this is particularly true of the Indian-dominated neighborhoods in old Dubai. India is *generated and lived* on a daily basis in old Dubai, as is evident in the texture of daily life within its neighborhoods and in how these spaces are—and are made into—distinct sites of urban citizenship. The movement within and between places in old Dubai constituted forms of Indian community and identity for my interlocutors. In its neighborhoods, residents (including myself) regularly spoke South Asian languages, consumed South Asian products, operated within the unpredictable temporality of what many of us jokingly called Indian Standard Time, and participated in South Asian social and cultural activities. Old Dubai was therefore experienced, despite the state of permanent temporariness in which foreign residents lived, as an extension of India. Its neighborhoods were largely familiar and comforting spaces for the Indians who lived, worked, and socialized there. Dubai's proximity to South Asia and the ubiquity of South Asian peoples, products, and cultural events, combined with its luxuries, higher standards of living, and increased cleanliness, led many to characterize the city as "a clean Bombay" or "India's westernmost state." The narratives, affects, performances, and experiences of Indians in old Dubai produced what Roger Rouse has called "an alternative cartography of social space."[2] My interlocutors often conflated old Dubai with all of Dubai and the UAE while also adamantly referring to the newer parts of town as foreign spaces, in effect pushing against the recentering of the city that had taken place over the previous ten years. The day-to-day world-making in these neighborhoods both blurred the line between Dubai and India and pushed against the more hegemonic national and international narratives of the cultural, geographic, historical, and demographic character of the emirate.

Indians in the downtown neighborhoods of Dubai are not easily definable as either "migrant laborers" or "expatriates," the most readily available categories through which noncitizen residents are made intelligible in scholarship, media, and government discourses about the city. In fact, the middle- and working-class Indians who occupied the downtown neighborhoods of Dubai in the mid-2000s were not privy to the luxuries and amenities of New Dubai and its wealthy "expatriate" clients, nor were they isolated like many low-wage "migrants" in work camps segregated from the city's centers. The cost of living in this area at the beginning of this century, however, was rising rapidly, despite the fact that its pace of development and change was nowhere near that of New Dubai and other parts of the city. Thus, while they were by and large left out of Dubai's boomtown projects, Indians in Dubai were in many ways the most impacted by them. My interlocutors felt left behind by Dubai's as well as by India's recent economic growth, both of which increased their ambivalences about migrating to Dubai, heightened their awareness of the differences between various Dubai residents, and awakened criticisms of the Indian state's privileging of certain parts of its diaspora while largely neglecting its nonresident Indian population in the Gulf. This twofold experience of Indians within daily life in Dubai's downtown neighborhoods—feeling more Indian than other emigrants and less Indian than those who live in India—challenges our understandings of the Gulf and South Asia as distinct areas of anthropological research and provides different narratives of emigrant life from those found in other studies of diaspora, particularly from the West. Ironically, as my interlocutors' stories bring into relief, it was the overwhelming *Indianness* of Dubai that framed Dubai Indians' experiences of liminality—as Indians, as emigrants, and as foreign residents in the city. Old Dubai was therefore a place of both intense belonging and intense exclusion.

India Extended: Geographies of Similarity and Difference

To fly from Delhi to my hometown it will take almost a day. From here, within five hours I am home. This is closer to home than some parts of India. For me it is an extension.—RAJESH, 32, *civil engineer, Kerala*

For many scholars who relocate to urban areas for research, the process of field-making begins with and is often shaped by the first few days and weeks in the city—the search for an apartment, finding the nearest grocery store and best eateries, mapping the easiest way to get from point A to point B, establishing contacts and making friends, and getting a feel for the ebb and flow of daily life in one's neighborhood and for the best hours of the day to conduct research, socialize, and run errands. In most parts of Dubai, residents think of the city as a series of distinct sites between which one commutes: from airport to apartment, from apartment to work, from work to the mall, from the mall to dinner with friends, and so on. The practice of commuting itself, often in air-conditioned cars, taxis, or buses, is therefore not as much a part of the process of living as it is a means toward an end.[3] The neighborhoods of Dubai where I lived and conducted the majority of my research, on the other hand, were marked by a vibrant street life in which the very movement within space—usually on foot—was integral to the formation of neighborhoods, social networks, and sense of community.

In contrast to New Dubai, downtown Dubai, where the majority of my interlocutors lived and often worked, displays a slow development and spread of urban space, starting with the congested alleyways and streets surrounding the mouth of the Dubai Creek and extending into more formally planned spaces like Al Karama and Golden Sands, which once constituted the "suburbs" or wealthier edges of mercantile Dubai. These neighborhoods house residential buildings, retail shops, wholesale trading markets, and an extensive range of other businesses, primarily based in the trade of South Asian and Iranian products, which still arrive daily on wooden dhows along the Dubai Creek. Services in downtown Dubai cater mainly to South Asians and include restaurants, money exchanges, night-clubs, beauty parlors, Internet cafés, Indo-Pakistani groceries, and other shops that sell a range of South Asian products and services. These neighborhoods are also some of the only walkable spaces in the city, and many people who live in downtown Dubai walk to and from social events, work, doctor's offices, grocery stores, and other activities. In addition, the paved walkway along the Bur Dubai side of the Dubai Creek is one of the only remaining places for public congregation in Dubai, as most parks require entry fees; on cooler evenings, many people can be seen taking exercise or just hanging out along the Creek (see figure 2.1).[4]

Navigating these neighborhoods without a level of familiarity is diffi-cult, as streets and alleyways are rarely called by their names and, unlike the high-rise spaces of New Dubai and Sheikh Zayed Road, not all build-ings are familiar to taxi drivers, delivery people, or even residents. While some historical and "heritage" tourist sites, like Shindaga, Bastakiya, and the Dubai Museum, are located here, these neighborhoods are rarely fre-quented by wealthier Westerners, who consider them "exotic" destina-tions for occasional tourism, and not integral to their experiences of living in Dubai.[5] As a researcher and resident, the act of walking through my day—both literally and figuratively—constituted my field site, teaching

FIGURE 2.1 · Hanging out by the Dubai Creek on a Friday. Photograph by Nitin Gogia.

me about the rhythms of daily life in the neighborhoods of old Dubai and allowing me to establish my own social networks and forms of belonging to the city.

During the first few weeks of 2006, when I was staying with Gautam and Reshma while searching for an apartment of my own, I began the process of field-making by moving through Bur Dubai with the family. My first Saturday in Dubai coincided with the beginning of the workweek for Gautam and the end of a school holiday for their young son, Vijay. I woke to the hustle and bustle of the family's morning routine. Gautam was simultaneously trying to talk Vijay into getting ready for school while shaving and dressing for work in the bedroom, and Reshma was preparing breakfast and saying her morning prayers in the kitchen, where she had a small Vishnu shrine. She played a tape of *bhajans* (Hindu devotional songs) while she conducted her morning routine. After breakfast, Gautam left for work and Reshma and I walked Vijay to his preschool, which was across Bank Street from our apartment building.[6] On the corner before we crossed, we ran into a woman with her two daughters in tow, a friend of Reshma's from college, a Muslim Bombay-ite who had only recently arrived in Dubai, and Reshma stopped for a quick conversation in Maharati.[7] After dropping Vijay off at school, where we chatted with a few other mothers about upcoming birthday parties, we ran some errands together, both Reshma's and mine. First, we walked around the corner to a passport photo and "Arabic typist" shop in order to get my paperwork for my residency in Dubai. As an American citizen, I was on a ninety-day tourist visa but needed a sponsored residency in order to stay longer and conduct research.[8] Typist shops and other services geared toward the needs of non-Arab migrants pepper the neighborhoods around the Dubai Creek, with signage in English as well as Hindi, Urdu, and Malayalam. After taking care of photos and collecting forms, we headed back across Bank Street to an Indian grocery, Choitram's, near the apartment. When Gautam got home, at 7 PM, we all headed to Al-Fahidi Street in Meena Bazaar near the Creek, where there is a Hindu temple and a Sikh Gurdwara off of the souk area.[9] After purchasing flowers in an alley with shops selling Hindu postcards, figurines, incense, flowers, and other devotional items, we deposited our shoes and climbed up to the temple floor, which was bustling with people. Prayers completed, we took *prasad* (sweets distributed to worshippers leaving the temple), then greeted at least a dozen family acquaintances on our way out. Though the day was organized around a couple of events, it was peppered with detours, lingerings, and small social interactions with other neighborhood people. This ordinary day highlights how the process of daily life and community-building were intimately tied to the geographic movement through the spaces of old Dubai, movements usually made on foot and not always with a clear focus on the destination. It was the journeys themselves that co-constituted identity, community, and space.

Middle- and working-class Indians in Bur Dubai and its surrounding neighborhoods are in many ways the quintessential Dubai residents; with a population of over 1.5 million, Indians form the largest national group in the UAE, and with other South Asians they make up the majority of the population and workforce.[10] Over two-thirds of the Indian population in Dubai resides in rented apartments, mostly in the densely populated city center.[11] While classified as temporary by the Emirati government, Indian communities in Dubai are well established and the Dubai Creek area has housed South Asian businesses and South Asian migrants for over a century. My informants considered these spaces mainly as extensions of India; in fact, many people felt that it was precisely the Indianness of Dubai that made it a favorable destination for migration. Thus, even though

Emirati national identity and citizenship were inaccessible to them, it was the access that Indians had to cultural and social resources in Dubai and the sheer number of South Asians in the city that made moving there seem less like international migration and more like being in another part of India. Charlie, for example, related his first impression of arriving in Dubai over ten years before: "My cousin lived in Karama and it is *all* Indian over there. In Bombay you see the railway quarters, Karama is like that, all the same buildings, same style, same, you know, clothes hanging in the balcony, wires dropping all over the place, and so you think, 'This is Bombay. This is India.'" Similarly, Bharati, who grew up in Delhi but whose family is originally from South India, explained that Indian cultures and languages are so prevalent in Dubai that she learned Malayalam after she arrived there. She also described Dubai as an extension of India, saying, "Dubai is close to India, an extension of India. Lots of Indians here, you don't miss India." The overwhelming Indianness of Dubai meant that, unlike in other diasporic locations, my conversations with my interlocutors in Dubai were not marked by nostalgia for homeland. While people certainly missed friends and family, they did not feel a lack of cultural resources or even a loss of community in Dubai.

The Dubai Creek neighborhoods offer many cultural activities and social clubs for Indians and Pakistanis of every region, language, and religion. When I interviewed Janice, a Christian woman in her forties from Pune, in a small office in Karama where she worked as a real-estate agent, she told me that not only were her social activities Indian-dominated, but her work life was as well: "Even now I talk, I deal with mostly Indians. Everywhere it is Indian. You don't really feel like you are going to another country. You don't miss Indians or India. Yes, you miss your roundabout or buildings or people. You are just out of India but you are in India. . . . Dubai is an extended city of India." What made these neighborhoods of Dubai feel like "home" and "extensions of India" for Charlie, Bharati, and Janice was the constant traffic in people, goods, and information between India and the Gulf. They, as well as several other interviewees, pointed out that Indian matrimonial sites even include the Gulf, and especially Dubai; families considered Gulf residents to be appropriate, perhaps even desirable, potential mates for their children, in part because living in places like Dubai was not seen to dilute Indian cultural values or to cause much "culture shock." Strolling through Meena Bazaar's retail areas, for example, one can hear Bollywood ringtones on cell phones, smell food cooking in small *dhabas* (Punjabi restaurants) and *chaat* (South Indian snack food) places, see Hindu deities displayed in stores and offices, and observe a wide cross-section of South Asian consumers, from women in saris shopping in groups for fabric, to British-Indian tourists bargaining over electronics, to Afghani and Pakistani men in pajama kurtas shopping for simple gold chains and bangles to send home. According to Janice, her fashion choices were still dictated by what was happening in India because the most current items from Mumbai and Delhi were always available in Bur Dubai's shops.

Dubai's closeness to India and intense, ongoing exchange across the Indian Ocean combined with my interlocutors' sense that Indian cultures and languages were in many ways accepted and integrated into Emirati life, particularly in old Dubai. They claimed they were not affected by Emirati culture except in "small" ways—following a different workweek, observing restrictions on eating in public during Ramadan—that they considered merely inconvenient, not challenging to their Indian identities. When I asked if Emiratis had been affected by Indian culture, however, all of my interviewees said Emiratis have been greatly impacted by Indian languages, food, dress, and popular media, and that they speak Indian languages sometimes better than they speak English. According to Indians in Dubai, "locals" speak Hindi, Urdu, and even Malayalam, local women love to wear Indian jewelry and salwar-kameez under their abayas, and Emiratis have a particular passion for Indian music and movies. The saturation of Emirati daily life with Indian popular culture can be seen throughout Dubai: first-run Bollywood films play at almost every theater; Indian television shows and channels abound on satellite television; and there are dedicated Hindi and other Indian-language radio stations. Money is still referred to as *rupiya* and *paisa* by older Arabs, and almost every hotel in the city contains at least one Indian restaurant. Jayant, a friend of Gautam and Reshma, called me of his own accord to request an interview once he learned about my project. He was adamant in our discussion that what makes Dubai—and by Dubai, it became apparent, he meant Bur Dubai, where he had lived for over twenty years—feel so Indian is that Emiratis have embraced Indian culture.

Did you see yesterday's Gulf News? They interviewed Emiratis about Indian movies. Emiratis have mentioned that they like to see Indian movies. It is fun for them. Emiratis enjoy Indian culture. They love

Indian food, you will find them in Indian restaurants on the weekends. They like to indulge in Indian culture, they would like to marry into Indian women, they would like to have contributions in Indian culture, they will mix together. . . . You find a lot of Emiratis who are speaking Urdu or Hindi. They enjoy spending time with Indians. Yes, when you think of living your life in Dubai, it helps to be an Indian. Most people speak the language, even Emiratis.

Although Dubai Indians felt that locals had absorbed their culture and language, particularly the older and less wealthy Emiratis who tended to live among them, they overwhelmingly thought of New Dubai's spaces as foreign, not only because they were difficult to access in a city with rapidly increasing traffic and no reliable public transportation, but also because, above all else, they were not South Asian spaces. Thus, while my interlocutors described Dubai as South Asian in their narratives about daily life, this "Dubai" was segregated and self-contained within the downtown areas and did not include newer parts of the city. In fact, the Dubai Marina, Jumeirah, Sheikh Zayed Road, and the city's various new free zones were just as "exotic" to my interlocutors as the Dubai Creek neighborhoods were to those who lived in New Dubai. In addition, these newly developed destinations were spaces that were infused with both anxiety and desire. The hotels, malls, nightclubs, and neighborhoods of New Dubai made many people uncomfortable, even though some worked there and others occasionally traveled to them to see new attractions, like malls or hotels, when they opened. Many nightclubs and shopping malls in New Dubai discriminate against South Asian "bachelors," and several of my middle-class informants and their friends felt uncomfortable going to these places. For example, Anita, a twenty-four-year-old office worker who grew up in Sharjah, said, "Most of the Indians are around Meena Bazaar. Most of Dubai is still very Indian. I would maybe not be as comfortable in the Greens or Jebel Ali, where there are more Europeans." And Charlie told me he mostly hung out in Bur Dubai and Karama, but was not comfortable in "New Dubai, Springs, Meadows, all white skin in those areas, they all look at you like what are you doing over here?" While some wealthy Indian socialites had chosen to move out of old Dubai, especially to areas near Jumeirah Beach, the Vohras—a wealthy Punjabi family who lived in Deira—had stayed in the same building for over a decade because of their sense of familiarity and comfort there. In fact, elite, middle-class, and working-class informants living in downtown Dubai all thought of Dubai's newer spaces as foreign.

My informants' experiences of Dubai as an Indian city thus centered on certain South Asian–dominated neighborhoods. Yet the residents of these neighborhoods used "Dubai" interchangeably to refer to particular neighborhoods, the city as a whole, the country, and even the Gulf. The slippage Indians made between Indian neighborhoods in Dubai and all of Dubai was a product of their own contemporary frame of reference and also of a long historical memory among Dubai's Indian community—one in which the heart of the city lay with the Dubai Creek. Newer areas were foreign not just to my informants, but also to Dubai. In stark contrast to diasporic communities who refer to "little India" in their respective cities, my informants claimed all of Dubai as first and foremost Indian cultural space. Their naming practices and the slippages within them produced the Indian-dominated neighborhoods around the Creek as the center of town as well as the "true" Dubai from which everything else has emanated. Calling these spaces "just like India" and the most authentic "Dubai," my informants often slipped between claiming old Dubai and the city or the emirate as a whole as Indian space. This imagined Indian Dubai, with its center in old Dubai, thus resisted government and corporate attempts to purify the city-state—both geographically and ideologically—of Indian historical and contemporary elements. Dubai's Indianness did not, however, preclude experiences of marginalization or hardship for its largely Indian middle-class downtown population. In fact, during the mid-2000s, the residents of downtown Dubai were largely removed from the benefits of megadevelopment and were experiencing rising insecurities around employment, remittances, and quality of life. Not only did my interlocutors not fit into the emerging dichotomy of "expat" or "laborer" that categorized foreigners in Dubai at the time, but their geographic and demographic liminality led to stark feelings of exclusion, both within the social hierarchies of the city and at the hand of the Indian state.

Neither "Expat" nor "Laborer"

During one of our very first meetings, Gautam encouraged me to consider moving to Dubai semi-permanently: "You and your husband would have a great life here in Dubai with your American passports. They give you everything if you are an American—a good salary, nice accommodations, even a car and driver! You would be living very well. You really should come." He told me that in just a few years in the Gulf I could save a lot of money for my future. I asked him about his life as an Indian expat: had he been able to live better in Dubai than in India and to save money as well? "No, not Indians," he said. "We don't have that kind of employment. But you are an American. You would love it here." Gautam's comments spoke to a system of migration, employment, and residency in Dubai that was very much dictated by nationality. While Gautam and my other interlocutors often faced financial insecurities and migration costs that exceeded those of their peers from Western countries, they also articulated urban citizenship and certain forms of privilege in Dubai that their low-wage Indian compatriots, particularly those who lived in labor camps removed from the city center, did not. Thus, middle- and working-class Indians in old Dubai fell somewhere between the categories of "expat" and laborer" through which foreign residents are most often understood in the emirate. In addition, while Dubai's boom was highly lucrative for many wealthier Western expatriates and for citizens, South Asians and other residents of the downtown neighborhoods of Bur Dubai, Deira, and Karama were facing new struggles and insecurities and were in most cases remitting less than they had before, due to increased costs of living. Not only were these neighborhoods becoming more segregated from the newly developed areas of New Dubai, but the people that lived there and their historical connections to the emirate were in a state of heightened uncertainty due to their increasing alienation from the rest of the city.

The quality-of-life differences between South Asian and Western expatriates are not only the result of a hierarchy of employment opportunities based on nationality, but are built into the process of migration itself. Unlike most Europeans and North Americans, South Asians need a visa to enter the UAE even as tourists, so they cannot stay in the country unless they are employed or are a dependent of someone employed there. This means that residency in the country is almost completely reliant on maintaining a steady job. Many Indians in Dubai procured employment through recruiting companies while still at home, a process that required giving large sums to headhunters for paperwork, visa processing, and travel expenses. Others arrived in the UAE on a visit visa to look for a job, then had to fly back home and return on a proper work visa. On arrival in the UAE, many of my informants had their passports seized by their companies (as protection from flight) and sometimes also found that salaries were lower than promised or garnished for a range of added expenses, resulting in a debt situation that prevented them from saving and remitting what they had expected for several months or even years.[12] Foreigners who cannot obtain a visa on arrival must return immediately to their home country for a minimum of six months on losing their job before they are allowed to apply for new employment. If a foreign resident tries to switch positions without the current employer's permission, s/he can be put on a "black list" that leads to deportation and the inability to land another job in the country.[13] Because of these rules and restrictions, South Asians are constantly and strategically maneuvering between the subcontinent and the Gulf as part of the practice of Gulf employment. This movement adds to the transient nature of Dubai's Indian communities, but also to the constant sense of connection that makes the Dubai Creek neighborhoods feel like extensions of India.

Companies in the Gulf often set pay scales based on country of origin, not on skill level. This was particularly true during my time in Dubai, though it has changed somewhat due to the UAE government's efforts to improve the migration system, especially for low-wage workers from Asia.[14] Employment ads at that time would openly advertise a preference for employees of certain nationalities, and accounts of job discrimination based on nationality or race were rampant in expatriate Internet communities, letters to the editor in newspapers, and day-to-day conversations among foreign residents of the city. Employers paid South Asians significantly less than they paid Westerners for the same jobs, usually without any of the housing, schooling, or other benefits that were normalized into the job offers that most North Americans, Europeans, white South Africans, and Australians received. Citizens of the UAE, even those who were less qualified, received some of the highest salaries, and companies were required to hire at least a certain proportion of citizens or pay higher fees for each employee's visa.[15] This set up a highly stratified racial, ethnic, and class system in the UAE, which spilled over into the social and cultural lives of my Indian informants, particularly at a time when megadevelopment projects and pushes for multinational investment were invested in "Westernizing" the face of Dubai by drawing in more white expatriates.[16] Thus, South Asians in Dubai lived within a tiered hierarchy of migration and employment where they had the least job security and the highest financial strain at practically any skill level and rank, whether office clerk or executive. The logic behind this system of employment, which also disadvantaged other Asian, non-Gulf Arab, and African groups, was that migrants were temporary and that they remitted all of their earnings. Therefore, they were paid according to the standard of living in their home countries, since they supposedly made more money in the Gulf than they would at home, but did not spend their money within the Emirates. This reasoning, however, actually produced remittance and saving differences based on race and nationality that were quite the opposite. While remittances by UAE Indians total over two billion dollars a year through official banks (and much more through unofficial streams), and while most of the Indians I spoke to were earning more in Dubai than they could in India, they were remitting only a small amount of their salaries.[17] In addition to the extra costs they accrued through the migration process itself, by having to rent their own apartments, pay for their children's schooling, cover transportation costs, and live without health insurance, most Indians in Dubai actually spent the majority of their income *inside* the UAE, which they often referred to as "indirect taxation" in our interviews.

That Indians and other non-Western groups accepted "indirect taxation" as part of the process of migration to Dubai challenges the popular conception of the UAE as a tax haven where these foreigners migrate solely for economic reasons and with no intention of settling. Moving to Dubai requires a considerable investment of time and money. Foreigners must pass a health exam, including an HIV test, in order to get residency. They must also undergo security screening, including retinal scans and fingerprinting. Every process that foreign residents in the UAE face, from opening bank accounts to setting up Internet access, requires extra fees, passport photos, and other time-consuming and costly bureaucratic steps that are not common practice in most people's home countries. A driver's license, for example, requires the applicant to complete expensive driving courses, in addition to passing an eye test and paying license fees. This means that mobility in Dubai is very much determined by nationality as well as class, particularly since Indians, unlike many Westerners, cannot acquire international driving permits prior to arrival and also cannot take unpaid time off to attend driving classes. Therefore, many Indians did not have cars, instead walking as much as possible and sometimes taking buses or informal taxis to get around town. The difficulty and expense involved in obtaining a driver's license and owning a car was one reason that South Asians, along with Filipinos and other lower-paid national groups, tended to segregate into tightly bound and densely populated geographic spaces. Western expatriates, in contrast, are provided with assistance at almost every level of the migration process, and many expenses—such as housing, moving costs, schooling, transportation allowances, healthcare, and visa fees—are included in their employment packages. Therefore, they often manage to save significant amounts of money in just a few short years in the Gulf, as was the case with many of the American and European expatriates I encountered during my time in Dubai.[18]

The insecurities of migration to Dubai and the UAE are shaped not only by nationality, but also by gender. For one, certain countries, such as Pakistan, do not allow single women to emigrate, and other countries, such as the Philippines, actively encourage women to migrate to the Gulf States. Therefore, demographically, even though the UAE is mostly male, it is imbalanced toward women among certain nationalities. Occupations in the UAE are often divided along the lines of gender and nationality as well, with companies actively recruiting employees from certain parts of the world for gendered occupations. The demographic of a particular occupation can shift rapidly, as employers look for cheaper sources of labor, or as middlemen establish new employment networks in different parts of the world. On repeat visits to Dubai, for example, I found that women workers in shopping malls had shifted from primarily Filipino to largely East African, and newer waves of construction workers were being recruited from Nepal and China instead of India. Once a man obtains residency in the UAE, he can sponsor his wife and children under his visa if he meets a minimum salary requirement.[19] Women, on the other hand, unless they are employed in certain high-level professions, like medicine, cannot sponsor family members. Often, companies have regulations against pregnancy among female employees, who are subject to immediate dismissal and deportation in the event. Fathers can sponsor their children under their residency visa, but boys can only be sponsored until they are eighteen years old or complete university; girls, however, can remain on their father's visa until marriage, at which time they can shift to their husband's visa. Thus, foreign resident women in the UAE are in a constant state of dependence, either on husbands and fathers, or on employers and home country regulations.[20]

South Asians in old Dubai, therefore, do not fit neatly into the category of privileged expat; nor, however, do they categorize themselves as migrant laborers or face the same challenges that unskilled or low-wage workers face. While economic and social divisions exist between Indians within the downtown areas, they are not as stark as the boundary between South Asians who live in labor camps and Indians in the rest of Dubai. For example, Jayant explained to me his take on how the Indian community in Dubai breaks down and how this affects where in the city people live and go.

NV: How does the community break down?

JAYANT: Yeah, economically. Four or five ways. Indian community that lives in labor camps. I doubt whether any of us gets to interact with them. . . . [T]hey lead their miserable life under-cared for. Nobody even knows who they are, where they are. Then another underbelly of Indians which serves the better-off people: office boys, watchmen, drivers, petty Man Fridays in shops, groceries, cafeteria. That is also a large chunk of people. Then clerical types in companies all over Sheikh Zayed Road or Deira or Bur Dubai. Then after a guy has been here five or six years, he is made a supervisor, and his salary just about crosses four thousand, five thousand, six thousand, and he is allowed to bring family, employer helps to cement bond further so he doesn't run away. Gets family status. There is that middle level. Transition between lower middle-class to borderline, but your wife has to work, can't have car and nice place on just your salary. Then middle guy, can classify by where he lives, probably lives in Sharjah, two-hour drive to work and back. Senior middle who works in Jebel Ali, Sheikh Zayed Road, has reasonably good income, and they stay in Bur Dubai, Karama, Deira. And of course there is this new league of people who are educated and are reaping the benefits of what other Indians have done by landing into jobs in Internet City, Media City, and they are living in Greens, Springs, Meadows, or New Dubai.

Jayant, like my other informants, reiterated the mapping of different classes and nationalities onto the geography of the city. The "new league of people" that Jayant referred to with disdain were professional expatriates entering Dubai with better pay and benefit packages than Indians already established in the city were receiving.[21] There was a general perception among most long-term Indian residents like Jayant not only that Westerners were doing better than they were, but that because of India's simultaneous economic rise, newly minted professionals on both sides of the Indian Ocean were much better off than those who had previously settled in Dubai. During the economic boom in 2006, when newspapers in the United States and the United Kingdom were running stories of expats who hit it big in the city, the Indian middle-class families I was interacting with on a daily basis in downtown Dubai were struggling more than ever, due to increased job competition and a higher standard of living. The costs for apartment rentals, food, parking, schooling, and other necessities had doubled or even tripled in just a few years, while most of my interlocutors had seen little increase in their salaries.

One afternoon in her Karama office, which overlooked a street packed with lunchtime traffic, Janice related the constant stress and worry that South Asians face in Dubai.

> Neha, you see, it's like this. Indians and Pakistanis when they come to Dubai they are healthy and fit, but when they go from here they either go in a wheelchair or in a coffin box. It's that highly stressful. Because of the expenses, from rent till petty expenses have doubled in last ten years. Especially those Indians Pakistanis who have stayed here, when they reach an age of sixty, they should retire by law. They start getting scared from sixty to sixty-five that their visa will not be renewed, that they will have to go back. Who will take care of their kids? This gives them a heart attack from the stress.

Due to the financial changes in Dubai, the perception that Indians remit the majority of their earnings was becoming less and less true, and the financial strain on foreign residents in downtown Dubai was impacting family relationships and people's sense of security in the emirate. Naveen, a civil engineer who had been raised in Dubai, completed college in India, and returned to Dubai in 1998, told me how, over the past few years, Dubai had changed "in leaps and bounds": "Ours was the only building on the street, now in three years, twenty to twenty-two buildings have come up. Growth is too fast. Rents are too high. Salaries are not keeping up with inflation. Everyone is suffering. We have seen people taking loans to pay rent. Parking is making everyone crazy. Four hundred to five hundred dirhams fine every month. No facility at all. Because of this inflation families are not having time for each other. Dad has two jobs, mom has to work, children and parents are suffering."

Despite the additional challenges faced by South Asians in downtown Dubai in comparison to expatriates living in New Dubai, and despite their rising costs of living, increasing insecurities and marginalization, and decreasing mobility in the city, these subjects continued to enjoy certain privileges that their less wealthy compatriots did not. In addition, while there were economic and social divisions between Indians within old Dubai, they were not as stark as the differences between Indians in old Dubai and the South Asians who lived in labor camps. My interlocutors practiced forms of diasporic and urban belonging, and they extolled the benefits of Dubai's amenities, luxuries, and cleanliness in comparison to India even as they lamented their sense of nonbelonging and constant state of temporariness in the Gulf. Indians in old Dubai, therefore, did not fit into either category—"migrant laborer" or "expat"—through which most foreign residents in Dubai seemed to be understood. Because the South Asian communities of the downtown neighborhoods of Dubai could not be neatly categorized, they were mostly invisible in governmental, journalistic, and scholarly accounts of the city. This liminality was not solely the result of Dubai's migration and employment system, however, but was also due to the way in which the Indian state hails certain subjects as part of its diaspora and effectively ignores others. Dubai Indians felt marginalized from the nation-state as well as from the rest of the diaspora in several ways. They articulated feeling left behind and ignored by the Indian government. However, regardless of their class status, they also pointedly did not refer to themselves as NRIS (nonresident Indians), a categorization that they reserved for Westerners like myself, people who had in their minds emigrated more permanently and left India behind.

Diasporic Identifications and Ambivalences

The neighborhoods of downtown Dubai are both extensions of India and spaces of diasporic community building, and both of these qualities enabled forms of urban citizenship for my interlocutors. The forms of belonging and identity experienced by Indians in Dubai resonated with as well as diverged from those found in scholarship about Indian diasporas in other parts of the world. These neighborhoods were spaces where people of different classes, religions, and regions came into contact and considered each other to comprise parts of a larger single Indian community, one that included, at times, non-Indian South Asians as well. Many of my interviewees tacked back and forth, for example, between a sense of diasporic community solidarity and national and transnational parochialisms through which they defined their social circles, potential mates, and the "quality" of the people who lived around them. Our conversations revealed a sense both of a single community and of several smaller ones, highlighting the way that identification and group boundaries were constantly shifting, negotiated, reified, and challenged—a phenomenon that anthropologists and others have observed among community formations in other South Asian diasporic locations, particularly in the West.[22] Despite my interlocutors' claims that Dubai was "just like" India, it was also a hybrid space for the production and performance of new identifications. Life in Dubai enabled diasporic affects and solidarities that were similar to those of Western South Asian diaspora groups, but Dubai Indians also articulated a vast divide between themselves and other overseas Indians. This sense of dissimilarity had to do both with Dubai's Indianness and with the perception that the Indian state cared less for its citizens in the Gulf than it did for its emigrants elsewhere.

Like Indian diasporas in other places, Dubai's Indian diaspora was a site both of new identifications based in the Dubai experience and of a reification of divisions between community members in the process of reproducing ideas about "home" and "nation." Naveen explained, for example, that while the Indian community was large and established, it was also deeply divided by religion, region, class, and length of stay in Dubai. The Indian community, he said, is a "very strong community. Large community and the oldest. But it is a toothless and very divided community. There is not [a] single entity and they have no singular representation. . . . [T]here are lots of formal and informal clubs based on economics, and then there are ethnic clubs based on religion or state that [an Indian migrant] comes from so at any given time he is having two to three affiliations."[23] But Naveen and others also emphasized feelings of community solidarity based on living in Dubai that bridged these gaps, solidarity that at times included other South Asians and at times did not. For instance, when I asked Gautam about Hindu-Muslim relations in Dubai, he said, "Indians will always help Indians. Not too much political-religious issues. Groups will have Hindu and Muslim friends and not much tension. Indians and Pakistanis do interact, but I think in the back of our heads they are always still Pakistanis." Sameera, a Pakistani woman I interviewed at a gold company in Deira, also talked about how Indians and Pakistanis were similar: "Indians in Dubai don't feel foreign [to me]. Eighty percent it is one culture. I have many Indian friends. Indian Pakistani we are like one." But she then, like Gautam, went on to emphasize that the two nationalities were also simultaneously different, saying, "Pa-kistani and Indian community are distinct. They do work and function separately but then they also come together really well."

Hindu and Muslim Indians also felt solidarity as well as difference with one another. While Muslim Indians expressed a sense of belonging to a transnational Muslim community (*ummah*), they also lamented the fact that they did not have the strong ethnonational social associations that their Hindu and Christian compatriots did. On the other hand, Hindus and Christians were often under the impression that Muslims from South Asia had advantages they did not and were able to assimilate with Emiratis, although no Muslim Dubai Indians confirmed this assumption. Hindu Indians in particular expressed differences between Pakistanis and Indians primarily as differences in religion; in so doing, they also participated in the process of reifying Indian identity as Hindu, even in a Muslim-majority country like the UAE. The length of time people had been in Dubai and their occupations also created cleavages in the community. Gautam elabo-rated on these differences, saying,

> First, Indians who have been here twenty-five to thirty years. [They are] almost a part and parcel of Dubai. They have been here mostly for business, they grew here, they have put in their money over here. Then the second class you will find people who have the second seat. The ones who have got appointed from India and they are staying here either in multinationals or in locally managed companies like Etisalat or Dewa. They are the second batch of Indians, salaried, they have their own way of life. Then there is a third grade of Indians, which you'll find the young Indians who had come after [19]85. I am in the last category, where Indians have heard that Dubai is a great place but by the time you got here you find that everything has gone on a bust and that is how you find Dubai.

Gautam's comments point to the historical presence of certain Indians in the Gulf, particularly merchants from western India, a presence that can be felt palpably in the neighborhoods surrounding the Dubai Creek. Middle-class Indians like Gautam felt that they were missing out on the perceived privileges and experiences reserved for those who had come to Dubai before and after them, especially as the housing and development boom made their costs of living increasingly difficult to manage.

While their simultaneous practices of community building and parochialism resonate with our scholarly knowledge about South Asian dias-poras in places like North America and Europe, my interlocutors were adamant that Indians in Dubai were not like those in the West at all. Primarily, Dubai felt less like elsewhere and more like an extension of India due to the historical entanglements between South Asia and the Gulf, the constant movement of people and goods back and forth across the Indian Ocean, the incorporation of Indian languages and cultural products into Emirati society, and the sheer number of South Asians in the city. This literal and figurative proximity made many Dubai Indians, de-spite the challenges they faced, feel that Dubai was a better migration destination than the West. Parents in particular were interested in raising their children with their values, and they felt that this was easier to do in Dubai. One afternoon, I was invited to lunch with Mr. Vohra and his family. Mr. Vohra was a business owner who lived in a fancy high-rise tower in Deira but still walked to his office near the gold souk and came home daily for lunch. He had two teenage daughters at home and an older son in college in the United States. With his wife and one of his daughters sitting around the table, he discussed raising children in Dubai.

> We are members of the India Club. We go probably four or five times in a year, only for the festivities. The girls like to dress up, we go all the seven nights for the *dandhya*. We have a Punjabi festival called *lori*, a harvest festival. For the last fifteen years all our friends get together in our house to celebrate lori, so it is an exposure we try to give them. I go to the temple every week. I go every Monday. She [gesturing to his wife] fasts on every Monday. If she can go to the temple, [that would be] good, at times we take the girls along. The Shiv temple in Bur Dubai. So we try to, twice a year we have the *havan* at home, after the *navratri*, us Punjabis we have the *ashtmi puja*, the eighth day, where we touch the young girls' feet, because we associate them with the *devi* [Goddess]. Everything we have back home we try to do it here.

My interlocutors cited the proximity of Dubai to India and the large number of Indians in the UAE as evidence of a stronger national and cultural identity among Dubai's Indian diaspora. However, the proximity of Dubai to India also meant that migrating did not feel like moving away, and Dubai Indians rarely expressed the sense of nostalgia or the anxiety over culture loss that scholars often associate with diaspora groups. Nor did Dubai's proximity to India create a situation in which the Indian state was somehow more interested in Gulf Indians than in those who had migrated further away; in fact, the Indian government's stance vis-à-vis Gulf Indians was quite the opposite. While my interlocutors most often referred to people like me—South Asians living in the West—as NRIS, this categorization does not apply to many South Asian Americans and was created specifically for Indian migrants to the Gulf. Created in 1973 by the Foreign Exchange Regulation Act, "non-resident Indian" status applies to Indian citizens who live abroad for a significant part of the year. They can, under this legal category, open bank accounts, deposit money through official channels, and own property. This law was designed to allow for greater remittances into India's struggling economy.[24] However, NRIS are not full citizens of India, for they cannot vote or have a political voice in the country under this status.[25] All Dubai Indians, because of their inability to naturalize in the UAE, are NRIS. In contrast, many South Asians in North America and Europe have naturalized. If they want citizen-like economic benefits in India, they can apply for PIO (Person of Indian Origin) status or, in some cases, for dual citizenship (Overseas Citizenship of India). Neither status comes with political citizenship rights. However, eligibility rests on having obtained citizenship—and therefore some level of political membership—elsewhere. It is the PIO who the Indian state is currently most interested in hailing as its ideal diasporic subject, a subject who can contribute to the country's economic growth while posing no threat to hegemonic understandings of Indian national identity as middle-class, Hindu, and patriarchal. In fact, some scholars have noted that Indian diasporas in the West are central participants in the production and preservation of this ideological Indianness.[26] In particular, the fact that those who migrated before 1950 or have previously held Pakistani (or other South Asian) citizenship are ineligible for PIO status reiterates this ideological investment by the state: Indians displaced into indentured servitude or into Muslim countries by partition are not welcomed into the fold of the newly imagined transnational India.[27]

Gulf Indians, in contrast to most other émigrés, have no permanent affective or political ties elsewhere in the eyes of the Indian state and thus do not have to be reincorporated into the nation. They are also, because of their time away from India and their ties to it, seen as a threat within the country. Indian gold "smugglers" from Dubai were considered a threat to postcolonial India's economy, for example, and the emirate is often associated with mafia and crime in Indian popular culture and discourse. While the NRI category was created by the Reserve Bank of India to make remitting easy for Gulf Indians, most of India does not want these emigrants to participate in the running of the country. It was not until 2006 that a bill was put forward to allow NRIS to vote. The popular backlash against NRI franchise was immense, and the bill has languished in committee.[28] The Indian state and Indians around the world conceptualize the "Indian diaspora"—what my interlocutors called NRIS—primarily through the figure of the North American, Hindu, male, patriarchal, upper-middle-class migrant and his dependent family members. Thus, regardless of their class status, those South Asians who are in the Western Hemisphere as a result of indentured servitude and those who have migrated to the Global South, such as South Asians in the Gulf Arab States, are not usually included in scholarly, state, and media representations of the NRI subject. Therefore, while the Indian government and Indian public culture view the Gulf in many ways as an extension of India, the people from South Asia who live there are perceived as seasonal, temporary, remitting migrants—and therefore not diasporic at all. This means that the Indian state, which is invested in neoliberal economic reforms and in economic and ideological investments by the diasporic middle class in Western countries, has for the most part neglected the needs of Gulf Indians, who are not hailed as ideal Indian citizens and whose specific concerns are often not addressed by consular programs.

Because the Indian economy relies heavily on remittances from Indians in the Gulf, and because Gulf countries are restrictive toward civil-society organizations, like Human Rights Watch, and NGOs, there is little formal organizing to assist Indians in Dubai in case of visa problems, arrest, deportation concerns, or abuse by sponsors. Many of my interlocutors were aware of the Indian government's passive stance toward its Gulf-based citizens and therefore did not expect that the Indian state would look out for their interests. They told me that overall the Indian state was less concerned about them than about "NRIS" in other parts of the world. The NRI categorization had, because of India's attempts to hail emigrant investment in the last few decades, come to represent those who were supposedly most successful abroad—professionals from North America and Europe—even though these groups had often naturalized in their migration destinations and thus were no longer technically nonresident Indians. Dubai Indians, who the category was meant to represent, rarely referred to themselves as NRIs, but rather told me they were simply Indians. Our conversations suggested, however, that they perceived themselves as both more Indian, in terms of cultural identity, than the rest of the diaspora, and less Indian, in terms of their relationship to the state, than Indians in India.

Over the course of several visits to the Indian consulate in Dubai, I met with a consulate worker, Mr. Roy, who was also a founding member of the Indian Association, a group of Indians who had organized themselves as a de facto replacement for the services usually offered by consulates. For example, they had created the Indian Community Welfare Organization to deal with issues concerning the labor force, housemaids, prisoners, and hospital patients, and to bring these issues to the attention of the local authorities and the Indian embassy. With over forty members who paid annual fees, the association had been operating for six years and was unofficially recognized by the Indian consulate in Dubai. However, its source of revenue was solely from community donations collected through fundraising drives, and it was supported financially by neither the Emirati nor the Indian government. Unfortunately, at the time of our meetings, the Indian Association was temporarily disbanded due to internal feuding, even though the volume of cases in the past year had risen. It was the only body of its kind doing work in conjunction with both the Emirati and Indian governments, and it provided services in place of both the home and host state. Mr. Roy told me that after thirty-five years, he felt more a part of Dubai than India. While India felt mostly foreign to him now, he also felt that "NRIs" from the West were very different than NRIs from the Middle East, mostly because in the Middle East there was no possibility of citizenship. A major failing of the Indian government, according to Mr. Roy, was that it did not adequately address the needs of its population in the Gulf, nor did it seem to want to. "Indians here are naturally returning Indians and more blue-collar while in the West they are permanent and professionals," he said. "The Indian government needs to address them differently, provide services instead of recruit money." This sentiment— that the Indian government neglected the specific needs of its Gulf population—was echoed by Charlie during a conversation I had with him over coffee one evening after he got off of work.

If I need help tomorrow, where do I go? Monmohan Singh [then prime minister of India] comes down here to meet expats, how many expats does he meet? Only the business guys, the rich guys. He is not meeting the laborers. I am in Alcoholics Anonymous. There was this thing in the Indian consulate, a day when they were going to have counseling. On a Thursday for four hours only. I called them and told them I wanted to help. I wanted to help and they acted as if I was intruding. I waited for an hour, and then they asked me all these questions. They gave me five minutes, said they will give me a call back. Never did. Then in Gulf News they said that the consulate had a very successful day with this panel, and that they had referred cases to AA, and they didn't call me at all. How can I even think that I will get help tomorrow? This is a fact that I face over here in Dubai.

Charlie pointed out that limiting the counseling sessions to a Thursday afternoon was essentially useless because Thursday was an official workday, which meant that most of the Indians targeted by this counseling would not be able to attend. The whole exercise seemed a futile one, more about show than about providing actual services. Like Charlie, many Dubai Indians did not consider the Indian government a source of help. It was therefore not just disenfranchisement that produced Gulf NRIS as second-class citizens, but their lack of access to the services provided to other citizens under the welfare state. Such inattention to the everyday issues faced by Indians in Dubai effectively removed them from diasporic subjectivity while including them within the rhetoric of the Indian nation; as part of India extended, but not as the privileged subjects of India's transnational initiatives, NRIS were expected to remit and maintain connections to "home," but were no longer under the Indian government's umbrella of care.

Liminal Diaspora, Liminal Nation

The older downtown neighborhoods of Dubai were in fact sites of everyday lived urban citizenship and belonging for Dubai Indians. The history of entanglement between the Gulf and South Asia, along with the experiences of constant movement of people, goods, and ideas back and forth across the Indian Ocean made for communities that were at once entrenched and transitory, extensions of India and spaces for new forms of identification and community-building. However, the difficulties of migration to the Gulf, the social hierarchies within which Indians lived, and the segregation of the Dubai Creek area from newer parts of the city also made the neighborhoods of old Dubai spaces where my interlocutors experienced and negotiated forms of exclusion. In addition, the uneven relationship between the Indian state and its overseas populations produced among Dubai Indians a sense of being simultaneously more Indian than other emigrants and unimportant to the Indian state. As the Dubai Creek area was becoming increasingly distanced from the rest of the city during Dubai's rapid development in the mid-2000s, Indians expressed increased anxieties about their quality of life and job security, but they also continued to claim Dubai as Indian cultural space, pushing back against iterations of the city that marginalized their existences. For Indians in downtown Dubai, the entrenched Indianness of the city easily coexisted with the ephemeral qualities of daily life that they experienced as so-called temporary migrants. This may seem like a contradiction: Dubai is *so* Indian that it does not feel like a different country, yet people cannot legally belong and are therefore "temporary." My interlocutors, however, did not experience this circumstance as a contradiction, because Dubai, while described to me as a place they did not belong, was also inside Indian national identity; even as they narrated their nonbelonging, middle-class Indians laid claims to Dubai as Indian cultural space above all else, and therefore described their reasons for being in the Gulf and their experiences there as impacted by more than just economic motivations. Although they considered Dubai an extension of India, they also mapped different national, racial, and class parameters onto the city's various neighborhoods. Thus, for my informants, Dubai as a whole was a site of belonging even as it included several spaces of nonbelonging. Space was thus a technology that produced both solidarity and difference across and between groups. It is through this understanding of belonging and exclusion as produced through place-making that Indians perform and articulate urban citizenship in Dubai. Their narratives, however, reveal that they are liminal to the Indian diaspora, to the Indian nation, and to the Dubai government's vision of the future.

Forms of belonging in old Dubai can be further understood by focusing, as I do in the next chapter, on one of its most entrenched groups, Indian merchants, who acted as unofficial citizens in Dubai while insisting that they had no interest in Emirati citizenship. Indian businessmen's forms of belonging to Dubai were changing in the early millennium due to shifts in Dubai's economy; the geographic and ideological move away from the emirate's mercantile past in the 2000s resulted in forms of nostalgia for a masculine Creek frontier of smuggling and illicit trade even as Indian merchants participated in producing Dubai as a neoliberal "global city" based in large-scale development and multinational businesses.

3 · BETWEEN GLOBAL CITY & GOLDEN FRONTIER

INDIAN BUSINESSMEN, UNOFFICIAL CITIZENSHIP,
AND SHIFTING FORMS OF BELONGING

One morning in March 2006 I sat at the large conference table that served as Mr. Soni's desk in Deira's gold souk. Through the glass divider that partitioned off his office, he could keep an eye on his traders while conducting several simultaneous meetings. I was there to interview Mr. Soni about his experiences as an Indian business owner in Dubai. Between more pressing appointments with key members of his staff, fielding phone calls in Gujarati, Hindi, English, and Arabic, and getting up to greet out-of-town customers, he told me about the gold industry in Dubai and the centrality of Indian businessmen, especially gold merchants, in putting Dubai on the map. "We built this country, you see," he said. "Dubai is rich today because it was a re-export center with no exchange controls or customs." Mr. Soni had been in Dubai for twenty-four years and was running the company his father had started in 1976. Many gold traders made their fortunes in Dubai back then, though much of the "re-exporting" was actually smuggling. "It was illegal to sell gold in India, but not illegal to send it from here. The Indian government says that no new gold entered the market during that time. How can that be true? Look at how much Indians are always buying gold for Diwali, for Eid, for weddings." Things had changed since the 1990s, though, due to the liberalization of India's economy and the lifting of gold controls. They were especially difficult at the moment, with gold prices at an all-time high. "People think less and less of gold jewelry as a store of value these days. Now it is all about diamonds and shopping malls and brands. We have to position ourselves differently."

Mr. Soni lamented the industry changes he had seen in his lifetime. What used to be an Indian-dominated market, he said, was now being taken over by locals, Iranians, and Syrians, and more recent changes in UAE business laws were even forcing him to hire Filipinos. His company had recently shifted production from India to the UAE to focus on styles that appealed to Middle Eastern and European tastes, and he was also a central participant in the Dubai Gold and Jewelry Group, an association of local merchants that had spent thirty million dollars in the last few years with the help of the Dubai government to brand Dubai as the "City of Gold" in order to draw more tourists into the once bustling souks surrounding the Creek. Despite these challenges, Mr. Soni insisted that his home was Dubai. Though his brothers in Bombay and Ahmadabad were currently thriving in the jewelry industry, he considered India a "holiday place," as did his children, and he stressed that it was India, not Dubai, that was a land of restrictions: "You never have a problem here as long as you look at freedom differently. . . . India is a country of restrictions. You don't miss the other freedoms it offers, to shout, to yell." Did he therefore consider himself an Emirati, I asked? Not at all, he told me: "I would not accept Emirati citizenship even if I could get it. I am an Indian tip to toe."

Like my conversations with Mr. Soni, my interviews with Indian gold merchants in the neighborhoods that lined the Dubai Creek contained within them disavowals of belonging to the Emirati nation, praise for the economic "freedoms" that Dubai offered, and claims to participation in a cultural and social milieu of mercantilism and trade that defined their identities as well as staked claims to Dubai's history. While gold-merchant narratives of Dubai's economic freedom seemed to resonate with the neoliberal global city model pursued by the Dubai government in the preceding decades, their nostalgic narratives of Dubai's golden past also gestured to the tenuousness of their positions as privileged expatriate subjects, and they recuperated masculine mercantile belonging in the telling of adventure tales about gold smuggling and re-exporting along the Dubai Creek. The colonial and postcolonial forms of Indian Ocean cosmopolitanism that Indian merchant narratives expressed, in which Dubai operated as a rugged lawless frontier of the subcontinent, both diverged from and overlapped with the forms of cosmopolitanism and neoliberal economic belonging available to wealthy expatriates during Dubai's boom period in the early millennium. The Dubai government's moves to shift the focus of its economy away from maritime trade networks into large-scale Western-style multinational development projects were threatening the forms of belonging that Indian merchants had carved out in the emirate during and after British colonialism in the region and before the liberalization of India's economy. However, Indian merchants were also to some extent part of these changes and acted as participants in the production of Dubai as an increasingly recognized international destination for trade and tourism. In addition, changes in migration and employment laws that resulted from Dubai's shift in economic focus simultaneously extended established patrimonial networks and challenged Indian merchant strongholds with regard to the gold industry and the Dubai Creek cosmopolitanisms through which they narrated their nostalgic belonging to the city.

Indian business owners, through their nostalgia for Dubai as a "golden frontier" of the subcontinent, interrupted hegemonic narratives of Emirati national identity and history as rooted in Arab and Muslim indigeneity, and in so doing claimed belonging to Dubai. Ironically, however, they were also integral to the legitimacy of the Emirati state through their practices of governance over other migrants. Indian merchants' affective and material practices and narratives therefore effectively produced them as unofficial citizens of the city. In three primary ways Indian merchants negotiated the multiple forms of belonging and freedom into which they were inculcated, particularly in terms of shifts away from the maritime trade history of re-export with the subcontinent toward global city models that focused on large-scale multinational development and tourism. First, Indian merchants' sense of belonging to Dubai was yoked not to their praise of the UAE's neoliberal economic "freedoms," but instead to a cosmopolitanism based in illicit maritime masculine trade, which they felt was disappearing in the city. Second, Indian merchants established their particular "freedoms" in the gold industry through political maneuverings with the state that maintained ethnic strongholds in the face of shifting forms of economic (de)regulation. Last, and perhaps most important, Indian merchants participated in the contemporary form of privatized, sponsorship-based governance (*kafala*) that defines Gulf migration systems. Kafala in Dubai, although thought to be in the hands of individual citizens, is in fact dependent on foreign resident managers and employers, who often act in the stead of citizens to perform the day-to-day practices of migrant governance that the Gulf States have designated as a civic responsibility of their citizens.[1]

Referring to my interlocutors as "Mr." in this chapter, as opposed to the first names I use elsewhere, is both aesthetically and politically deliberate.

For the most part, I addressed Indian merchants as "Mr." or, in some cases, "uncle." Such address indicates my own relationship to the merchants as a younger South Asian diasporic woman who was often treated in a paternalistic way, and it also reflects the highly masculine character of the souks, offices, and other venues within which I conducted this portion of my research, where I was often the only noncustomer female present. In addition, by using slightly caricatured industry surnames like "Soni" (literally "gold" or "gold worker"), I attempt to protect anonymity for a small community where merchants could easily be identified by more precise caste, regional, or religious markers.

Freedom, Cosmopolitanism, and Re-export: Indian Ocean Networks

Mr. Soni's insistence on Dubai as a site of freedom depends both on the differential forms of governance deployed by the contemporary Emirati government, which allow certain foreigners to belong through consumption, trade, and the accumulation of wealth, and on a nostalgia for a colonial and postcolonial past in which Indian merchants held privileged positions in relation to other expatriates.[2] In fact, his understandings of "freedom" as directly in contrast to postcolonial India's economic restrictions were a product of Dubai's historical economic reliance on South Asia and the nonliberal paternalistic ethnic networks that proliferated among Indian small business in Dubai, even though they were articulated in terminology that appeared to be consistent with the contemporary neoliberal discourses and practices of the Dubai government. There were therefore two competing but overlapping forms of economic freedom and cosmopolitanism circulating among Indian merchants in Dubai at the time of my research: the neoliberal global city model espoused by the state and made visible through economic projects of megadevelopment; and the nostalgia for the Dubai Creek as a golden frontier built on male camaraderie and smuggling. These competing and overlapping forms of "freedom" derive from a combination of the historical relationship between India and Dubai, the changes in Dubai's economy implemented by Sheikh Mohammed in the last decade, and the role of Indian and other merchants in producing Dubai as a regional hub for "re-export" before the adoption of the newer economic models through which Dubai's boom (and subsequent "bust") are understood today.

Like Mr. Soni—and unlike many less affluent Indians—most of the businessmen I spoke to in Dubai articulated their reasons for settling there in terms of the restrictions imposed by the Indian government. Dubai for Indian businessmen operated in effect as India's "offshore," a location that provided a haven for entrepreneurs from the restrictive economic policies of the Indian government while remaining close enough to "home" to allow for transnational businesses and the management of capital flows between Dubai and South Asia.[3] After independence in 1947, India had a "closed" economy, restricting imports and focusing on national industry.[4] In addition, in order to protect its gold reserves, the Indian government outlawed gold bullion possession by individuals. Dubai had always been a trade center that attracted merchants from the subcontinent, and without such restrictions on trade it drew even more Indian merchants and strengthened the networks already established in the region. Trade in textiles, gold, electronics, dry goods, and other products—mostly illegal on the Indian side—flourished between Dubai and India between the time of South Asian independence and the liberalization of India's economy in the early 1990s. While oil played a large part in the development of Abu Dhabi, the Emirati capital, commercial trade was the backbone of Dubai's economy both before and during British colonialism in the region.[5] Even after oil was found in Dubai, in 1966, it was mostly re-export to the subcontinent, particularly gold re-export, that made fortunes for both citizens and expatriate businessmen alike. After 1991, when India relaxed restrictions on trade, Dubai's gold industry slumped because gold in India was no longer more expensive than the international standard. However, gold and other trade industries still rely on the economic interdependence between South Asia and the Gulf.[6] And with the recent boom in India's economy, the UAE is actively courting bilateral trade agreements between the two countries, hoping to eventually make the UAE India's "top trade partner."[7]

In explaining the history of gold in Dubai, Indian gold merchants, especially those who had been in the Gulf for several decades, repeatedly pointed me to one source—Robin Moore's *Dubai*, if I could find it. It would not be easy to find, they said, because the novel was banned in Dubai, but if I did, I would learn all I needed to know about what life was like for them back then. Apparently Robin Moore, who published the novel in 1976, had come to Dubai and done extensive research on gold smuggling, including speaking to some of my interlocutors. The book, readily available in the United States (though out of print), centers around the life of an American named Fitz, who, after working in the American embassy in Iran, goes to Dubai to make a fortune smuggling gold and then opens a restaurant cleverly called the Ten Tola Bar.[8] Moore's novel depicts Dubai's world of re-export, which was well organized and operated under the watchful eye of Sheikh Rashid (the former ruler of Dubai and Sheikh Mohammed's father), who made a lot of money off of each successful dhow trip to India.[9] The gold trade across the Gulf relied on sophisticated networks between Bombay and Dubai that often involved politicians and police. Moore describes in detail the processes of smuggling gold and how networks of knowledge and capital functioned transnationally. My informants characterized *Dubai* as a historical account of India's heavy reliance on the illicit gold supplied by the Gulf. According to the novel and my interlocutors, gold demands were constantly rising in the 1960s and 1970s, weddings in India and Pakistan were postponed until new gold shipments could arrive, and rich Indians were desperate to convert their American dollars and sterling into gold. Gold that cost $35 per ounce in Dubai could either be sold for over $100 in India or traded for silver, usually at close to 200 percent profit. Throughout the book, the characters' actions move between legality and illegality: they operate openly in front of certain authorities and institutions, such as Sheikh Rashid and the Dubai police, but have to be diplomatic with Indian officials and the press. The ambivalent space occupied by gold smugglers in Dubai is what Carolyn Nordstrom has called "il/legality."[10] She argues that all economic networks function through a blend of legal and illegal means. Without a focus on the extralegal, it is impossible to understand the functioning of power and money in the contemporary world. Indian merchants used il/legality in the narratives they related to me and in their repeated references to this novel as a mode of belonging. They felt that, through their networks of semi-illicit trade between the Gulf and South Asia, they were responsible for producing the successes of contemporary Dubai.

The contemporary UAE state, despite its focus on economic diversification and global business, emphasizes that foreigners are a temporary and necessary evil of post-oil development, effectively erasing pre-oil, colonial, and pre-national cosmopolitans from official state histories. Due to its relative newness as a nation and the increasing demographic imbalance between citizens and noncitizens, the UAE is interested not only in policing the borders of citizenship but also in "Emiratizing" the economy to reduce its reliance on foreign workers. It would appear that citizens, or "locals," are the most privileged group in a country like the UAE, but in fact the government deploys multiple logics of citizenship that provide differential privileges and access to wealth accumulation for different groups. Among other things, the UAE government makes allowances for neoliberal expatriate subjects, like Indian merchants, who are offered belonging through economic participation but who are also complicit in preserving the boundaries of national identity through disavowals of formal citizenship in the country. While the legal status of such expats renders them officially transitory, several scholars have noted that migrant communities in the Gulf States are also quite entrenched and that both "foreigners" and "citizens" contain within them forms of hybridity that make these categories actually much more porous than the Gulf States would have them be.[11] Indian merchants' narration of Dubai's cosmopolitan history, however—unlike that of other expats, like those I discussed in chapter 1—also directly pushed against the idea that cosmopolitanism in Dubai was new and a result of oil wealth. Their constant insertions of Indian masculine achievements in the making of modern Dubai destabilized the idea that cosmopolitanism was a Western, modern, or "new" product that has arrived only recently in the Gulf region.

The Creek Frontier: Mercantilism, Masculinity, and Nostalgia

As I sat on a worn leather couch in Mr. Menon's office in Bur Dubai's Meena Bazaar area, I noted on the wood-paneled walls the numerous photographs of Mr. Menon, a South Indian who had been in Dubai's gold industry for over forty years, either shaking hands with Emirati royals, standing in front of the India Club with other suited Indian men, attending camel races, or participating in what appeared to be opening ceremonies for retail shops. Placed in a particularly prominent position was a black-and-white photograph of Mr. Menon standing next to Sheikh Rashid; it was most often through Sheikh Rashid that older Indian gold merchants established their belonging to the emirate and especially to the trade history of the creek. Although photographs chronicling merchants' *wasta* (influence) and connections to Dubai's past were common in the offices of my interlocutors in the business community, to actually be photographed with Sheikh Rashid was a rare honor. Regardless of whether they had actually met him, however, my informants universally described Sheikh Rashid as fair, as particularly connected to Indian culture (his

teachers, advisors, nannies, and servants were often Indian), as a "democratic" man whose *majlis* (council chamber) was open to anybody, and as
someone who relied on the business expertise of the Indian community in
order to plan Dubai's future. In short, they deemed Sheikh Rashid a man
who shared their belief in market "freedom," but with a position of favor
accorded to Indians. Indian merchants' nostalgia for a past in which they
held a more respected and exalted place in society resonated with Emirati
narratives of national identity as rooted in biographies of the sheikhs,
which portray them as visionary leaders who single-handedly produced
profitable stable countries in a short period of time.[12] While official state
histories tend to write out the pre-oil Indian mercantile presence in Dubai, Indians insert themselves back into this history through similar individualistic narrative devices. For example, the biographies of board members of the prestigious India Club depict Dubai in the 1950s as a backwater
where Indian merchants had to struggle to make a living without the luxuries they have today and without their families.[13] The bustling Creek
atmosphere of pre-oil Dubai emerges in these biographies and in merchant narratives as a frontier of the subcontinent, where industrious men
went to look for fortune, overcame hardships, and paved the way for the
drastically different Dubai that the rest of us can enjoy today—with its air-
conditioning, luxury living, family atmosphere, and feminine spaces of
consumption.[14] As individualistic narrative forms, biography and autobiography were used to assert this particular masculine entrepreneurial
belonging to Dubai's rough-and-rugged past. And the frontier metaphor in
my informants' retelling of Dubai's past mirrored official state discourses,
which valorize patrilineal rule through the faces and stories of individual
men's visionary acts.[15]

Through Mr. Menon, I was connected to a gold bullion trader named
Mr. Zaveri, who, according to several of my interviewees, was the inspira-
tion for a main character in Robin Moore's *Dubai*.[16] Over the phone, I
explained to Mr. Zaveri the reason for my request to meet with him: I was
an anthropologist studying Indian business in Dubai and wanted to know
more about the gold industry. He took a few seconds to answer, "I would
like to see all of the questions you are going to ask me first. Please bring
them to my office." Expecting a glitzy office in a tall building, I was
surprised when I finally found Mr. Zaveri's small office door wedged
between a shop selling shawls and a falafel joint on a street that was well
removed from the main thoroughfares of Deira's gold souk. An employee

buzzed me in and escorted me in a cage elevator to Mr. Zaveri's office, which was decorated with 1960s metal office furniture, dirty white lino-leum tiles, and a Hindu deity calendar hung next to a real-time digital display of commodity prices. About a dozen men were busy answering phone calls about the day's gold rates. Mr. Zaveri, an unassuming man in a wrinkled short-sleeve shirt who appeared to be in his late sixties, was sitting among his employees, himself answering the phone from time to time while also texting on his mobile. He requested my sheet of questions and told me to come back the next day. When I returned, Mr. Zaveri ushered me into his private office, offered me tea, and then pulled out my sheet of questions, which was covered with notes in his handwriting. He asked me about my background: where did my parents come from? Was I married? Did I celebrate the Hindu holidays? After apparently ascertain-ing that I was a "good" girl (married, Hindu, and not a reporter), he told me that the information I was seeking was very sensitive and that he had to be careful because the history of gold in Dubai had "not always been that savory." During the course of our conversations, I came to believe that Mr. Zaveri's aura of secrecy was primarily about appearing important, for the information he shared did not diverge significantly from that shared by other merchants: personal gold sales were illegal in India until the 1990s, so people hired wooden dhows to smuggle it past the Indian au-thorities; guns were necessary to arm boats "just in case"; and there are probably "kilos and kilos" of gold at the bottom of the Indian Ocean, dumped there by smugglers who wanted to avoid being caught.[17] Mr. Zaveri then told me that, as a bullion trader and money changer, he was currently physically moving seven to eight million dollars a day through his office. To prove his success (and to dazzle me, as I undoubtedly was), he took me to a vault on the floor above, which was stacked with ten-tola and kilo bars of pure gold, and with trash bags full of currency, both dollars and dirhams (see figure 3.1).[18]

Mr. Zaveri had diversified away from jewelry in the past decade and was also participating in a new free-zone project called the Dubai Multi-Commodities Center. He, like other gold merchants I spoke to, was proud of what he had accomplished during his time in Dubai, but he also in-dexed the need for propriety in speaking about smuggling and other quasi-legal dealings. The space occupied by Indian merchants in Dubai as risk-taking entrepreneurs on the edge of legality was used in their narratives as a mode of belonging: they felt that it was through a unique relationship

FIGURE 3.1 · Gold bars, worth about $1 million USD, on display at a Dubai Gold and Jewelry Group meeting, 2006. Photograph by Neha Vora.

between India and Dubai, which they had single-handedly created, that Dubai had wound up on the map at all. The successes of contemporary Dubai in terms of commerce and development had as their basis this open secret of smuggling, the sharing of which produced a sense of community between Indian businessmen and a sense of belonging historically to the emirate.

Indian merchants, even as they asserted claims to Dubai's past as one that was particularly Indian, participated in the erasure of South Asian elements from Emirati national identity through their production of community and of "Indian" identity. Despite their insistence that Dubai is actually a freer place than India and that they put Dubai on the map, Indian businessmen echoed Mr. Soni's sentiments that while they preferred Dubai to India in many ways, they were Indians and nothing else. They claimed to have no interest in belonging politically to the UAE via citizenship or other legal rights. Thus they contributed to their own exclusion from official citizenship while proliferating other forms of historical and contemporary belonging to the emirate. They lived, worked, and socialized almost entirely within the South Asian-dominated neighborhoods of Bur Dubai, Deira, and Karama, and referred to Dubai as an "extension of India," a "clean Bombay," and "India West," terms that circulated in my interviews with non-elite Indians as well (see chapter 2). Indian businessmen were actively involved in Indian social, cultural, and religious organizations, reproducing what they called Indian "tradition" in Dubai, and providing a platform from which to educate their children about Indian customs, language, and history. In fact, their communities were even more tightly knit and patriarchal than those of my middle- and working-class interlocutors, because of their historical entrenchment in the emirate and the passing on of businesses from fathers to sons; since their business, family, and community lives overlapped to such a degree, Indian merchants often had little or no daily interaction with people outside of their religious, ethnic, regional, and linguistic circles. The ability to self-segregate and to police the boundaries of their communities was something that Indian elites preferred about Dubai, in contrast to Western countries, where they felt the cultural identities of their children would be threatened. For example, Anand, a high-level Punjabi engineer, described the merchant communities as both tightly knit and segregated from the rest of Indian Dubai: "Like all the Sindhi and Gujarati businessmen who live in Bur Dubai and Deira. They just don't move anywhere else. It is them only. It makes no difference to them whether you are in one part of Bombay or brought here, there is no change in their lifestyle. They eat the same food, they move in the same circles, they only move in their own community, they do business in their own community. To them it doesn't make a difference."

In order to preserve cultural identity, the Indian businesspeople I spoke to sent their children to Indian schools, and they tried to maintain at least one Indian language in the home. They also had live-in servants and nannies, many of whom did not speak English, which furthered the Indian-language skills of their children. Most of the people I spoke to were quite religious (primarily Hindu, Jain, or Muslim) and kept shrines in their homes, displayed Hindu or Muslim images and items in their offices, and observed religious festivals, fasts, and *pujas* (Hindu devotional ceremonies) on a regular basis. While these practices and ideologies resonated with those of middle-class Indians as well, they were followed more strictly among the business communities of Dubai.[19] As feminist scholars of South Asian diasporas have noted, diasporic communities often draw the boundaries around gender roles tightly and police the mobility and practices of women, who are considered responsible for teaching cultural values to children. Among Indian elites in Dubai, I also found a gendered and patriarchal construction of Indian culture. In most families, it was not wives but rather servants, cooks, and nannies who were responsible for housekeeping and childcare; boys often followed in their fathers' footsteps and joined the family business; marriages outside of the community were restricted, and arranged or semi-arranged marriages were common; and shopping was a central part of women's lives. Many high-end boutiques and five-star restaurants cater to Dubai's Indian elite. On any given evening, well-dressed Indian women can be seen purchasing diamond jewelry in Damas, a Gulf-based luxury jewelry retailer, or designer salwar-kameez in Meena Bazaar, or shopping at one of Dubai's many expensive malls. Charity lunches held at major hotels are attended by couples dressed in Armani suits and the newest Delhi sari styles; Bollywood stars are regularly spotted at events in Dubai; and Indian families throw lavish weddings and parties at which members of the Emirati royal family often make appearances. While business-community families often lived in high-rise apartment buildings or villas surrounded by nationals and expatriates from many other countries, they tended to maintain a nondiverse social circle, sticking to those they felt formed part of their community, usually based on religion, region, language, and class simultaneously. Their cosmopolitan sensibilities were therefore also infused with a number of parochialisms, both of which simultaneously defined their sense of belonging and identity.[20]

Because they defined their own ethnic identities so narrowly and worked so vigilantly to maintain "culture," Indian merchants and their families did not challenge Emirati national identity and citizenship; rather, they helped cement the idea of an Arab nation-state by distilling Indian and Emirati national identities into distinct, mutually exclusive forms. During my interviews, Indian businessmen told me that they did not have political influence in Dubai, that neither they nor their children considered themselves Emirati in any way, that Emirati culture and UAE citizenship were closed to foreigners, and that they were nothing but Indian in their "hearts and minds." These subjects, however, were ambivalent and rehearsed several discourses, practices, performances, and affects of belonging that went past their scripts of being in Dubai solely for economic accumulation, and they exhibited a nostalgia for a disappearing form of Indian Ocean cosmopolitanism through which they defined their identities. Most prominently, while naturalization is officially impossible for Indians, and Indian businesspeople were adamant that they themselves were not Emirati, many people told me that there do exist Indians who *have* become Emiratis. These "Indian Emiratis"—if that is what they would be called—were described as community leaders who have contacts with the royal family or have completely adopted Gulf dress, culture, language, and religion. The existence of such Indian Emiratis would come up in conversation without my encouragement, usually right after I had asked a merchant whether he felt limited by his own lack of citizenship. The interviewees often responded, in essence, "But of course there are Indians who have become citizens." When then asked if they could refer me to Indians who had naturalized, they commonly answered that they did not know any personally, but that "they are there."

I never did find this mythical Indian Emirati, and a little research among expatriates who were familiar with the naturalization process suggested that there are only a handful. The specter of this figure, however, played a significant role in allowing Indians to assert belonging while simultaneously disavowing it. By claiming that Indian Emiratis exist, Indian businessmen established that naturalization was not closed to them, that their nonbelonging was in fact voluntary. Thus, it was not just the state but also Indians themselves who were producing distinct divisions between Emirati and Indian national identities.[21] My interlocutors expressed their desire to maintain Indian citizenship in terms of nationalistic pride, their satisfaction with the economic status they already enjoyed in the Emirates, and an insistence that Emirati citizenship was not such a wonderful thing at the end of the day. As Mr. Menon told me and as his colleagues echoed in different words: "Why would I want to be a citizen? I can't vote." Mr. Menon's interests here clearly lie with the economic rights provided by Dubai's neoliberal economy and not with liberal-democratic political participation through activities like voting. His colleagues similarly emphasized that their noncitizenship was voluntary, not due to state restrictions, and in so doing they established their role as partners with the state in producing their status as elite *foreigners* in Dubai. They chose to remain outside the realm of national identity and solely within that of the economy. In this way they displayed political power and engagement with the processes of governance while disavowing more formal modes of belonging to the Gulf. Although I was unable to confirm claims about the privileged positions that sheikhs afforded to Indians or about Indians who naturalized as Emiratis, the truthfulness of these accounts is less important than the simple fact of their circulation among Indian elites in Dubai. Such narratives formed a central part of the way in which this group spoke about historical and contemporary belonging in the emirate.[22]

Maneuvering Neoliberalisms:
Monopolies of "Freedom" in Dubai's Gold Industry

Indian merchants' group-based associations were often extensions of the transnational economic networks that formed the basis for their monopolies over Creek-area retail and wholesale trade. The established hold that Indian merchants had on certain sectors of the Dubai market made it easier for them to make higher profits than did newer entrants into those sectors. In Dubai, according to Mr. Soni, you can be a "big fish in small sea." Although he acknowledged that certain policies could not be changed, like those of citizenship and access to political rights, Mr. Soni, along with other Indian merchants, was quick to tell me that the government is mostly benevolent toward Indian business. Indian businessmen were particularly proud of what they could accomplish in a "free" place like Dubai and articulated their membership in Dubai society in terms of how Dubai lets them realize their full economic potential, without restrictions. I was often told why Dubai was a better place for Indians than were America and other parts of the West. Indian merchants believed there was more discrimination in the West and in India than there was in Dubai. They suggested, for example, that in India college quotas for scheduled classes were a form of discrimination, as were the pressures put on children to assimilate in the West. They also considered economic restrictions on foreign business in the West discriminatory. "In other countries you pay taxes!," one shop owner declared. Freedom for these Indians was thus narrated primarily in terms of economic deregulation. As Mr. Mirani, a prominent Sindhi trader in Bur Dubai told me, "It is very easy to open a business over here and make the money if you have the ability to. But that is not being an Indian, you can be anybody. Dubai welcomes anybody who has the finances to do that." However, in their definitions of freedom, Mr. Mirani and the other Indian businessmen I spoke to did not always acknowledge their role in the manipulation of Dubai's market in order to benefit their own businesses or the specific advantages proffered to them by the Dubai government. Indian merchants' successful (and not so successful) attempts to work with the government to produce economic regulations and loopholes preserved their own monopolies while also allowing for limitations on foreign business that favored Emiratization. Most literature on ethnic entrepreneurship has considered how transnational and diasporic networks maneuver around the restrictive and often racist policies of states through informal economic practices.[23] In the United Arab Emirates, and in Dubai in particular, however, Indian entrepreneurs worked in conjunction with governmental institutions to produce the legitimacy of the state, through a blend of formal and informal business practices. In fact, the ability to combine informal and formal business practices with minimal government interference was a central component of my informants' definitions of Dubai as a place of "freedom."

While the UAE assesses no income tax, has very low import and export duties, and touts its openness and investment opportunities, foreign businesses are hampered by the UAE Commercial Companies Law, under which foreigners can only own up to 49 percent of any business and must conduct banking, hiring, and other activities in their citizen partner's name.[24] However, Mr. Menon told me, the Dubai government takes measures to alleviate the impact of these restrictions on expatriate businesspeople. In fact, all my informants spoke about the open proliferation of loopholes and ways to get around the system of privileging citizens. Established Indian entrepreneurs had been relying for decades on networks of knowledge and expertise, as well as long-standing relationships with prominent Emiratis, including many in the ruling family, to maintain monopoly-like ethnic strongholds on gold and other industries.

In order to establish a limited liability company (LLC) in Dubai, a prospective business owner must submit its name to the Licensing Department of the Department of Economic Development for approval, a process that can take a little or a *lot* of time depending on whom one knows. The foreign businessperson also needs a certificate that shows at least 300,000 dirhams in the bank, which a local partner can provide for a short period of time for a fee.[25] Only then can the business be issued visas for employees. This system also requires personal contacts, because in order to secure a larger number of visas, one needs an influential partner. Officially, the business is owned 51 percent by the citizen, 49 percent by the foreigner. However, Indian merchants related both official and unofficial ways to change this balance. Several of my interviewees told me that they had obtained through their contacts with government officials and their relationships with their business partners an official memorandum notarized by the Dubai government through which they owned 80 percent of their business. Others had obtained official power of attorney over the company. This meant that while the majority of the company was still in the local's name, the local owner had no real access to the company's finances or any way to make major decisions that affected the company.[26] Unofficially, every gold merchant I spoke to who had been in Dubai for over a decade had some form of "side agreement" in which his sponsor either agreed to a lesser stake in the company, a specific annual payment, or to bequeath inheritance of the company to the foreign partner.[27] In addition to the quasi-legal agreements used to circumvent 51 percent local business ownership, long-standing businesspeople in Dubai and those with wasta found other ways to operate outside the UAE's restrictions on foreign business. First, while most businesses had to convert to the new system when the law of local partnership passed in 1984, some that had connections to the royal family remained wholly foreign owned. Therefore, certain businesses currently operating in Dubai outside of free zones have 100 percent foreign ownership, including several Indian-run firms that are major fixtures in the Creek neighborhoods of Bur Dubai and Deira.[28] Additionally, in order to open a shop in the souk areas, one requires "key money," usually thousands of dirhams, to be paid over and above the annual rent due to Indian merchants and their sponsors in order to set up a new shop. Because of the networks of influence and ethnic monopolies in Dubai, in some cases shops can be obtained only through word-of-mouth recommendations from other merchants, which sets up and maintains a system in which the Creek-area retail industries, especially gold, electronics, and textiles, are controlled mostly by Indians.

While these "loopholes" work to the benefit of established Indian businesses in Dubai, recent government pushes to lure multinational corporations through the establishment of free-trade zones have put pressure on Indian small-business owners, who are struggling to maintain their established strongholds in the face of major competition. Mr. Soni's disappointment in the changes that had taken place over the last two decades in Dubai was echoed in my interviews with Mr. Menon. Mr. Menon had owned several businesses since the 1960s, both retail and wholesale, but had recently decided to switch tracks and work as a representative of South African gold suppliers to the Dubai wholesale market. The market, he told me, was too saturated, and the jewelry business was shifting away from Bur Dubai and Deira to higher-end shopping malls in newer neighborhoods populated by European expats. "Branding is the only way for you to make high margins now. People are consolidating and the small guys will disappear. They can't market that easily. Emiratization and the middle class are hurting the industry." Mr. Menon, like other merchants, explained that while working-class Indians were still buying simple gold bangles and chains to take home as remittances, the true money nowadays was in diamonds and 18 karat "fashion" jewelry, which was not Indian-run in the same way as the old souk areas that specialized in 22 karat gold for South Asian tastes. The rise of Damas as a coveted Middle Eastern brand; the entry of DeBeers, Tiffany & Co., and other high-end luxury retailers; and the opening of a gold-and-commodities exchange (*sukuk*) were shifting the gold trade away from Indian merchants and into the hands of multinational corporations that defined the global city Sheikh Mohammed envisioned in his plans for the emirate's future. Simultaneously, new regulations on employment of nationals and foreigners were challenging the Indian ethnic stronghold on gold. But, Mr. Menon insisted, locals still preferred to do business with Indians, and Indians were managing to work around these changes.

An example of new neoliberal market technologies implemented in

Dubai—and Indian businessmen's attempts to utilize them to their benefit
—is the Dubai Multi-Commodities Center (DMCC). The DMCC, started in
2002, is designed to be a production and re-export zone, and offers 100
percent foreign business ownership, a fifty-year tax holiday, and other
incentives to lure foreign businesses to Dubai. In 2006, when I conducted
my fieldwork, the DMCC already had 760 registered companies. Gold and
diamonds are two of the largest segments of the DMCC, and the DMCC also
has an active gold exchange, the DGCX, which operates in collaboration
with businesses in India and other parts of the world. While free-trade
zones are considered to be distinct areas with different forms of sovereignty than the nation-state at large, the borders of free zones in Dubai are
much more porous than they appear, and the role of Indians in the DMCC is
an attempt to continue political engagement with the state in ways that
privilege Indian strongholds in the gold industry. While it is advertised as
an area designated for export activities, the DMCC is actually the brain-
child of Dubai-based gold merchants and caters in many ways to the retail
and wholesale needs of established gold and jewelry companies in the city.
In 2006 the advisory committee for the DMCC's gold sector was comprised
mostly of expatriates, and six out of the thirteen members were prominent
Dubai Indians. Seventy percent of gold that passes through Dubai goes to
the subcontinent, and in 2006 the DMCC was already responsible for about
50 percent of Dubai's entire gold trade. While the DMCC had a refining and
manufacturing center within the government-provided free-zone area already running, the office buildings for the DMCC did not have an official
date of completion. Consequently, for four years the DMCC, whose members are mainly established local gold merchants, had been operating *vir-
tually*, out of offices located mostly in the Creek area.

As Aihwa Ong has noted, free zones are geographically bounded spaces
in which normal governance is suspended in favor of neoliberal market
forms.[29] However, in the case of the DMCC, this supposedly restricted
space for full foreign business ownership in fact permeated the emirate,
requiring of the Indian merchants who participated in it little or no
change in day-to-day operations. Because of the lack of restrictions both
inside and outside of the free zone, the free zone operated as a way to
maneuver around some of the restrictive policies of the state in a way that
satisfied both locals and expatriate businesspeople. For instance, a foreign
businessperson could own one company inside the free zone under 100
percent ownership and one outside of the free zone as a 49 percent part-

ner to a local. He could then offer goods on consignment from inside the free zone to outside; he thereby legally owned all his products, which reduced his economic dependence on his local partner. In this way foreign businessmen were circumventing economic restrictions on ownership, but the rentier state structures of what many Indians I spoke to called "indirect taxation" remained in place: local sponsors still collected annual payments, the hiring of nationals was still favored, and the industry as a whole brought more money into Dubai. While this process appears to be the workings of a neoliberal free market, the DMCC brought into relief the state's willingness to work with expatriates in ways that further relaxed the restrictions on foreign business ownership in all of Dubai, consolidating the hold that existing gold players (most of whom were Indian) had on the sector, and making it difficult for newcomers to establish a foothold.[30] While Indian merchants defined freedom and belonging through neoliberal discourses of relaxed regulation and entrepreneurial opportunities, they were simultaneously threatened and challenged by the newer neoliberal market forms that were circulating in Dubai. Their understandings of belonging and practices of citizenship therefore were based on their narratives of maneuvering the system as a form of "freedom" and privileged belonging to Dubai.

Noncitizen Kafeels

The gold shops in the souk areas of Dubai have security cameras designed to keep an eye on customers but particularly on employees. Because the shop employees have a sense of being under constant surveillance, I had a hard time striking up conversations with them about their experiences working in the industry and living in the UAE. As I made my daily rounds through the souks, I was nevertheless able to piece together information on the working hours, salary levels, and housing conditions of the almost exclusively male South Asian staff in gold retail shops. The men that I spoke to told me that they had arrived in Dubai through familial and community networks or had been recruited by headhunters in their hometowns. They had either paid money in India for jobs promised on arrival in Dubai, or they had arrived in Dubai on a visit visa, stayed with friends and family members, and ended up finding jobs within companies and industries that were already employing their relatives and acquaintances. Therefore, many had family members or friends already working in the gold industry, sometimes in the same company or shop. In Indian-dominated industries like gold and textiles, staff members are often housed in cheap accommodations near work or even on the work site. Employers also provide them with canteen-style food, and thus lower the cash wages they pay, because housing and other costs are taken directly out of the employee's paycheck. Employers maintain lower costs through these services, and they are able to pay employees less without facing resistance because the wages are often still much more than migrants would be able to receive in India. In one retail shop in Deira's gold souk, on a particularly quiet afternoon when the owner was out of the office, I managed to sit down with Ram while the other employees gathered around and chimed in to add to his narrative. Ram told me that about 60 percent of his family was in Dubai and that the workers in his shop shared rooms in a company villa in Sharjah and were bused in for a shift that started at 10:30 AM and ended at 10:00 PM, with a couple hours off in the middle of the day. He had every other Friday off and made 1,500 dirhams per month, much more than he would have made in India, even with his economics degree. (Others who had been there longer told me they made up to 2,000 dirhams per month.) Ram had originally come to Dubai on a visit visa and acquired this job, but had to return to India for a few months when the visa expired; he was now paying off debts accrued from the process of traveling back and forth. He was also earning less than he had been promised, and his employer had possession of his passport. The employees, he told me, while some of the others nodded in agreement, were "all like part of the family" because they were mostly from Bombay, lived and dined together, and spent their time off together as well. In fact, aside from the shop customers, he had no interaction with "locals" (Emirati citizens). "Dubai is part of Bombay for me," Ram said, but he also added that "the culture of India is much better than here," for in Dubai it was all work—work to feed his wife and two children back in India.

Perhaps the most significant way in which Indian gold merchants legitimize the state and perform citizenship in Dubai is through their governance over the Indians and other noncitizen employees—like Ram and his co-workers—who work in their factories and shops, in effect acting as kafeels by proxy for their citizen business partners, who often exist on paper only.[31] In fact, without the large number of expatriate employers and managers in the Gulf, the kafala system of migration sponsorship that underpins Gulf economic and political systems would not be able to function as it does. Certain foreign residents are therefore responsible for the maintenance of the very citizen-noncitizen binary through which they are interpellated. However, most scholarship on migration in the Gulf focuses too heavily on the differences between citizens and noncitizens at the expense of exploring the role of noncitizens in the production of social hierarchy and exploitation in the region. In his work on migration in Bahrain, for example, Andrew Gardner argues that Indian elites face structural violence similar to a "transnational proletariat," which includes the Indian laborers in the Gulf.[32] While Indian elites do face certain limitations on their behavior and restrictions on business due to sponsorship and partnership regulations, the differences between elite and nonelite discourses about these problems are stark: elites, while hampered by the system in some ways, are invested in that very system as a risk-benefit analysis in which they have come out ahead. Gardner, like many other scholars of the Gulf States, relies too heavily on the citizen-noncitizen split in Bahrain as the primary form of social and economic structure, instead of considering other forms of belonging: the relationships between Indian elites and Indian workers, for example, mirror in many ways the "structural violence" he identifies as part of the kafala system in Bahrain.[33] However, the divisions *within* national groups in the Gulf, and particularly within "Indians" as a group that is present and numerous at every economic level, are equally if not more important than a focus on the citizen-noncitizen binary, especially when it comes to the living and working conditions of so-called migrant laborers—low-wage, unskilled, or semi-skilled foreign residents, mostly from South Asia.

In order to satisfy expatriate businesses, Dubai government discourses and policies grant businesspeople formal and informal ways to practice governance over other populations, usually working-class South Asians like Ram and his fellow employees. The Dubai government both has an official policy of Emiratization and touts a cutting-edge global business model that is open to all nationalities; in order to accomplish both goals, it has installed a three-tiered classification system in which employers have to pay more to maintain "older" styles of ethnic businesses. An employee visa costs more if a company does not employ a diversity of foreign nationalities, and it costs even more if a company does not employ a certain percentage of Emiratis (see table 3.1). Thus Mr. Soni's comment that he was "forced" to hire Filipinos. However, most Indian owners I spoke to were happily paying significantly more per employee visa to keep their

TABLE 3.1 · Transaction fees in dirhams per visa category as of 2005.

	CATEGORY A (>30% ONE NATIONALITY)	CATEGORY B (31–74% ONE NATIONALITY)	CATEGORY C (>75% ONE NATIONALITY)
Labor permit for PhD and MA	1,500	2,500	3,500
Labor permit for BA or equivalent	3,000	3,500	4,000
Labor permit for all other groups	5,000	5,500	6,000

Source: Embassy of India website, www.indembassyuae.org.

workforce exclusively Indian. The extra costs for visas were deflected by money saved in lower employee salaries and company housing. In this way, migration from South Asia is in effect privatized into the hands of individual expatriates, not simply Emirati sponsors. Indian businessmen maximize profit from this situation, while the state relegates responsibility for the well-being of lower-class migrant workers to their own compatriots.

Informal or "flexible" economic practices that are employed by Indian businesses in Dubai are often extensions of similar practices in India. While my informants complained about the challenges they faced due to India's liberalization, Barbara Harriss-White argues that, instead of creating more formalization within the economy, liberalization in post-1990s India has actually "catalyzed" a nexus of collective action by local businesspeople, politicians, and other actors that has furthered informal sector activities, increased accumulation among elites, and resulted in an economy that is actually less "free" because of the very neoliberal reforms that promised freedom.[34] For example, charging employees for setting up jobs, withholding salaries, and utilizing family members as unpaid labor all allow for larger profit margins. These processes also keep employees in an insecure position where they are beholden to employers and have little actual access to forms of resistance. Joint family firms and credit-sharing situations are common to the Indian economy, and many of these practices have been in place for quite some time, through generations of family members and transitions in local politics.[35] These organizational structures allow for low labor costs (often lower than the market) and they also reinforce patriarchal relations. Many of these patriarchal informal economic forms are reproduced in the transnational space of Dubai-India business relations, where (male) Indian merchants actually rely on economic practices that exploit the labor of other (male) Indians in order to maximize wealth accumulation. Money extracted from poor migrant workers adds substantially to the income of elites in the Gulf. For example, although exact figures are difficult to confirm, it is estimated that rent extracted from migrants in the Gulf is a billion-dollar industry.[36] While technically citizen business owners are responsible for the conditions of employment, in practice it is most often their expatriate partners who exploit South Asian migrant labor in Dubai. Thus, certain forms of governance are relegated to expatriate populations, and it is through these practices of governance that foreigners are in fact part of the production of the state's authority.

Though I asked every merchant I interviewed who owned factories or housed his own employees if I could tour these spaces, only Mr. Soni agreed, picking me up from my apartment one day in his black Mercedes and driving me to his jewelry manufacturing plant in industrial Sharjah. His workers were housed at the factory in small dormitory rooms furnished with bunk beds (see figure 3.2). Four to six men shared one room. They were provided meals in a canteen where Mr. Soni had hired a live-in Indian cook, and they had to shower outdoors. This is an example of "good" housing conditions for laborers in the Gulf, for Mr. Soni was happy to show me how well he took care of his workers in comparison to his friends and colleagues in Dubai.[37] His workers were like his family, he told me, and he cared about them. Mr. Soni's and other merchants' references to "family" and to ethnic diversification laws as losses of the "freedom" Dubai offers to entrepreneurs combine neoliberal narratives of deregulation with patrimonial business practices to showcase the particularities of Indian merchant belonging in Dubai. By disarticulating political and cultural belonging to the UAE while also participating in practices of governance and political engagement with the state, Indian businessmen act in some ways as citizens, extracting rents from other migrants, influencing decisions that maintain their primacy in the market, and exercising governance over laboring classes. Mr. Soni and his colleagues espoused certain neoliberal market values and postcolonial liberal ideas about citizenship while participating in nonliberal forms of patronage and exploitation that

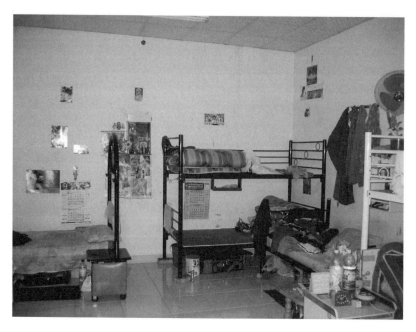

FIGURE 3.2 · Dormitory room in Mr. Soni's Sharjah factory. Photograph by Neha Vora.

reproduced social stratification among the Indian communities in Dubai. They therefore reified an Arab and Muslim nation-state to which they could never officially belong. However, their claims to belonging through historical narratives of masculine mercantile sociality also challenged and exceeded the neat temporal, cultural, and legal distinctions between citizen and foreigner in the UAE, thus recuperating the South Asian presence within Emirati national identity and imaginations of its heritage and history.

Conclusion

While it might at first seem that Indian merchants were rehearsing a form of neoliberal globalization in which they functioned as participants in the market but not in the nation, if one looks more closely at their narratives and practices, one finds that their assertions of belonging centered more on forms of economic freedom and cosmopolitanism that were specific to an Indian Ocean mercantilism that extended from colonial relationships with the Gulf and articulated with the postcolonial Indian state, and thus were not direct products of the neoliberal "global city" market form that dominates contemporary accounts of Dubai's boom (and recent bust). While UAE government narratives place migrants within a post-oil temporality and define them as a temporary but necessary evil of economic development, Indian merchant narratives reveal colonial and postcolonial hybridities that include Indian identities in the production of the contemporary Emirati nation. However, Indian businessmen also participate in the recuperation of their foreignness by disavowing formal modes of belonging to the UAE. The convergence within state and Indian merchant discourses of neoliberal rhetorics of choice and free markets in Dubai contributes to a lack of intervention into the exploitative conditions under which the majority of Gulf Indians live. Both official Emirati state and Indian business discourses emphasize laborers' "choice" in coming to Dubai, the "benefits" to them of Dubai over India, the freedom that workers possess to return home if they are not happy, and an assumption that employees now have more rights than employers in the UAE. With these narratives, both the state and Indian businessmen deny responsibility for the unsafe, unsanitary, and unsatisfactory conditions under which many people in the UAE live. By relegating governance over laborers to wealthy elites, the Emirati state has abdicated its responsibility for worker wellbeing; by narrating belonging in nonpolitical and nonnational terms, expatriate business owners mask their own practices of citizenship and governance. Indian businessmen in Dubai are integral to the production of the Emirati nation-state as a legitimate and distinct entity, apart from the economy and apart from the foreign residents who make up the majority of the population. Without the citizen-like practices of expatriates in the UAE, the state would not function as it does, and the concept of national identity as purified of foreign elements would be threatened.

Indian businessmen can thus be considered unofficial citizens of the UAE, and of Dubai in particular. Through narratives and practices of belonging that went beyond the confines of neoliberal markets, they both challenged hegemonic understandings of citizenship in the UAE and reified the division between citizen and noncitizen. Their narratives, as well as those of the middle-class Indians I introduce in the next chapter, point to a need for scholars to understand how multiple logics of belonging and citizenship circulate not only in the Gulf, but within all contemporary spaces. Indian businessmen disavowed the illiberal modes of citizenship in the UAE, which they claimed to have no interest in because they confer no "rights." In so doing they produced themselves as outsiders to the UAE nation. However, they also challenged the liberal modes of citizenship in India, where people have too much freedom "to shout and yell," and in the West, where immigrant cultural identities were supposedly under threat. Indian merchant narratives in the Gulf may reflect emergent modes of transnational citizenship that rely on territorially oriented nationalisms but simultaneously reify as well as challenge the limits of geographic spaces, the distinctions between liberal and illiberal states, and our contemporary understandings of what constitutes "freedom" and belonging. Middle-class Indians participated in similar rhetorics and practices, but their emergent forms of belonging and politicization in the Gulf also produced forms of substantive citizenship that diverged from and challenged those of elite expatriates and business owners.

4 · EXCEEDING THE ECONOMIC

NEW MODALITIES OF BELONGING AMONG

MIDDLE-CLASS DUBAI INDIANS

In May 2011, I was in a large ballroom in one of Singapore's five-star hotels, listening to a panel of experts debate the future of the Gulf. An Emirati academic had the stage. He had just presented a fascinating paper about social networking in the UAE and was addressing a question from the audience about the possibilities of the "Arab Awakening" reaching his country.[1] His response was aimed at dispelling the idea that Emiratis were nonpoliticized and complacent. He emphasized how the economic benefits of citizenship do not erase other issues faced by Emiratis, issues surrounding censorship, access to civil society, education, and employment. Another audience member, a South Asian historian, raised her hand: "What about the political role of the migrant population, especially those who have been there for their entire life [sic]?" The Emirati academic responded, as many readers may now be anticipating, by stating that migrants had no political role, that they were temporary, that they could always leave if dissatisfied with the UAE, and that in any case they made much more money in the Gulf than they could at home. While his presentation pushed directly against common assumptions that Emirati citizenship is determined through the economic advantages proffered by the welfare state, he recuperated market fundamentalism in his definition of migrant lives, effectively negating the possibility of any affective or political belonging to the UAE nation by noncitizens through the very assumptions he had previously criticized. The structural evidence presented by other scholarly and media accounts of the Gulf overwhelmingly support the Emirati academic's conclusion that migration is temporary and economic, and that migrants do not belong. This economic reductionism serves to erase migrant daily lives from our understandings of the Gulf, even when used to champion against labor abuses and so-called modern-day slavery.[2] In fact, economically driven narratives of noncitizen experiences in the Gulf rehearse their own violent exclusions by producing foreign residents as exceptions to citizenship and national identity; these exclusions are ironically complicit with the interests of the Gulf States in policing the boundaries of formal membership to the nation and its attendant rights.

Nevertheless, in this chapter I explore, perhaps counterintuitively, how middle-class Indian foreign residents' own descriptions of migration stressed voluntarism, economic opportunity, and market participation. Economic migration rationales and beliefs in market fundamentalism by middle-class Indians contributed to the idea that noncitizens were outsiders to UAE culture and society. However, their middle-class subjectivities and neoliberal ideologies actually produced belongings that *exceeded* the economic and that staked political and affective claims to the city.[3] Indian narratives of economic migration contained within them a belief in market fundamentalism that appeared to mirror that found in governmental and scholarly discourses. Their narratives were actually essential for the production of a split between market and nation in Dubai, a split that allowed simultaneously for a national identity purified of foreign elements and a neoliberal economy in which foreigners were welcomed. By exploring the narratives and daily activities of middle-class Indians in Dubai, I consider the ways in which my interlocutors themselves enabled the emergence of a globalized economy in Dubai that appeared to be distinct from the UAE nation-state and from Indian "culture," while enabling new forms of belonging that challenged the very division between nation and economy in Dubai that they themselves were complicit in producing.[4] Specifically, the processes of migrating, living, and working in Dubai enabled two substantive forms of urban diasporic citizenship among middle-class salaried Indians in Dubai—racial consciousness and consumer citizenship. These emerging forms of belonging created a sense of distinction from Indians in India, and they both produced identifications with other South Asians in the Gulf and revealed fissures within Dubai's Indian diaspora.

Middle-class Indians developed racial consciousness through their experiences of systematic discrimination and racial hierarchies in Dubai. However, while they experienced discrimination based on race and nationality in almost every aspect of their lives, they also expressed very particular middle-class identifications, identifications that relied on their belief in a neoliberal free market economy. On the surface, racism should be contradictory to the idea of a "free" market, in which all people regardless of origin or circumstance are welcome onto a level playing field of economic opportunity.[5] Dubai Indians' pervasive experiences of formal and informal racism did not negate their belief in the emirate's free market; rather, these experiences actually catalyzed their belief in—and production of—an "open" economy distinct from a "closed" nation. Indians in Dubai also exhibited forms of consumer citizenship, creating belonging through practices of consumption, which further bolstered the division in Dubai between economy and nation. While staking public claims to Dubai and articulating affective attachments to the city through consumption, these practices were considered to be purely economic—just buying things or enjoying services—and therefore outside of the purview of identity and politics.

Expatriate, citizen, scholarly, and governmental discourses at the beginning of the millennium converged to produce a narrow and closed form of citizenship in the UAE as well as its exceptions. Through two primary mechanisms—racial consciousness and consumer citizenship—Dubai Indians rehearsed citizenship to Dubai while disavowing interest in belonging to the Emirati nation. The distinction in Indian middle-class beliefs between nation and market effectively worked to produce the two as distinct domains, and this distinction was utterly necessary for the functioning and legitimacy of the Emirati state. With a large demographic imbalance toward noncitizens, of whom South Asians constitute the vast majority, the absence of politicization by South Asians vis-à-vis formal citizenship claims to the UAE, and their acceptance of an existence that is defined solely through economic migration, is essential for the continuation of the UAE's national identity, welfare state, and infrastructural "post-oil" development. Dubai Indians, therefore, are not simply passive exceptions to citizenship, but are integral to bounding a form of citizenship against which they frame their own subjectivities and positions within the UAE. In light of recent changes in Dubai that reduced their opportunities for financial success, Dubai Indians' narratives of economic freedom and middle-class achievement came into conflict with the hierarchical racial and national divisions within the city and brought into greater relief these new forms of subjectification and claims to citizenship.

"Dubai Is Like a Bus, an Air-conditioned Bus": Economic Migration and Middle-class Ideology

Tucked behind a main thoroughfare in Satwa, a neighborhood sandwiched between the wealthy areas of Jumeirah and Sheikh Zayed Road and populated primarily by middle- and working-class residents from Asia, I found Rohit's cozy villa, where he and his family had been living for almost twenty years. As an architect for a large state-owned construction company, Rohit was involved in several of Dubai's new high-rise projects. Over the course of his thirty-plus years in the UAE, he had worked for an oil company in Abu Dhabi and part-owned two consulting-and-design firms. He had just recently switched over from independent consulting to a corporate position in order to ensure greater job security and make more money for his retirement. Like other Dubai Indians, Rohit, despite having spent his entire career in the Gulf, considered himself a temporary migrant. He was raising his daughters with the Hindu cultural traditions of his Punjabi hometown, and he was remitting money to family in India while also slowly furnishing a home there in which he expected to retire. Rohit in many ways exemplifies the Indian middle-class "dream" in Dubai: he had managed to accumulate wealth during his time in the Gulf, had improved the living conditions of his family, and was setting himself up for a comfortable retirement in India. When I asked him how he felt about living in the Gulf after having been there for so many years, his response was one that resonated with the narratives of my other middle-class salaried interlocutors: "I say I am an Indian. I live and work in Dubai. People say we have immigrated. I always say no, we have not immigrated. I am here as an economic immigrant; I came because opportunities are here to make money and save money. I work here and that is why I live here. All human movement and immigrations are based on economic factors. Very few—U.S. is different because they give you professional enhancement—but this place is all economic immigration."

Rohit, a self-identified middle-class Indian, made a strong distinction between "immigration" to other diasporic places like the United States, where people settle, and the Gulf, a place solely for economic betterment, not for putting down roots. Rohit's preference for Dubai over other countries was due, in addition to its cultural and geographical proximity to India, to its neoliberal market, which he fiercely believed in—a market in which anyone could succeed with enough patience and hard work, and where one was not beholden to the state in the form of taxes or civic duties. Like the business owners I interviewed, he perceived that living in the United States would confer certain benefits, but he preferred the economic "freedoms" of Dubai. He likened the city to a bus, one that was fast-moving and also more luxurious than India, saying, "Dubai is like a bus, an air-conditioned bus. Get onto the bus, don't bother if you get a seat or not, then gradually you will settle down, things will move on." Rohit's metaphor of Dubai as a bus is extremely poignant, for it summarizes the sentiments expressed by many of my interlocutors about their migration and daily lives in Dubai. It is not coincidental that a middle-class Indian who feels he is an "economic migrant" chooses the image of a bus to describe Dubai; a bus is primarily a middle-class mode of travel, utterly unromantic and without attachment, merely a conduit from one place to another. That the bus is "air-conditioned" suggests that Dubai offers amenities and luxuries that might not be available in India. And that the passengers in this image may be initially unsure whether they will get seats or not speaks not only to the economic challenges of moving to Dubai, but also to the certainty that eventually the city will be worth the ride. Dubai's neoliberal market, therefore, contains risk and certainty, and it is a means to elsewhere, not an end unto itself. Unlike media representations of Dubai, in which the city is symbolized by its skyscrapers, hotels, and shopping malls, Rohit's metaphor speaks to an alternate experience, one that is far removed from the very projects he is helping to construct, and one that acknowledges the ephemerality of Indian existences in the UAE. Moreover, the image of the bus exemplifies a mobility that is particular to Dubai; it is constantly moving and people are constantly getting on and off. This is different from the forms of immigrant mobility that shape our understandings of migration in other places, like the United States, where family movement supposedly ends in settlement, and where being "mobile" implies the ability to climb a ladder of social status. Thus, the types of belonging and identity that form through mobility in Dubai, as Rohit emphasizes in his comments, are not the same as those we often imagine within our scholarly and popular understandings of migration and its effects in other South Asian diasporic locales.

Salaried Indian middle-class workers, like Rohit, and their families narrated their migration in terms of economic mobility, claiming participation in Dubai's market as a means rather than an end, thereby disavowing any belonging to the Emirati nation. The salaried Indians I interviewed were both single and married, with and without children, and hailed from a range of fields, such as advertising, aviation, marketing, information technology, education, human resources, administration, management, and media. Most had income levels that allowed them to have families in the UAE if they wished and that provided them with at least a modest amount of disposable income. Most important, all self-identified as middle class and distinguished themselves both from Indian business elites and from low-wage laborers and service workers. While middle-class Indians felt restricted in Dubai, particularly due to recent economic changes in the city, and described experiences of discrimination, they also praised the leaders of the UAE for creating an environment where foreigners have many opportunities to accumulate wealth. Their presence in the emirate was more tenuous than that of the business owners I interviewed, for they were tied to renewable short-term work contracts. But unlike young people who were born and raised in the emirate, this group of Dubai Indians claimed no desire for belonging to the Emirati nation even as they rehearsed forms of substantive citizenship that exceeded their own narratives of economic migration.

Unlike South Asians in other parts of the world, who often claim hyphenated identities that link together homeland and place of settlement, Dubai Indians did not assert belonging to the UAE, but defined themselves and their sense of belonging primarily through Indian nationalisms, as well as in terms of Indian regional, linguistic, and religious backgrounds. My interlocutors assessed the benefits of Emirati citizenship primarily in economic terms, and while they expressed a certain desire to be eligible for those benefits, they were not willing to sacrifice their Indian identities or even their Indian citizenship, evincing a patriotism to India that they did not have toward their host country, even though they were at times conflicted about their relationship to the Indian state. Neil, a software engineer from New Delhi, explained, "I might hate Indian politics, but I am fiercely patriotic when it comes to India. I love India; that is where I want to die. God forbid if the Emirates takes sides, I would be with India. . . . I would never renounce my Indian citizenship. If they have dual [citizenship], great. But citizenship would be like a membership card, like you are a member of an automobile club. Not something that would change your identity." Interestingly, Neil also used a vehicle metaphor for life in the UAE; citizenship to him was like membership in an automobile club, free of affective attachment, desired solely for the ease of access and economic benefits it could potentially provide. Because they deemed the UAE to be outside of their imagined communities, it would seem that middle-class Indian expatriates, like the Emirati government and like many academic accounts, did not consider themselves as immigrants at all, but rather as temporary workers.[6] My informants, therefore, rehearsed discourses and practices through which Dubai's economy, the Emirati state, and individual expatriate national cultures emerged as mutually exclusive and separable forms. However, Neil's comments also suggest an affective pull toward the UAE; his fear of having to "take sides" in a conflict suggests that Dubai represented more than the form of economic benefits a membership card in an automobile club would provide, being also a "home" where he had deeper connections that he worried might come into conflict with his Indian nationalism.

While constantly claiming their own subjectivities as unchanged by the process of migration, Dubai Indians centralized change in their narratives about living and working in the Gulf. They focused on change to express deterioration in circumstances and opportunities, and resulting uncertainties about jobs and futures. Most middle-class Indians suggested that it was only in the last five to ten years that they had seen Dubai change for the worse. These changes presented a conflict between their middle-class neoliberal ideas about success as individually achieved and the structural inequalities within which they were increasingly embedded. As Neil said about his recent experiences in the city, "Laws, accommodation, rents, living conditions have gone down, can't afford the same you had few years back, racism has increased, especially in working culture, a lot more fake stuff. The culture we follow is you work hard, you make your money, you enjoy your life. It is not like you ride on someone else's back always." That's really hurting over here, showing on a lot of people." Dubai Indians felt that the city had once been a profitable place to work, a place where they could save money in order to build a home in India and to travel to India easily for vacations or family emergencies. The claiming of belonging through nostalgia for Dubai's past was in some ways similar to the narratives of Indian business owners, even though middle-class nostalgia was expressed with the intention of highlighting new forms of economic hardship. Those who had been in Dubai for several years were purchasing less gold jewelry and other investment items, for example, while working longer hours to cope with the changes and keep up with Dubai's rising costs of living. Middle-class Indians felt that property owners and business managers were taking advantage of Dubai's new international notoriety by inflating rents, actively recruiting white Westerners who provided companies with a better "image," and raising prices on consumer items so that it was practically impossible to save money.

The changes in Dubai were infused with a profound sense of geographic segregation and isolation. Skyrocketing rents forced people to move into smaller places in less desirable neighborhoods, either closer to congested downtown areas or to the outskirts of Dubai or to Sharjah. Simultaneously, companies were moving further out of the city, which added hours of daily commuting. Planned developments named the Greens, the Meadows, Emirates Hills, the Springs, and Dubai Marina—all quite ironic for a desert city—had sprung up in New Dubai. These communities housed wealthier expats who worked in offices in Jebel Ali, Media City, the Dubai Marina, and other free zones, which had been built in previously undeveloped areas on the former outskirts of the city. Free zones had been growing at a quick pace in Dubai. They had created thousands of new jobs, and many multinational companies had set up branches in free zones or even moved their headquarters to Dubai.[7] New Dubai seemed a world apart from the congested and less planned downtown core of the city surrounding the Dubai Creek, and the newest free zones incorporated residential, commercial, industrial, and leisure spaces that did not require wealthier expatriates to ever venture into downtown Dubai. Due to traffic, the few kilometers from old Dubai to New Dubai sometimes took close to an hour to drive. These two parts of town were becoming more distinct as they became more spatially segregated. This segregation reflected change in the minds of my informants not only in spatial terms but also in terms of increasing hardships for Indians and other older residents of the city.

Middle-class Indian workers attributed the recent changes in the city primarily to the functioning (and failure) of Dubai's market. They felt that their current challenges were due to Dubai's economic mismanagement, and that this mismanagement had resulted in the emirate's failure to integrate into a globalized world where economic opportunities were merit-based and superseded the boundaries of national belonging. One Bengali information-technology worker complained, for example, "There is no logic, no rationale behind this kind of rent increase and things like that. Public transport is pathetic. Those kinds of things are not really becoming of a global city." In order to express the failures of the Emirati government and of business managers (usually European) in supporting a truly "free" market in Dubai, my informants often compared Dubai to India, which they pointed to as a recent success of globalization. While, according to them, manual labor from India was a stream that would never dry up, Dubai was at risk of losing its Indian middle class, who, they said, worked harder than other expatriates, were more skilled, and worked for the least amount of money. They suggested that it was increasingly difficult for companies to attract professionals from India given the salaries they were offering, and that salaries had not kept up with inflation. In fact, many told me they were thinking about returning to India, that the same jobs now command higher salaries in India, and that many people in their companies have already gone back. To them, the recent negative changes in Dubai indicated that the country was in the midst of a mismanaged and false economic "bubble" that would eventually have to burst. As Rohit explained, "Every graph has a self-correction, and Dubai will have a self-correction. Cost is increasing, salaries are not, frustrations are building up, you spend a larger part of your waking hours on the road and not doing anything productive. All of this is going to drive people to the point of frustration where the value that you are getting from this country is not really living up to the life that you are living over here."

The narratives of Dubai Indians worked in two ways: they focused on the economy as the defining factor in the lives of Indian migrants, and they reflected a belief in a globalized free market in which workers followed the jobs. For my informants, then, being in Dubai was considered a matter of "choice," based on a risk-benefit market analysis. However, in reality this choice was not always available. It was unclear whether jobs in India were truly commanding salaries competitive with Dubai, whether it was actually becoming harder to recruit educated Indians, or whether more skilled Indians were in fact permanently returning to India than in previous years. Moreover, despite feeling that the recent changes in Dubai were negatively impacting their lives, many Dubai Indians were, like Rohit, employed by the development companies working to produce Dubai as the global city that Sheikh Mohammed imagined for its future. Choice, therefore, was more a discursive assertion of agency and neoliberal market beliefs than a practice that my informants could actively deploy at will.

Middle-class Indians indexed Dubai's deteriorating economic freedom primarily through accounts of racial discrimination. They thus exhibited a racial consciousness that was derived from their experiences of living and working in Dubai, a diasporic subjectivity that came about through the experience of migrating from India and forming new communities elsewhere. Rather than undermining their beliefs in market fundamentalism, however, this racial consciousness actually relied deeply on middle-class neoliberal understandings of the market and on middle-class identification. It was therefore a subjectivity that, instead of indexing the impossibility of "free" markets devoid of social power dynamics, reified a global economy and presented racism as a failure to integrate into that economy. However, racial consciousness, infused with a nostalgia for prior egalitarianism and anger toward "new" entrants into the city, was also a politicized claim to belonging in Dubai that went beyond economically driven narratives in order to assert specific roles for Dubai Indians in the making of the city.

Racism and the Failure of the Free Market

By claiming that racism in Dubai had increased with the influx of multinational corporations and Western expatriates, middle-class Indians both highlighted a sense of frustration with Dubai's failed market freedoms and asserted a claim to the city that they felt had not been earned by newer migrants, in particular white expatriates who were hired to fill managerial and other positions in large companies and who were populating the spaces of New Dubai. Middle-class Indians used a range of terms to describe the group they felt was responsible for the majority of the discrimination they faced, especially in the workplace: European, Westerner, British, and, most often, gora, which literally translates in Hindi-Urdu to "fair-skinned" or white. They felt that goras received preferential treatment, were openly racist at times, and made generalizations about all Indians. Charlie, an engineer from Bombay who works for Emirates Airlines, told me about the workplace privileges he felt whites were getting over him.

> I deal with some customers. We go into meetings with a gora manager. You know they are talking rubbish in the meeting. You are trying to convey the right message. They will shine you up [try to make you look bad]. They make it like you are not important. If there is another gora in the same grade and same category, if I say something he will shine me up, but if he says something it is acceptable. Performance appraisals, you will get a good, they will get an outstanding. If you go and complain or ask, they say they will look into it, that's all.

Charlie concluded our conversation about workplace experiences by stating, "It is racist, horribly racist. Not the locals, it is the whites who come here, British most of them. They come here and make rules for their benefit. It is not the locals. The locals are very accommodating."

Joyce also expressed her frustration at the new group of expats and referred to whites as "foreigners," indicating that they were not among the foreign residents with whom she shared a sense of nonbelonging in Dubai, but rather direct contributors to her experience of being overlooked and taken for granted. She explained the work hierarchies between "foreigners" and other expats in Dubai: "The same job that we do the foreigner is always given more money for that. Like if I earned for six thousand, the person from U.S. or U.K. will always get ten or twelve thousand, almost double. They get all the perks, like if we apply for leave once a year they question us like 'Why do you want to go now?' Like if we want to go in December, they say 'It's a busy period,' but if a foreigner wants to go at that time during Christmas, they can go. Everywhere they are given preference." As a Christian, Joyce considered the Christmas holidays the most important time of the year, but she felt that her managers considered the needs of white and Western expats more important than her own.

Dubai Indians blamed whites for discrimination more than they blamed Emiratis, who were the official owners of companies, or even Arab and Indian elites, who often held high-level positions in well-established local companies. Nadia spoke of her frustrations about working in a city where skillset and experience were not valued equally for all nationalities.

> There is a person in the office. She doesn't even have a degree, from London, doesn't have any real experience, and she gets paid as much as I do. It makes you wonder, I am a manager and she is supposed to be helping me with my work. It makes me think if they can pay her so much, and she just started, why can't they pay me? We have editors in the office, Indian and English. There is a big difference in the way they are paid. You could see when my husband was going for interviews, racism is a big problem. They would say, "You don't speak Queen's English," and he would say, "Well you can't say that." But they do it.

Nadia's observation that less-qualified whites earned more than she did echoed claims I heard many times in my interviews. Many told me that they were working in jobs for which they were overqualified, simply because higher-level jobs were not slated for Indians or other Asians. And, just as they claimed that whites got more pay for less skill, Dubai Indians also related many incidents in which the standards that white and Emirati workers were held to were much lower than those to which they were held, as was reflected in Charlie's comments about evaluations. Discrimination is embedded into the employment structure in terms of salary and benefits, and into migration procedures, making South Asians feel they have the least ability to negotiate or protest against company demands, as they have higher levels of job and visa insecurity. Other forms of racism in Dubai were less institutionalized. For example, my interlocutors claimed that companies often rejected South Asian applicants for reasons like those levied against Nadia's husband, whose English skills were questioned, even if the applicants had been educated in the United Kingdom or United States. Experiences of discriminatory practices within the workplace were common. As one employee of an Internet company told me, "The autonomy of the person to be respected, to be given that basic right, is definitely not there. Westerners and Arabs get treated with so much more respect."

Like their business-owner compatriots, salaried Indians felt that a special relationship between Indians and Emiratis had once existed, but that it was deteriorating as Dubai attempted to raise its international profile. They characterized racism as new to Dubai. Temporality was therefore a component of my interlocutors' claims to Dubai and of their racial consciousness—from their point of view, Indians had not always been embedded in a national racial hierarchy of employment; rather, they were *no longer* paid based on their education or skillset. According to my interviewees, with Dubai's "boom" many companies chose to employ Europeans, even when they were less educated and less skilled, because company leaders thought having European employees would improve their image for clients and customers. Middle-class Indians expressed nostalgia for Dubai's past, for a time, they claimed, when Indians were treated with more respect. Arun, who works in advertising and had spent time in Saudi Arabia as well as in the UAE, told me that locals had a special attitude toward Indians, but that other Dubai residents did not share this sentiment: "If it is a local company, there is a chance that an Indian will get [the job], because they like Indians. They have grown up with Indians and lots of times their nannies, their grannies, they must have been Indians. Either Indians or Malaysians, Asians. So they have a conviviality, if I might say, for the Indians. They indulge their culture, they like their movies. You would never see a Lebanese going for Indian movies or hanging out with an Indian. So this kind of racialism I saw." That Indian foreign residents emphasized the historical connection between Dubai and India—the Indian "grannies" and "nannies" that some Emiratis may have, for example—spoke to affective ties that had developed over generations and preceded the current economic boom in the city. Indians who had been in Dubai for several years or decades almost always spoke about increasing challenges they faced with the boom and the rise of Dubai as a global city. Emirati attitudes toward Indians seemed to have shifted as a result of the UAE's turn away from its maritime connections across the Indian Ocean as it embraced more Westernized and "international" business models, with the corresponding influx of non-South Asian expatriates into Dubai.

While in the workplace Indians were most disdainful of racism by whites, they also attributed the racial and national hierarchy in Dubai to government institutions and to Asian and Arab expatriates who participated in keeping Indians out of certain spaces and certain positions. My interlocutors reported that in government offices "the Westerner would literally be invited to the front of the line" and that Emirati government officials would literally "throw" passports and documents at Indians instead of handing them over politely.[8] They described numerous incidents in which they felt the police automatically gave Europeans and other Arabs the benefit of the doubt. And they described a number of cases in which they or their friends were not allowed into bars or nightclubs, or were ignored in restaurants and shops; the bouncers and servers who treated them this way were often Indian, and my informants attributed such behavior to rules passed down from non-Indian "higher-ups." Dubai Indians' sense of being targeted by racial discrimination thus extended beyond the workplace into all aspects of their lives. They acknowledged that the government had made attempts to systemize bureaucratic processes, especially those around migration, such as outlawing employer retention of employee passports. They were also happy that the local media had started to actively "name and shame" establishments that excluded single South Asian men. However, they considered these gestures to be minor, and they thus continued to feel consigned to a lower stratum in Dubai.

My interlocutors experienced discrimination systematically as well as through individual incidents, which caused them to feel that, no matter what their jobs, salaries, or achievements, they were trapped and underappreciated. Thus frustration and rising insecurity were at the core of every one of our conversations. Middle-class Indians in Dubai developed a racial consciousness that emerged directly out of their experiences of living and working in a Dubai that was attempting to establish itself as a global city. This subjectivity was a product not simply of the hierarchical hiring and employment practices in the UAE, which had been in existence for several decades, but of the process of comparing experiences with members of other national and racial groups inside and outside the contemporary workplace with nostalgia for a past in which Dubai had purportedly been a less discriminatory place to live and work. In particular, increased racism was attributed to the influx of white expatriates into Dubai. The racial consciousness of Dubai Indians, however, was not at odds with their middle-class subjectivity, and in fact both worked hand in hand to produce the idea of a neoliberal market that was distinct from race, culture, or nationality. The nostalgia my interlocutors had for Dubai's past and their praise of India's current economic successes hinged on the idea that those who worked hard enough should and would succeed given an even playing field, an ideology they continued to espouse even as their direct experiences contradicted it. This market fundamentalism, however, overlooked the many advantages that the middle classes in Dubai and elsewhere had over their compatriots, and in fact reified middle-class exclusionary practices while also staking political claims to historical and cultural belonging in Dubai as an established and uniquely connected expatriate community.

Race and the Making of the Middle Class

While racial consciousness among the Indian diaspora emerged from shared experiences of discrimination in Dubai, it also hinged on middle-class subjectivity. Race and class were co-constituted in a way that perpetuated a set of exclusions even as they produced forms of solidarity. Thus, while the challenges of life in Dubai led to an identity that was imagined to include people from a number of national, regional, religious, and linguistic backgrounds, such challenges were also understood as specifically middle-class concerns. In fact, most of my interlocutors found themselves defining racial consciousness both with and against other Dubai Indians and South Asians. Jayant, a journalist who had moved to Dubai after postgraduate work in Delhi, conveyed themes that were present in my other interviews as well, themes that both reinforced and undermined a shared identity, saying, "The sense of identity is strengthened because there is a sense of discrimination against all Indians simply because a good number of Indians here are unskilled and not too well qualified and get paid less, so I tend to get the feeling, the discrimination that I sense makes me want to identify as an Indian, to show them that India is not what they think it is, that there is a lot of diversity. For every two people who are unskilled, there could definitely be at least one Indian that is very skilled."

As Jayant's comments illustrate, middle-class Indians were ambivalent toward other Indians. They often expressed solidarity and compassion for Indian laborers, who hailed mainly from the southern states of Kerala and Andhra Pradesh; many of them could not help but feel angry when they saw the working conditions of Indian "laborers," and they often assumed that locals or other expatriates could not feel the same level of compassion because they were not Indian themselves. But middle-class Indians also blamed migrants for the racism they experienced in their own lives, arguing that because uneducated and unskilled workers constitute the majority of South Asians in the Gulf, people assume all Indians are uneducated and unskilled. Therefore, my informants' racial consciousness was invariably qualified by an assertion of middle-class status, a status that made them feel superior to lower-wage migrants and therefore less deserving of racist targeting.[9] Embedded in this process of differentiation was the idea that Indians often bring discrimination on themselves; the system, many suggested, might be less discriminatory if all Indians were to practice self-management and possess greater self-respect. Thus, while criticizing a racist system, my informants also placed some of the blame for that system on Indians—but only on certain groups of Indians, who they counted as distinct from their own identities, subjectivities, and levels of achievement and status. The term *Indian* thus carried with it several shifting and contradictory meanings. In any one interview, an interlocutor might use *Indian* to indicate a sense of shared racial identity based on experiences within Dubai; to indicate and perpetuate stereotypes that others had of Indians; to distinguish themselves from "Indians" who were supposedly responsible for these stereotypes; and to claim the identity as a form of patriotism and connection to India. My conversation one afternoon over tea with a married couple, Rami and Ritu, in their high-rise apartment near Lamcy Mall (a popular South Asian shopping center), exemplified these ambivalent and multiple uses of *Indian*. Ritu is Hindu, and Rami Muslim. They met in university, married, then moved to Bahrain in the

1980s. After spending several years in Bahrain, they moved to Dubai, where they had been living and working as administrators in higher education for over twenty years.

NV: Tell me about Indians in Dubai. What kinds of jobs do they usually have?

RITU: Indians, there are too many here and in every job, from cleaning the roads, clearing garbage to bank directors, biggest doctors. I think in all the fields Indians are more prominent.

RAMI: Because most of them are laborers and low-category employees, so people think Indians are all poor and illiterate and good for nothing.

RITU: Yeah, like they will take any sort of thing without questioning, they will accept it. They will not be like Britishers.

RAMI: And we accept anything so we get that treatment. But there is discrimination in my workplace.

As the conversation continued, I asked Rami and Ritu whether discrimination was common in Dubai, and they said yes, then explained why.

RAMI: As long as Indians don't respect themselves there will be no respect for them. We accept anything, we accept any salary, we accept any job, we accept any crap, and we are responsible for it. We have lowered our levels. We have lower-level standards, and that's what we are paying for. You won't find a white man sweeping the roads or cleaning the drains but Indians will willingly do it. And ten guys will do it cheaper than ten other guys.

RITU: Maybe he [the white man] is a taxi driver over there, but over here he won't show that. He won't be a driver over here. There are too many of them [Indians], that is the reason. Keralites, all of them.

RAMI: We have lowered our standards all over the world. It is compulsion. They are compelled to get out of the country, compelled to take whatever they get, so there is no future for Indians in this country. It will get worse.

In the constant slippage between *we* and *they*, Rami and Ritu both acknowledged certain modes of shared identity and perpetuated some of the very stereotypes that they did not like to have used against themselves.

Ritu and Rami lamented the fact that they were forced into a system which "other" Indians helped to create, and thus removed themselves from the production of a discriminatory system in which Indians received lower salaries and less respect. Instead, they claimed, it was because other Indians did not manage themselves, either by not challenging an unfair system or by behaving according to stereotypes, that they themselves were mired in a system that they could not challenge and within stereotypes that they could not surpass. This roundabout logic emerged from the simultaneity of two contrasting modes of identification among the Indian middle class: as neoliberal participants in a free-market economy, and as a systematically oppressed and disenfranchised racial group. Thus, the necessity to distinguish between Indians was just as strong as the necessity to identify with them.

The idea that all South Indians are uneducated laborers was repeated especially in my conversations with North Indians. Rohit, the Punjabi architect and self-described "economic immigrant," told me that he was always careful to remind people that he is North Indian.

> Whenever some discussion comes up, especially with Western expats, you have to identify that you are a North Indian, because the mindset mostly with Western expats is with the South Indians, because they are the majority here and unfortunately they are doing the menial work, the low strata, so to the Western expat everybody is a typically South Indian—Maloo, Malabari. I have nothing against them, but this is a mindset of a Western expat and even Arab expatriates. That everything is from the lower stratum. So you have to say yes, I am from up north, I am a professional.

Not only did middle-class Indians distinguish themselves from low-wage foreign residents through such ethnic, educational, and regional parameters, but they also felt that they were quite distinct from the Indian elite. My interlocutors felt that Indian business owners, because they were employers, contributed to the oppression of other Indians. Elites were supposedly not as hardworking as middle-class and working-class Indians, relying instead on their longevity in the Gulf and their connections (wasta) with powerful Emiratis to bypass the difficulties of migration and life as foreign residents. Thus, they did not participate fairly in Dubai's free market. Middle-class stereotypes of Indian elites were similar to their stereotypes of Emiratis: they were excessive consumers, lazy, and got wealthy off the labor of others. Through their narratives, middle-class Indians in Dubai reified neoliberal technologies of belonging and subjectivity in which the ideal citizen is an entrepreneur of him or herself, and in which, under the condition of a free market, states should give preference to self-governing individuals.[10] This neoliberal ideology accompanies a shift in global discourses and technologies of governance from biopolitics to ethicopolitics, which focuses on risk-taking, enterprise, and self-management over the responsibilities (and control) of the state over its citizenry.[11] Belonging among middle-class Indians was therefore claimed on two levels: they saw themselves as the ideal subjects of Dubai in that they were hardworking, self-sufficient, and educated, but they also saw themselves as part of a racialized majority that was not treated equally. In this way, their diasporic racial consciousness was constantly constituted alongside a neoliberal outlook and a belief in market fundamentalism.

Middle-class Indians felt they were exercising free-market choice in coming to Dubai to work, but that the racial hierarchies into which they were inculcated restricted their ability to choose or negotiate. Complaints about mistreatment in Dubai were almost always accompanied by explanations of why Indians could do nothing about this mistreatment. At the same time, my informants had no immediate plans to move or change jobs. They often referred to India's economic boom, and many suggested that they could probably now earn more money in India than they were earning in Dubai. They also claimed that newer Indian migrants were "not allowing themselves" to get stepped on because they were less desperate to leave India. For example, Joyce felt that because of her visa issues and financial insecurities she could not challenge discrimination by her bosses, but she was confident that India's economic growth would make Indians less likely to accept inferior working and living conditions in today's market.

> Once upon a time in India we never had the options. Today we have the best of options. People are paid better salaries than they are paid in Dubai and they have their own home, they don't have to pay rent, water, electricity, buy a visa, be in the fear of losing a job. There if you lose your job you get another job the next day. People who have the skills are in high demand. You have the options of buying properties, vehicles, get married, everything on bank loans, so people are not going to be living here long if they have to scrape through life to live here. So Gulf countries should really think twice before just keeping on increas-

ing their rents. Lots of people are going back and are very happy, doing well.

Like Joyce, other middle-class Dubai Indians asserted their options, even as they complained about Dubai, as a way to showcase their choice and agency as self-managing subjects who participated in creating their current life conditions. Such claims were intended to demonstrate, to themselves and to those around them, that their sense of being trapped in Dubai was due to practices of calculated risk, choice, and self-management, by which they chose to stay despite racist hierarchies, rather than returning to India or moving elsewhere. Dubai's disadvantages did not negate their belief in Dubai as a potentially free market that could offer extensive economic opportunities. They attributed their negative experiences of being Indian in Dubai to the failure of Dubai's free market and a foreshadowing of immanent collapse of Dubai's bubble, to free-market forces being impeded by whites and locals, and to the Emirati government's inaction with regard to the recent imbalances between resident groups. Racial consciousness that emerged from their experiences of discrimination was a new subjectivity for Indians in Dubai, but it did not challenge their middle-class identifications or their belief in a free-market economy. In fact, racism, as it was attributed to the failure of globalization in Dubai, was a catalyst for further bounding the economy as distinct from culture and nation. Through a racial consciousness firmly rooted in middle-class identification and a neoliberal self-representation as "self-managing" subjects, middle-class Indians in Dubai actually participated in the production of a globalized economy that was distinct from race, nationality, culture, and the state. In so doing, however, they also asserted a form of belonging to Dubai that could not be contained by economic definitions, and that included staking geographical, historical, and cultural claims to the emirate.

Another interlinked form of identification emerged among middle-class Indians as a result of their migration experiences—consumer citizenship. My informants considered consumption, unlike racism, to be an economic practice that signaled market success. However, through their narratives and their practices around consumption and commodities, Indians in Dubai created forms of public and affective belonging to Dubai that distinguished them from Indians in India. While consumption of foreign brands and the transnational movement of products might seem to reify a globalized economy and disrupt the boundaries of nation-states, consumer citizenship practices among middle-class Indians in Dubai instead reinforced the idea that national identities were territorial. Like racial consciousness, consumer citizenship was a claim to the city even as it was a disavowal of belonging to the UAE nation. Thus it was a mode of urban citizenship that both reified and challenged the economic underpinnings of Indian daily life in Dubai.

Consumer Citizenship, Choice, and Claims to the City

Like Rohit in his comment likening Dubai to an "air-conditioned" bus, which implied that the emirate was wealthier than India, Dubai Indians explained the differences between India and the Gulf largely in economic terms. They described the conveniences and luxuries of life in Dubai, including air-conditioning, better cars, cleaner restaurants, reliable utilities, better electronics, lower crime, and well-maintained streets. I regularly asked my informants if India felt different now when they returned for visits, and most said yes, focusing on the difficulties of readjusting to electrical blackouts, heat, overcrowding, unregulated traffic, beggars, and the attitudes of their friends and relatives, who expected money and brand-name gifts. Bharati related her sense of comfort living in Dubai in almost exactly these terms, saying, "There are no power cuts, any other problems, no water problem, you can still have a housemaid, you can use a.c. twenty-four hours and not worry. From that point of view you are comfortable. It is difficult to move back to India once you get used to this, people have difficulty adjusting." While Bharati frames her preference for Dubai in terms of luxuries, she also claims it as a home by mentioning the potential difficulties in "adjusting" to a return to India. The experience of Dubai as a space of luxury and comfort relative to the hardships of India constituted a form of belonging that I call consumer citizenship—one that was integral to shifting identities among Indians in Dubai, and one that led to affective and political stakes in the city that were in fact irreducible to the economic terms through which they were often framed.

Liberal theory assumes that identity is based on citizenship in terms of territorial belonging to a nation-state and democratic rights. However, as Inderpal Grewal argues through her study of South Asian diasporas, contemporary identities are often transnational and defined through consumer practices. In the 1990s, for example, consumer culture made certain subjectivities possible for South Asians in the United States, and "discourses of individuality yoked freedom to participation in consumer culture and associated political freedoms with self-improvement."[12] Indeed, each of my middle-class interlocutors expressed a change in their own subjectivity through a reference to Dubai's "conveniences" and to the choices they made to consume products and services available in the city.[13] These conveniences and the practices of consuming them were not only part of the production of Indian foreign resident citizenship in the city, but they were also central to the production of middle-class identifications and ideologies that reified market fundamentalism and a distinction between Dubai's "global" economy and the UAE's autochthonous nation. My interlocutors felt they were consuming Dubai based on economic opportunity and the "freedom" to showcase style and preference, and that it was their level of economic opportunity alone that produced forms of difference between them, the people they had left behind in India, and both elite and working-class Dubai Indians. As Mark Liechty has argued, however, middle-classness is less about income and more about consumer desires and practices which exist "in-between" the imagined poles of wealthy and poor.[14] Consumption produces middle-classness as a subjectivity infused with ideologies about cosmopolitanism, neoliberalism, and modernity. Similarly, my middle-class informants associated consumption with social status, freedom, and a more "international" attitude than their counterparts. Though rising costs in Dubai were making remittance practices more difficult for Dubai Indians in the mid-2000s, the simultaneous rise of consumer culture in Dubai through branding, shopping festivals, and lotteries also made commodities and consumption practices more central to people's lives, and led Indians to think of disposable income as a mode of diasporic "freedom."

When I visited Dubai for the first time, Gautam's wife and family were in India for the summer, and although he was working most of the time, he found a few evenings to show my husband and me around the city. For Gautam, driving us around Dubai and showing us shopping malls and luxury hotels was a form of hospitality—he was showing us *his* city. And he insisted it was his home we were visiting; therefore, even though he was clearly overworked and underpaid, he refused to let us pay for meals, drinks, or souvenirs. Every evening we spent together, he took us to a shopping mall and showed us what was on offer in Dubai. He told us about lotteries in which people buy in for 500 dirhams (a lot of money for middle-class Indians) but have relatively good chances of winning a kilo of gold or a BMW or free rent for a year. He often participated in these lotteries, though he had never won, and his friends and colleagues did as well. Lotteries, which were quite commonplace in Dubai and incorporated into the marketing campaigns of several companies, were representative both of the idea of the "dream" of becoming rich in Dubai and the economics of risk and chance through which middle-class Indians understood their existences in the Gulf. Other interlocutors similarly took me to shopping malls for weekend outings after I had met them for interviews, and they often spent these outings pointing out products and services Dubai offered that made it distinct from both India and the United States.

Introducing one's Dubai life to outsiders involved showing off the various consumption venues around the city and their over-the-top spectacles. But most of my interlocutors could not afford to consume the things they were showing me. They took me to malls with designer European labels, but rarely entered the shops. They drove me to fancy hotels, but entered only as far as the lobby. They purchased lottery tickets, but seemed never to win the expensive items that they otherwise would never be capable of buying. Dubai's consumer culture provided ways in which middle-class Indians could participate in activities around the city without having to feel that they were excluded due to a lack of resources. In fact, the only "public" spaces remaining in many parts of Dubai are shopping malls, where people can congregate without having to pay.[15] Coffee shops require that one make a purchase, and even parks have entrance fees and are therefore not "public." For example, Za'abeel, an extravagant park that opened in Karama in 2006, with light-up sidewalk tiles, twenty-foot-tall animal balloons, and a gigantic children's play area, cost five dirhams for entry. Therefore, during cooler evenings, many South Asians who lived nearby exercised by walking around the perimeter of the park, where they could proceed without having to contend with traffic signals and cars.

Public space and consumption were thus inextricably connected in Dubai, for congregating, socializing, and leisure activity most often required inhabiting the city's various consumer spaces. Through the process of moving around through the city and interacting with its material offerings, middle-class Indians carved out their identification with Dubai; they showcased the options, but rarely partook of them, and the spectacle of consumption constituted a cultural practice in and of itself. My informants consumed the consumer culture of Dubai and formed their belonging through this culture, even more than through the actual consumption of material goods. Their practices of engaging with these sites were therefore less about spending and more about staking claims to the city as their home. While they did spend money on children's toys, eating out, movies, and clothes—money that they would not have been able to spend in extended family situations in India—their belonging to Dubai was to a site of consumption rather than to the commodities themselves. This kind of "consumption" of Dubai's consumer culture in effect transformed the city's seemingly exclusive private shopping malls and hotels into new kinds of "public" spaces that constituted middle-class belonging in Dubai, even as they remained, nonetheless, like all publics, exclusionary.[16]

Friends and family back in India also considered Dubai a site of consumerism, which was in part why my interlocutors felt increased pressure to return with commodities like electronics, clothing, and gold jewelry as gifts. Dubai's brands and shops are so well known in India that family members ask for them by name. Many scholars of migration have noted how the consumption of Gulf culture in the form of commodities and remittances is changing social status and family relationships in South Asia.[17] As one South Indian salesperson told me, "Kerala is very much Dubai, and Dubai is very much Kerala." The rising familiarity with and consumption of Gulf products in India contributed to the claiming of Dubai as an Indian cultural space, but also created tension between Dubai Indians' desire to consume personally and their sense of material responsibility to remit in the form of money and commodities. Indians in Dubai often felt that Indians in India, most often members of their extended family, did not understand them; family members assumed that because they lived in Dubai they were well off, pressured them for money, and did not understand the hardships of living in the Gulf. My interlocutors claimed to have become more open-minded since coming to Dubai, where they were exposed to other nationalities and cultures, and that they had difficulty relating to the close-mindedness of friends and family back "home." Thus, the consumer culture of the city extended even in their own narratives beyond economic access to goods and services; rather, it produced a marked shift in middle-class Dubai Indian identities, to the point that they now felt out of place in India.

Middle-class Indians particularly differed in their experiences of consumer citizenship based on gender. My women interlocutors, while acknowledging employment-related stresses, were more likely to say that

Dubai offered them increased freedom. This freedom was twofold: they felt safer, and this increased their mobility and independence. For example, Shalini, who is divorced and lives alone, said, "It is very safe compared to other countries. I feel Dubai is really, really safe. We used to go for movies before marriage and never had any problems, second show after we finished work in the hotel. . . . We used to go, just girls, and come back— absolutely safe." According to Shalini and many of the women I interviewed, one could more freely move around in Dubai than in India and could socialize and spend leisure time more easily. The greater independence and mobility women felt in Dubai was also due to the lack of extended family, who they felt often kept an eye on them, did not let them go out as much, and criticized their actions. Being in the Gulf was a way for some women to work outside of the home, have access to new experiences, and keep disposable income for themselves and their immediate nuclear families.[18] Ruba Salih, in a study of Moroccan women workers in Italy, argues that commodities create home spaces for Moroccan women, who think of Morocco as home when in Italy, but do not feel at home when actually in Morocco.[19] Thus, practices of consumption can highlight tensions about where home really is. And, as Mark Johnson has documented in the case of Filipina workers in the Gulf, the consumption of certain commodities like clothes and fast food is oftentimes a form of resistance against other kinds of consumption that inculcate women into particular gender and family dynamics, like the buying of gold and gifts for family members back home.[20] Similarly, for Indian women in Dubai, certain forms of consumption increased their personal power, while others tethered them to family obligations. Many middle-class Indian women, for example, purchased brand-name clothing and other items for themselves and their children, and they ate in restaurants with their families; at the same time, however, they spent a lot of money building and furnishing houses in India that they rarely got to see, as well as a lot of time collecting gifts to distribute on return visits.

Men sometimes struggled with the very things women found liberating. For example, some men told me that Dubai and its material "freedoms" put pressure on families. Charlie, who had divorced soon after arriving in the Gulf, felt that living in Dubai was especially stressful for men, saying, "A lot of guys that want to make money, they keep their families back, so that is also a lot of stress, and I know a lot of families breaking up here, more cases of Indian marriages not working out. It is very open market here, it is very free, and people get into all sorts of stuff, and back home they are sending money and they get used to that. I know loads of people that have changed after coming here." Both men and women lamented the fact that Dubai had fewer "family values" than India, pointing out the prevalence of commercial sex-work, the number of people they knew who were having affairs, the lasciviousness of Arab men, and the promiscuity of European and East Asian women as threats to the family. However, the issue of family values was a more minor concern for women, and they were inclined to highlight the good things Dubai offers. While men's narratives usually revolved around racial consciousness and shared experiences of discrimination, middle-class women more often asserted consumer citizenship as a form of belonging. However, men also practiced consumer citizenship, and all of my informants felt torn between a sense of responsibility and obligation to family members back home and a desire to assert their independence through practices of consumption. Their understandings of consumption were also filtered through a middle-class neoliberal subjectivity that focused on choice and management. They were therefore preoccupied with the need to self-manage disposable income, and they often critiqued other people's consumption in terms of bad choices, focusing, for example, on how Emiratis and wealthy expatriates were "wasting" their wealth on cars and designer clothes instead of responsibly investing it.[21]

Emiratis themselves also practice consumer citizenship, but their assertions of propriety over the UAE as a country are primarily made in terms of formal citizenship—rights and territoriality—and less in terms of urban belonging.[22] This reifies the Emirati nation-state as distinct from its economy, for foreigners can exist within the economy, but the nation-state is the sole purview of citizens. However, by similarly asserting their belonging in terms of their own nationalities—where they hold formal citizenship—and by denying the social and cultural aspects of consumption, Indian foreign residents also produced the UAE nation and national identity as based in rights and territoriality. Consumption, for my informants, was seen as integral to their participation in neoliberal market practices, not as a form of belonging to Dubai, even as their narratives and practices of consumption produced urban and diasporic citizenship that exceeded the economically driven rationales of choice and freedom through which they were interpellated, and through which they themselves defined their actions and motives.

Conclusion

Consumer citizenship and racial consciousness among middle-class salaried Indians in Dubai simultaneously produced Dubai's economy as global and neoliberal and national identity as based in official forms of territorial and patrilineal belonging to the nation-state. But in so doing these subjectifications also created forms of belonging for Indians in Dubai that exceeded the economic framework within which they were supposedly migrating, working, and living in the city. These forms of belonging undermined definitions of migration and identity as based on separated, abstractable domains like "market," "nation," and "culture," and thus required the constant performance and reiteration of practices and discourses that solidified the boundaries between them, not only by the state and by the Emirati citizenry, but, more importantly, by Indians, the primary exceptions to citizenship in the UAE.

My middle-class interlocutors self-identified as Indian based on their nationality and their lack of citizenship options in the UAE. They articulated their migration solely in economic terms and developed a racial consciousness that, while posited against their differential treatment by whites and Arabs, was inseparable from class, and in fact rehearsed middle-class identities and a belief in supposedly middle-class values and practices. Middle-class Indians believed in market fundamentalism and the possibility of economic success based in meritocracy, and they policed their own and others' practices in order to be self-managing subjects. Their racial consciousness relied deeply on separating themselves from both working-class laborers and business elites. They were therefore neither "those" Indians who took abuse and worked in demeaning positions, nor "those" Indians who flaunted their wealth and exploited their compatriots. Practices of consumption were also important to middle-class Indian life in Dubai, but my informants had to constantly negotiate a tension that allowed them to assert consumer citizenship in the UAE and independence from family in India on the one hand, and to fulfill the economic responsibilities and obligations of migration on the other. In fact, it was the ability to successfully manage this tension that contributed to middle-class Indians' understandings of themselves as self-managing subjects. However, my interlocutors viewed consumption as an economic practice that was separate from UAE national identity and from their own social and cultural identities, which contributed to producing the economy as distinct from the nation, thereby reinforcing the notion that belonging in the UAE, like everywhere else, is passport-based and territorial, even as their consumer citizenship practices resulted in diasporic subjectivities and claims to the city's "public" spaces that superseded their legal status as outsiders.

Many accounts of middle-class migrants around the world and many accounts of migration to the Gulf assume the primacy of the economic in people's migration choices, life chances, affects, and attachments. However, the economic is not separate from or fundamentally more essential than other domains of human undertaking. In fact, the economic fundamentalism of migration representations—whether they come from states, extranational organizations, scholars, or migrants themselves—work to elide the human elements of daily existence for transnational populations. To take the assertion of "economic" migration and passport-based belonging at face value is to ignore the ways in which the narratives and practices of middle-class Indians in Dubai, like transnational migrants everywhere, *produce* economic migration and passport-based belonging while simultaneously exposing the instability of these paradigms.

5 · BECOMING INDIAN IN DUBAI

PAROCHIALISMS AND GLOBALISMS

IN PRIVATIZED EDUCATION

When your mail came around it was like, this is my chance to say what I feel about the place, so I think you will have lots of people excited to talk about it. Because nobody talks about Indians and nobody cares. I mean, fine, you have it in your head that you are here to do what you have to do, and you have to go back someday, so that is there. But you have lived here, you want to do something here.—AMINA, *24, office worker, American University of Sharjah class of 2004*

In her now canonical work on transnationalism, Aihwa Ong explores how citizenship in an era of neoliberal globalization is "flexible," and she points to how certain privileged Asian youth are "astronauts" or "parachute children" who can move easily across borders and reside in several locations due to their parents' wealth and business connections.[1] In Dubai I met several young South Asians who might fall into this category: their parents were middle- or upper-class business owners, executives, managers, or professionals, many of whom owned homes in South Asia; they were fairly well traveled; and they attended college and graduate school either in India, the West, or in newer branch campuses of American universities in the Gulf Arab States. Ashish, an interlocutor who became my good friend during and after fieldwork, is one such young person. From an upper-middle-class Sindhi family, Ashish was born and raised in Dubai. His father owns a garment company that does business across the Middle East and South Asia. After attending Indian primary and secondary schools in Dubai, Ashish went to the American University of Sharjah (AUS), which is affiliated with American University in Washington, D.C. After graduating from AUS, he entered a prestigious master's program in the United States. Ashish speaks with an impossible-to-place accent that seems at once Indian, American, and British, exhibits a cosmopolitan knowledge of different parts of the world, and is an avid photographer, erudite budding political analyst, and active blogger. When I met him, before his trip to the United States for graduate school, his aspirations for the future were to work for the United Nations or at a policy-oriented think tank that focused on the Middle East. However, Ashish's seemingly global "astronaut" orientation consistently brushed up against forms of immobility and parochial identifications through which he was also interpellated, both in Dubai and in the United States. While he aspired to live and work in the United States or the Gulf, his ability to reside in both of these places, to move between them, and to build the future that he desired were not always possible because of his Indian passport and because he had reached an age when he was no longer guaranteed residency in Dubai. In other words, there were times when his parachute did not open.

One such time occurred a few days before Christmas in 2007, when I was living in California. I received an unexpected phone call from Ashish, who was in the midst of his master's program in Washington, D.C. He wanted to know if it was too late to take me up on an offer I had extended to visit me during his winter break. "But I thought you were going back home to Dubai," I said. "I was," he responded, "but I have been to the airport twice so far and they won't let me get on the plane." It turns out that Ashish, who holds an Indian passport because he is unable to naturalize in the United Arab Emirates, and is no longer considered his father's dependent, not only needed a visa to return home, but the American-based airline he was flying also wanted to see his actual paper visa—the faxed copy from Dubai that he had was not sufficient for the airline staff. The original visa was waiting for Ashish at the Dubai airport per common Emirati procedure, but the rules of the airline were such that people of certain nationalities were not allowed to board a flight to the UAE without an official visa in their passport. Given that it was the weekend and right before Christmas, the Emirati embassy in the United States was closed, and Ashish was unable to clear up the matter. As I listened to him express his anger and frustration over this incident, I thought back to several conversations we had had in Dubai about his identity as a second-generation foreign resident of the emirate. In our first interview, when I asked him to describe his identity, he referred to himself as "Indian by default." I asked him to explain, and he said, "I basically feel that as an Indian I would never be a full equal over here. I am discriminated against. I wouldn't be able to get equal pay for equal work. I am always going to be second-class even if I were to get citizenship somehow. I would never be accepted as one of them."

Ashish's sense of second-class identity was a politicization that grew out of his inability to transcend a parochialized Indian existence in the UAE and elsewhere, but it was also a diasporic claim to citizenship and racial justice in Dubai, the only "home" that he had ever known.[2] Several scholars of diaspora have highlighted the cultural "in-betweenness" or "confusion" of second-generation South Asian immigrants that stems from two distinct identity pulls; I approach this population through a different yet interconnected lens of in-betweenness—the production of parochial and global identities through privatized education in the United Arab Emirates; more specifically, the rupture between the experiences of South Asian youth in primary and secondary education on the one hand, and in Western universities and American branch campuses on the other. Ashish and the other young people I introduce here understood and expressed their identities, belongings, and futures differently from their parents and even from South Asians raised in the Gulf a few years before them—the Dubai Indians whose experiences, narratives, and claims to belonging I have already explored. Newer generations of young people raised in the UAE were thus articulating a reconceptualization of South Asian diasporic identities in the mid-2000s, a reconceptualization that can be traced in large part to a seemingly insignificant but quite consequential shift taking place in the Gulf. Over the last decade, there has been a dramatic influx of American and Western-style universities into the Gulf Arab States, universities that are particularly attractive to middle- and upper-class noncitizens, who otherwise would need to leave the Gulf in order to obtain higher education. These universities, which were stark contrasts to their primary and secondary schools, were providing new experiences, encounters, and vocabularies by which second-generation youth could express and understand the process of becoming Indian in Dubai.

Forms of higher education have only recently become available to noncitizens in the Gulf, through the influx of Western university branch campuses and for-profit degree programs. Globalized higher education in the Gulf is among state incentives to diversify away from oil wealth into "knowledge-based" economies, and it is attractive to ruling families as a way to train citizens to be locally and globally more competitive in order to reduce the current reliance on foreign labor.[3] Ironically, however, these universities are attended most often by middle- and upper-class foreign residents. While branch campuses are often understood as indicators of the erosion of the values of the Western university—particularly academic freedom, critical thinking, pedagogy, and disinterested knowledge production—the classroom and social interactions within these campuses are proliferating new forms of citizenship and belonging for Gulf residents. Branch campuses have a particularly important relationship with emerging forms of racial consciousness and claims to belonging among noncitizen members of diaspora groups that have long-standing ties with the region. These universities extend the length of time noncitizen children can stay in Gulf countries. In them, too, South Asian students, despite having grown up in a "global city" like Dubai, often have their first experience of sustained contact with Emiratis or other foreign nationals. This is because primary and secondary schools in Dubai, like the geographic spaces of the city, regularly segregate foreign residents both from citizens and along national lines. Private education at the primary and secondary level therefore produces foreign residents as temporary migrants and as nationals of their homelands, effectively cutting off the possibility of their belonging to the UAE nation.[4] The university experience was one of dissonance and rupture between the parochialized forms of education that South Asian youth went through in primary and secondary school and the multicultural and supposedly egalitarian platform of the Western university, where they received liberal, neoliberal, and "global" forms of citizenship training. In particular, because these universities were located within the very "home" that South Asian youth knew, the dissonances created by moving from a parochial insular lifestyle to one in which they had sustained intimate contact with Emiratis and other nationals made "home" an increasingly unstable and politicized concept.

In this chapter I explore the conditions of middle-class South Asian young people's existences in Dubai as "in-between" subjects whose identities both overlap with and diverge from those of diasporic youth in other parts of the world. I also consider how growing up in Dubai produced a different sense of self and home for the second generation than their parents articulated. Moving from parochial to neoliberal and globalized forms of identity production enabled new and unexpected diasporic subjectivities, definitions of belonging, and even politicizations, particularly among students who attended university within the UAE. Indian and Pakistani students who attended schools like American University in Sharjah articulated identifications that were extensions of their South Asian noncitizen positionality in Dubai, but these identifications were also differently enabled and mobilized as they experienced first-hand the promises and failures of global and neoliberal citizenship that Western universities in the Gulf deploy. The narratives and experiences of these young people challenge the forms of belonging and exclusion through which South Asians in Dubai have historically been interpellated and through which my other interlocutors expressed their understandings of citizenship, migration, and identity. The emerging forms of politicization and claims to "second-class" citizenship by South Asian university students point to potential larger-scale shifts in the relationship between Gulf States and their foreign resident populations, and to new claims to the city, the Emirati nation, and the region within South Asian diasporic futures.

DBCD: Dubai-Born Confused Desi?

The histories of South Asians in the Gulf, the forms of citizenship and governance that contemporary Gulf states deploy, and the regulatory regimes into which foreigners in the Gulf are imbricated challenge us to think through what diasporic citizenship means on the level of daily life for different immigrant communities in these countries and how this is changing with the influx of educational options that allow for more settled existences. Indian middle-class communities do not neatly fit into the category of "expat" or "migrant," for while they participate in certain neoliberal rhetorics of Dubai's economic freedoms and disavowals of formal belonging, they also both have a long history of trade and settlement that pre-dates oil, and they struggle within contemporary racial hierarchies that present them with economic and social difficulties that their European or Arab peers often do not encounter. In the UAE and in other Gulf States, the ability to migrate with family members is based on minimum salary requirements for the male head of household (at the time of my research this was 4,500 dirhams, or a little over $1,200).[5] Therefore, the young people I discuss were able to grow up in the UAE because their parents had achieved some degree of middle-class status. Foreign children are sponsored by their fathers, and their ability to reside in the UAE is predicated on this sponsorship. Foreign children are ineligible for naturalization and retain the nationality of their fathers, regardless of whether they were born in the Gulf. Boys can be sponsored on their fathers' visas only until they turn eighteen or graduate from university; girls, on the other hand, are considered dependent until marriage or until they find employment that provides them with their own visa sponsorship. Second-generation futures in the UAE are therefore profoundly uncertain, and these uncertainties are highly gendered as well. This uncertainty—combined with the ubiquity of South Asian peoples, products, and services in the downtown neighborhoods of Dubai, where the majority of the South Asian diaspora lives—led South Asian youth to develop understandings of identity that were both oriented toward South Asia and firmly rooted in Dubai. Young people born and raised in Dubai shared some forms of identification and nationalism with their parents and with Dubai Indians of older generations, but they also differed from these groups in their sense of belonging to Dubai. To some degree, South Asian Dubai-born young people exhibited characteristics scholars have noted among diasporic cultural productions, narratives, and community formations in other parts of the world. Much of the work on South Asian diasporic identity focuses on the dissonances and challenges of cultural duality that second-generation migrants experience.[6] The term ABCD, for example, which stands for American-Born Confused Desi (*desi* being a colloquial term for South Asian), has become common jargon among South Asian communities in the West as well as in Indian cultural productions, like Bollywood films. Dubai-raised young people's narratives also contained elements of "confusion" or biculturality, but in ways that were specific to the Dubai context.

I regularly asked Dubai-raised young people how they identified themselves, and while they all said they were Indian or Pakistani and not Emirati—a feeling they shared with most of their older compatriots—they also qualified their identities quite strongly with "Dubai," stressing that South Asian cultures and communities are different in Dubai than in South Asia. In fact, they felt a sense of foreignness when they traveled to the subcontinent, even as they experienced Dubai as a South Asian sociocultural space. For example, Ashish told me he identifies as "Indian in Dubai as opposed to someone just from Dubai. The Indian part of it would be relatively important even though I don't particularly strongly identify as an Indian per se, only because I never actually lived in India." Thus, his statement that he is "Indian by default." He did not feel the nationalistic pull toward India that many older Indians and newer migrants expressed, but he also had no other available options in terms of identification. Similarly, Haneefa, who grew up in a Shi'a Indian community in Dubai, told me that she considers herself Indian, but finds India itself very unfamiliar: "When I go back I feel I am an alien and I don't know why. And my friends feel the same way. They are so self-conscious about themselves that they only wear Indian clothes. I ask them if it is because they want to get in touch with their Indian culture, and they say 'No, we are just self-conscious because people look at us.'" Haneefa and her friends were more out of place in their "home" countries than in Dubai. Even while feeling like strangers in South Asia, however, young people had a sense of connection with their nationalities and were patriotic to varying extents. Nadia, who had spent her whole life in Dubai but held a Pakistani passport, was both loyal to Pakistan and ambivalent, like Ashish and Haneefa, about actually living in South Asia: "I am proud to be a Pakistani. I love Pakistan. I love my country. Pakistan is Pakistan. I will definitely choose a Pakistani to marry if I get one. What should I call this feeling I have? Of course when I go there I feel like a foreigner. I don't know anything, I don't know where to go, where to shop from, which road to go if I want to go to my uncle's house. Here I know everything." Despite their patriotism and identification with "homeland," my young interlocutors found South Asia unappealing as a place to settle permanently, unlike their parents who, regardless of years spent in the Gulf, were perpetually planning for return. It was Dubai that was home for those born and brought up in the city. Despite her affection for Pakistan, Nadia said, "If anyone tells me now go to Pakistan and get settled there I would not do it. I love Dubai. I did O levels, A levels, everything, graduated in Dubai. No tension, all my siblings are, Ma'shallah [thank God], here. My home is Dubai. I am born here, I did everything here. I feel Dubai is my country."

Nadia's comments may appear contradictory: she says both that she loves "her country," Pakistan, and that "Dubai is my country." However, a dual sense of identity emerged in almost all of my interviews with South Asian youth in Dubai; they articulated that they were Indian or Pakistani in Dubai, but that they were not Indian or Pakistani in the way people who lived in those countries were. The feelings of cultural duality expressed by South Asian youth in Dubai mirror what scholars have found among diaspora populations in Western countries, where people do have some access to permanent residency or citizenship. In other words, Dubai-born Confused Desi (DBCD) self-identifications were not too far removed from the ABCD ones that circulate in literature, scholarship, and popular media.[7] However, my informants also felt that they were different than people like myself, an American of South Asian origin, and they addressed this difference openly in our conversations. When I asked Amina about Indians in Dubai and Indians in other countries, she stated that they were quite different from each other because "Indians in Dubai are conformist with what is happening in India. They have not lost their identity. People still wear the traditional clothes, not like we have given up our culture. Even young people growing up with me, you can see them going to *dhandhia* [a popular form of Gujarati dance] or *Diwali* [the most important Hindu holiday]. They still celebrate it over here. . . . My dad's brothers have settled in Canada and England, their kids are different because they have lost all cultural identity. Here people retain. They speak the language, retain the culture. They have knowledge."

Like their parents, second-generation Dubai Indians associated Western diasporics with a lack of culture; unlike their parents, however, they envied the citizenship and political rights available to immigrants in countries like the United States, Canada, and Australia, and many expressed a desire to eventually have permanent citizenship in the Gulf or in the West. They were quite aware that their positions were more tenuous than mine, despite our similar class backgrounds and parental occupations. These young people associated greater rights with living in North American or European countries, or perhaps in Australia or South Africa. They felt that they would also have more freedoms in India, but did not find it appealing as a place to settle. While older middle-class and elite foreign residents associated "freedom" with economic opportunities, Dubai-raised youth connected it to Western values and systems of government, a connection that may have resulted from the forms of citizenship training that they received in Western institutions of higher education. While they were critical of the West for eroding people's cultures and culturally preferred Dubai, the West inevitably came up in our conversations as a possible future home, reflecting both the lack of rights they felt in Dubai and the international education systems to which they had been exposed, which often prepared them for life abroad. For my informants, the West was a site of desire but also of necessity: they craved increased rights, were accustomed to certain commodities, and knew they might have to leave the Gulf. For many of these young people, the West was therefore the best option available.[8] They considered Dubai home, but were not comfortable living their lives in perpetual uncertainty. Haneefa explained, "What if something happens to my dad and I am not married? Of course I am working and can go through my work, but how long can one go on like this? There should be a stop somewhere. People are going to be, like, 'I am not going to take this anymore.' This is why when I get married I would prefer to go abroad." Even though Haneefa considered Dubai her only home, she was aware that her life there as an unmarried woman was precarious and was therefore preparing herself for a future abroad. Haneefa was also adamant that she would not want to raise her children in Dubai, a sentiment many of her peers also shared. They wanted their children to have the juridico-legal rights that came with citizenship, and they were also concerned that Dubai was too materialistic. So, even as they laid claim to Dubai as their home, second-generation South Asians were ambivalent about whether to remain there indefinitely.

The question of where to settle and raise a family points to another major realm of uncertainty for many young Dubai-raised South Asians—marriage. As Haneefa's comments highlight, marriage questions brought up the gendered nature of belonging and exclusion in the UAE. The young men I spoke to had a sense of insecurity because they needed to find jobs immediately after finishing school if they wanted to stay in Dubai; however, many of them were expected to work in family businesses after graduation, which would secure their residency. Young women, on the other hand, experienced insecurity both in terms of jobs and in terms of marriage prospects. I had a long conversation over coffee one evening with Priti and Anjali, two women in their early twenties who had just completed college, Priti in Australia and Anjali at an Australian university in Dubai. I started by asking how they identify themselves, since both had been raised in Dubai by Indian foreign resident parents.

> ANJALI: Indian. In Dubai you don't get the "Dubai Indian" thing like you guys have [in the United States]. If we lived in Australia we would have another tag, but here you are just Indian because you don't merge with the locals.

> PRITI: You are always on a temporary basis; you have to go back at any time. You don't get the benefits like free schooling. You don't feel like you are actually part of the city. But you do know you live here. This is home for us. If I had to say where I was from, I would say Dubai. So it is sort of a two-pronged thing. With everyone here you would say Indian

and with everyone abroad you would say . . . like when I went to Australia I'd tell them I'm Indian but I've grown up in Dubai. So I'd still mention the Indian part and I wouldn't just identify myself as Dubai.

Our conversation revealed how identity for Priti and Anjali was relative and difficult to pin down, but the gendered aspects of tenuously belonging to Dubai became even more apparent when, during our conversation, Anjali's boyfriend arrived. A Pakistani national raised in Saudi Arabia, Umer was attending university in Dubai, where he met Anjali. Since I was recording the discussion, I observed the formalities, which included explaining to him that everything he said would be anonymous if he chose to participate in the interview. Anjali jokingly commented, "Yeah, and tomorrow our names are in the paper—my dad goes, 'You're not on my passport anymore.'" The other two laughed nervously in response. Anjali's comment showed not only how normal the insecurity of "home" was to these young people, but also the very gendered ways in which women's futures were tied closely to the decisions their parents made for them about marriage. While Dubai-based interethnic marriages are becoming more common, they are still considered undesirable by Indian parents, and therefore Anjali, a Hindu Indian, had not told her parents about her relationship with her Muslim Pakistani boyfriend and did not intend to, even though the pair had begun to seriously discuss marriage. When I asked Priti how important nationality would be for her parents, on a scale of one to ten, when it came to a future son-in-law, she answered, "52," as Anjali and Umer chuckled in agreement. It was not just older Indians who pressured their children about the importance of nationality and cultural identity, however; young people themselves often echoed these sentiments. Their sense of being Indian and maintaining Indian cultural and religious values included marrying other Indians. But, for women especially, where they ended up geographically was intricately tied to marriage. While many people do find Indian matches in Dubai or other parts of the Gulf, most girls grow up expecting arranged and semi-arranged marriages with Indians in India or in other parts of the diaspora.[9] Therefore, the young women I spoke to—all of whom were unmarried, some of whom were working—were unclear about where they would be even a year down the road. They expressed a desire to marry eventually, but no urgency about the matter.

It is noteworthy that when asked where their homes were, my young interlocutors invariably said Dubai, never the United Arab Emirates.[10] For them, as for other Dubai Indians, Dubai was a space apart, different from the rest of the Gulf because of the large Indian population and the ubiquity of Indian languages, food, commodities, and social groups. Their sense of belonging was thus framed by urban citizenship, not by nationalist sentiment toward the UAE. Yush, who lives in Sharjah, the neighboring emirate, said that Dubai was unlike other places in the Gulf and the UAE: "If you go out of the country, you say I am from Dubai; you don't say I am from the UAE." Dubai for Yush and for his peers was above all a South Asian— and especially an *Indian*—social and cultural space. After all, they had lived most of their lives in communities that were nationally segregated through the city's geographic and social mappings of belonging and exclusion. The sense of Indianness that infused Dubai was additionally strengthened for those raised there because they were taught Indian citizenship and belonging through a privatized education system that produced foreign residents' future orientation toward a return to South Asia or migration out of the UAE. Ashish's comment that he was "Indian by default" reflected his sense that he had no possibility for any other national identification. His comment also was indicative of how Emirati forms of governmentality, belonging, and exclusion operated in the production of second-generation youth as Indian "by default." In fact, this notion of South Asian identity was produced not only by proximity to India and parental denial of official belonging, but also by the ways in which state and corporate interests worked together to teach specifically Indian forms of citizenship and identity to children through the segregation of foreign groups from citizens in privatized education and through the promotion of nation-based learning options for migrants. In the UAE's primary- and secondary-education systems, citizens receive free public education in Arabic (and, more recently, in English), while noncitizens attend private schools most often based on their nationalities. The separation in education based on nationality—and not only the demographic and cultural ubiquity of India in Dubai—is integral to the production of parochialized South Asian identities among second-generation youth.

Producing Parochialisms through Education

Among the welfare benefits instituted by the UAE government following independence was free access to public education for all citizens.[11] In contrast, foreign residents have no access to public education and rely on an ever-expanding range of private educational options for their children. While some expats can afford to send their children to expensive international schools—which are often subsidized by their employers—most foreigners in Dubai send their children to less expensive private schools that are nationality-based. These schools tend to cost less than Western or international schools, are usually close to the ethnic neighborhoods that foreign-resident groups reside in, and are attractive to parents interested in preserving national "culture" for their children. In Dubai more than a hundred schools cater specifically to national groups, the majority of them Indian. There are also schools that cater to Filipino children and teach a Filipino curriculum, French schools, Russian schools, Iranian schools, Arabic schools, Australian schools, British schools that prepare children for O and A level exams, and American schools that prepare children for the SATs. Most Indian schools teach an Indian curriculum and prepare students for CBSE (Central Board of Secondary Education) exams and for exams from a particular state, like Kerala. Some Indian schools teach an American or British curriculum. Indian students in Dubai are therefore educated to attend colleges in India or in other parts of the world. In fact, the UAE government is committed to expanding the "quality" of education for Indian students, but in a way that maintains this parochial orientation toward India and keeps Indian students segregated from citizens. While teaching is in English, many schools offer Hindi and regional languages, and also teach aspects of Indian history and culture.[12] Arabic is now required at private schools, but most Arabic training is cursory. The Dubai-schooled foreign residents that I interviewed spoke Arabic only at a very basic level, and most of them (particularly non-Muslims) could not read Arabic script.[13] Indian schools do accept non-Indian students; however, they make up a tiny fraction of the student population, usually one or two per grade. Indian and other private schools are run mostly by foreign residents and also employ mostly noncitizens, usually from the same national background as the school itself. For example, Our Own English High School, a highly regarded Indian curriculum school, is staffed primarily by Indian teachers.[14] It is owned and managed by GEMS Education Solutions, a subsidiary of the Varkey Group, which is owned by an Indian businessman in Dubai and is one of the largest private-education corporations in the world.[15] The Varkey Group began by establishing Indian schools in the UAE and has since expanded to include international schools that teach

British and U.S. curricula throughout the Gulf, in India, and in the United Kingdom. The schools started by Varkey in the late 1960s were among the first private schools for foreigners in the Gulf, and they have set the standard for the nationality-based structure of private education in the region.

My middle-class informants referred to private education, among other things, as "indirect taxation." Even though Dubai is supposedly tax free, many Indians were subject to hidden costs of living in the Gulf, a major one being private education, which is a necessity for foreign residents raising their families in Dubai. My interlocutors argued that "indirect taxation" affected Indians disproportionately, for their Western expat co-workers regularly received free education for their children as part of their employment packages. Private education in the UAE, if one pays out of pocket, is expensive. In addition, the fees increase drastically based on the curriculum taught, which means that only wealthier expatriates can afford Western education that prepares students for international universities. Costs for schools like Our Own English High School start at 400 dirhams per month for kindergarten students and reach over 800 dirhams per month for high-school students. Add to this fees for busing, uniforms, books, and registration, and many middle-class Indians, who usually do not receive free education for their children as part of the perks associated with their jobs, pay close to if not over 1,000 dirhams per month for each child enrolled. Considering that most middle-class Indians in the UAE that I spoke to made between 5,000 and 10,000 dirhams per month, education fees represented a significant portion of their income. For a British or American curriculum school, the fees range from around 10,000 to over 50,000 dirhams per year (for ten months of schooling), not including uniforms, busing, or books. However, many families with children in the more expensive schools received education as part of their employment package, therefore even further widening the wealth gap between elite and middle-class foreigners, and between Western and non-Western migrant groups in the UAE.[16] For those who had to pay out of pocket, fees were increasing faster than incomes, which decreased the amount of money people in the Gulf could save or remit. There are less expensive schools available to Indians, the most famous being Indian High School, which is subsidized by the India Club and the Indian government. However, such schools have lengthy waitlists, and many admissions are decided by lottery. Newspapers regularly report parents queuing overnight just to get a number to enter their children in the lottery. While I was in Dubai, Gautam had to take a precious unpaid day off work in order to acquire a lottery ticket for a well-regarded Indian kindergarten near their home; he left at midnight and returned in the late morning with the coveted lottery ticket, which made his son eligible for the drawing. Most non-elite Indian parents, therefore, must allocate a significant portion of their income and their time to their children's education if they want to raise a family in the Gulf.

Private education is integral to the production of the citizen-noncitizen divide in Dubai and to the production of parochial national identities among foreign resident children, who are trained to claim belonging not to the UAE but rather to the "homelands" represented by their passports. First, the division of schooling into public and private, which relegates noncitizens to private schools, instills and solidifies a sense of nonbelonging in expatriate children. Students in private schools are not taught in Arabic, have little sustained interaction with Emiratis, and learn Emirati culture and history only as outsiders to that culture and history. In addition, they are most often prepared for higher education outside of the UAE and therefore expect their tenure in the UAE to have an end date. Second, private education produces national identities; because most children are segregated into national groups and taught national languages and histories, students develop identities that are based primarily on their parents' country of origin. In addition, nationally segregated schools work in conjunction with nationally segregated communities to create in children tightly bound social and cultural identities that are defined by nationality, region, religion, and language. However, private education in Dubai not only produces parochialized national identities and the foreignness of noncitizens, but also traffics in neoliberal and cosmopolitan ideologies of citizenship that are rooted in capitalist market values. For example, students are educated primarily in English and are trained to be transnational subjects who expect to reside in several places over the course of their lifetimes. This is a function both of the neoliberal economic policies of the UAE, which include education as a commodity offering, and of the middle-class South Asian diasporas in the Gulf, who articulate their migration choices largely in terms of economic opportunities. Students at Indian schools therefore learn to be Indian, but also to look toward what they themselves describe as "Western" models in order to learn about forms of economic, political, and cultural citizenship. Course offerings, for example, often include Western political theories and history, and

European foreign-language training is encouraged. This "global"—but decidedly Western—orientation was extended in the recent influx of American branch campuses and Western-style higher education into the Gulf. But the transitions from secondary schools to these universities were also moments of rupture and dissonance for students, for their parochial Indian forms of learned citizenship and identity came into contact with the specific ideologies and practices that underpinned the integration of supposedly global and "universal" forms of education into the existing social fabric of Gulf countries.

Globalized Higher Education in the Gulf

Institutions of higher education are relatively new to the Arab Gulf countries. Until 1977 there were no universities in the UAE. Government-sponsored public colleges and universities for citizens first appeared, in 1977, with Emirates University in Al Ain. Today, there are several universities in the UAE dedicated to the higher education of citizens, like Zayed University for women and the Higher Colleges of Technology.[17] Much public higher education in the UAE is vocational and aims to train students in fields such as computer technology, banking, and restaurant management.[18] Before these universities were established, UAE citizens had to study abroad. Many went to India because of the historic connections between South Asia and the Gulf; highly qualified students often went to the United Kingdom or the United States. At the time, the UAE government paid all costs for the international education of its citizens. Today, some citizens are still fully funded to study abroad through competitive scholarships, and higher education for citizens in UAE universities is free. The quality of public education in the Gulf is improving, but many citizens opt to attend one of a growing number of private Western universities in order to be more competitive on the job market when they graduate. Over the last decade, there has been a rapid increase in foreign (usually Western) universities opening branches in GCC countries. The United Arab Emirates has greatly expanded its higher education options with the American University of Sharjah (AUS), the American University of Dubai (AUD), and the University of Wollongong, and more recently, with the opening of the Harvard University School of Government and Michigan State University in Dubai, and of New York University in Abu Dhabi.[19] This is a trend in other Gulf States as well. For example, branch campuses of Texas A&M,

Virginia Commonwealth University, Georgetown, Cornell Medical School, and other prestigious U.S. universities have opened in Qatar; the American University of Kuwait (AUK), which counts Dartmouth among its American partners, recently graduated its first class; and the opening of the King Abdullah University of Science and Technology (KAUST) in Saudi Arabia marks one of the largest investments by a Gulf state in Westernized education models.[20] These campuses, as well as the for-profit educational options proliferating in the Gulf, are part of state-sponsored moves away from oil to diversified economies, which include the promotion of knowledge as a commodity and investment in high-quality education to produce citizens as managerial transnational subjects.

Several scholars have noted how neoliberal ideologies have affected the American university system and its expansion abroad. Aihwa Ong, for example, explores how the spread of American and American-style universities in Asia as profit-making enterprises coincides with post-9/11 American attitudes toward migration from the Middle East and Asia, attitudes that have caused the number of international students enrolling in universities in the United States to decline.[21] American-style universities provide training for neoliberal forms of global citizenship, in which "calculative individuals" learn skills to succeed in the market. Kris Olds and Nigel Thrift argue, similarly, that global corporate education is part of a neoliberal capitalist orientation that focuses on the "government of the soul" and on producing "enterprising" subjects.[22] They discuss how states align with these kinds of educational projects both for revenue and because producing neoliberal subjects is considered an investment in economic growth. While foreign universities take part in this process, they encounter unique issues in terms of balancing the tenets of academic freedom with the opportunity for profit. This is particularly evident in the specificities of higher education in the Gulf. By providing free zones in which limits on speech are at least partially suspended, Gulf rulers satisfy their own nationalist agendas while pursuing economic growth.

The recently opened Dubai Knowledge Village (DKV) exemplifies the trends in global education that Aihwa Ong and others have discussed.[23] A kilometer-long, for-profit free zone owned by Dubai Holdings (a public-private company with ruling family interests), DKV is located in the heart of "New Dubai" and borders the free zones of Dubai Media City, Dubai Internet City, and the Dubai Marina. It markets itself as a "one stop shop for all educational and business needs" and lures international institutions by providing 100 percent business ownership and a tax holiday.[24] Several foreign universities are housed in DKV, including schools from the United States, the United Kingdom, Australia, Belgium, France, and India, along with locally based institutions. They provide both general education and specific professional training in fields like medicine, fashion design, computer programming, engineering, and management to UAE national and expatriate students, and they also recruit students from other parts of the Gulf and around the world. These programs and degrees are accredited in the home countries of the universities and therefore train students for careers either in the Gulf or abroad. Several online universities are also based in DKV, as well as what it calls "academic service providers." The latter are companies that work in conjunction with DKV universities to provide vocational and business training to students. As a free zone, DKV also benefits from relaxed regulations in terms of censorship. Internet access, for example, is not filtered by the government to exclude certain websites.[25] Dubai Knowledge Village represents a site in which state interests in economic growth, corporate interests of international institutions, and the neoliberal entrepreneurial goals of middle-class and elite consumers converge. As with private primary and secondary education, foreigners make large profits from higher education in the Gulf, particularly since many institutions are designed around global market needs for specific skills. There are no formal systems of financial aid for noncitizen students, and zones like DKV provide tax-free environments with low startup costs. Academic hubs are a burgeoning trend in the GCC, and there are "cities" like DKV devoted to education in Sharjah, Qatar, and other parts of the Gulf. These institutions provide the bulk of private higher-education options for expatriates, and they are integral to Gulf state initiatives to develop non-oil revenue streams through knowledge economies.

Many scholars have connected the globalization or transnationalization of American universities with other trends in the university system geared at profit-making enterprises. Due to a reduction in federal and state funds to both public and private universities, a rise in competition from for-profit ventures, and increases in distance and online learning, American universities increasingly partner with corporations, promote patenting of research findings, divert funds away from humanities and into science and engineering, and expand their offerings overseas in order to generate revenue.[26] In addition, the number of corporate universities in the United States has dramatically increased, which has affected traditional curricula and forms of measuring academic success.[27] These trends, which began in the 1980s with a significant decrease in state funding to universities, have left many scholars unsettled about the future of tenured positions and academic freedom within American universities. Many have also noted an increase in the use of market language to speak about the university: students are considered "clients," educational offerings "products," and extracurricular and other options "value-added," for example.[28] The marketization of education is by and large considered negative, perceived to detract from the "liberal arts," "moral," and "spiritual" aspirations of the university, which, note Sheldon Rothblatt and Bjorn Wittrock, "is the second oldest institution with a continuous history in the Western world, the first being the Roman Catholic Church."[29] While scholars acknowledge that the university has never been monolithic, has never codified uniform ideals, and is not easily distinguishable from the state or the market, they generally still lament the contemporary commoditization of higher education, which is indexed in part by the increasingly transnational nature of universities and the neoliberal orientation of international curricula.[30]

Additionally, the globalization of the university is considered by some to threaten the principles of academic freedom, especially since the relationship between states, markets, and academic institutions is neither clearly defined nor internationally standardized.[31] Projects such as Education City in Qatar and Knowledge Village in Dubai thus seem to exemplify this process, particularly in light of recent World Trade Organization negotiations to further liberalize the General Agreement on Trade in Services (GATS), which specifically includes higher education as a commodity service. Philip G. Altbach, however, places these trends within a longer history of geopolitical power struggles, colonialism, and imperialism.[32] He argues that universities have always been global institutions, that most of the non-Western world's "indigenous" universities are modeled on Western higher education, and that the American university itself is an amalgam of multiple influences. The recent trends in globalized higher education, therefore, must be considered as part of larger processes of neoimperialism across the world. Altbach points to the dominance of English as a language in university settings, the privileged position of the U.S. academy worldwide, the fact that international students pay their own way,[33] and the colonial and missionary roots of many contemporary international universities, such as the American University of Beirut. In sum, we can consider the current multinational university as a "union of unequals." Altbach says, "When institutions or initiatives are exported from one country to another, academic models, curricula and programmes from the more powerful academic system prevail."[34]

There are thus two sides to the debate circulating both within and outside of the Gulf region on the emerging distributed-knowledge economy that American branch campuses represent. On the one hand, the university caters to global market demands and potentially improves the economies and citizenry of the Gulf States, and on the other, globalization of the university perpetuates a history of global power imbalances that threaten individual local cultures with American hegemonic ideologies. Both sides of the debate do seem appropriate when applied to the Gulf context. Gulf countries, invested in diversification and neoliberal business models, aggressively court American universities and often pay the setup and operation costs, as with the Qatar Foundation (QF), a philanthropic arm of the Qatari government that funds all universities in Doha's Education City, including Cornell, Georgetown, Virginia Commonwealth, Northwestern, and Texas A&M.[35] These schools receive millions of dollars in management fees from QF, which are channeled directly into their U.S. home campuses. The line between nonprofit and for-profit globalized higher education, therefore, is a blurry one.[36]

Middle- and upper-class expatriate parents in Dubai see in these universities an opportunity for their children to stay close to home—therefore preventing the "erosion" of cultural and religious values associated with the West—while they learn skills that will supposedly make them more globally marketable. Because these options are so new for foreigners in the Gulf, Indians raised in Dubai who are past their twenties went abroad for higher education, usually to India and in some cases to Europe or North America, with uncertainty about whether they would return. The youth I interviewed had educational experiences that were substantially different than those of Indians just a few years older, for they were able to stay in the Gulf for the duration of their schooling. Only now, in their twenties, were they facing the possibility of living abroad. The complexities of how foreign resident students engaged with the newly available educational offerings and the constructs they bring with them are an understudied but important element of the literal and figurative extension of the American university. Specifically, the experiences of South Asian young people in Dubai who attended branch campuses of Western universities highlight some of the unexpected effects that these schools are having on diasporic populations in the Gulf, and muddle easy dismissals or celebrations of the practice of globalizing higher education.

Dissonance, Discrimination, and Diasporic Subjectification

Western-style universities in the Gulf, while producing transnational and neoliberal subjects, also produced forms of localized politicization and claims to belonging for South Asian youth that they did not have prior to entering the university system. By entering a university space that is modeled, in most cases, on American academic institutions, young people are placed on equal footing with each other, at least theoretically. However, my interlocutors recounted many incidents that posed challenges, even problems, in their transition to this type of egalitarian space. Although they had lived in a "global city" for much or all of their lives, most of the students at American branch campuses and other Western institutions experienced diversity in more intimate ways than they ever had. For example, while primary and secondary education in the UAE tends to follow national lines, privatized higher education is diverse; AUS is home to students of over seventy nationalities.[37] Thus, many South Asians raised in Dubai first interacted in a significant way with Emiratis and Arab and Western expatriates when they entered university. The experience of higher education in the Gulf in particular put South Asian students in direct contact with the discriminatory and hierarchical models through which their belonging and exclusion were defined in the country, creating dissonances between the ideologies that shaped their curriculum and their everyday interactions and experiences of being university students. The uncertain futures that South Asian youth faced came into stark relief for them only after they entered university, and their experiences of higher education, both inside and outside the classroom, marked a rupture not only from their childhood, but also from how they had come to understand their identities and their place in the world.

Most of the young people I interviewed were attending or had attended branches of Western universities in Dubai or Sharjah. When describing their childhoods and their primary and secondary education, my interviewees recalled happier times. They spoke of a Dubai that was smaller and more community-oriented, where people got along, and where it was easier to be Indian. They had grown up almost exclusively in Indian social and cultural circles, mostly in the neighborhoods of old Dubai. Their family friends, their neighborhoods, their peers, their schools, their leisure activities—all produced for them a sense of Dubai as an Indian ethnic space in which they felt they belonged to a specifically Indian community and within which they did not have much reason to contemplate their lack of UAE citizenship. The university setting was in stark contrast to this ethnically segregated childhood. When my interlocutors began to interact with Emiratis and other expatriates, they developed a more concrete sense of the citizen-noncitizen hierarchy in the UAE and of the fact that they were effectively foreigners in their home, which produced nostalgia for happier times and a better Dubai. It was within the space of the academy that South Asian students learned their difference from other groups, for they experienced direct racism and practices of self-entitlement from their peers, often for the first time. These experiences produced disillusionment with the place they considered home and further reinforced an imagined past in which Dubai was more open to Indians, a nostalgia that resonated, albeit derived from different experiences, with the narratives of my older interlocutors. South Asian university students said that what they found most difficult was the behavior of Emirati and other Gulf Arab nationals, not of goras, who their parents' generation complained about, for example. They spoke of incidents in which "locals" cut in front of them in cafeteria lines, expected them to share notes and even homework, and spoke in Arabic in mixed Arab and non-Arab social gatherings in ways that made them feel excluded. It is unclear the extent to which social hierarchies outside of the university impact the planning and execution of Western branch campuses, but while students are afforded more equality in the university than they would be under the UAE's legal system or in the workplace, distinctions between groups inevitably seep into the university structure itself.

How school mission and daily, lived experience diverge in American branch campuses is exemplified at AUS. While AUS has a stated policy of nondiscrimination, houses students of all nationalities together, and attempts to enforce egalitarianism in terms of grades and even rules against cutting in line, the staff and faculty pay structures are still nationality-based. Of course the university's official stance supports fairness, but several people I spoke to at the university, both Western and South Asian, claimed that Indians get paid less for the same jobs than do Americans, particularly those in administrative positions.[38] Low-wage work, such as landscaping and cleaning, is done almost exclusively by South Asians, who become, as in other parts of the country, invisible even when in plain sight. Because AUS is in Sharjah, it follows Sharjah's strict decency laws. Men and women are housed in separate dormitories on different sides of the campus, and women must follow a curfew or they will be reported to their parents. Tank tops and short skirts are banned from campus, as are public displays of affection between men and women, which include any form of touching; police-in-training from the nearby police academy patrol the campus to enforce these rules. Thus, the gender-integrated campus life that most American universities intend for their students is not commensurate with what AUS's home institution would provide.[39]

In the classroom itself, which sometimes included members of ruling and other influential Emirati families as students, faculty members recounted practicing a certain amount of self-censorship. They tended not to criticize social and economic hierarchies in front of their students because they never knew how influential or connected their students might be. During my time in Dubai, several faculty members at different institutions were deported or reprimanded for bringing the controversial Danish cartoons of the Prophet Mohammed into class for discussion.[40] American universities in the Gulf do not provide tenure, so jobs are still bound to visas that can be revoked at any time for any reason.[41] At these universities, too, American and European history and politics are often placed at the center of liberal arts learning. As one Egyptian graduate told me in 2011, after the revolution, "I learned to think of 'left' and 'right' in terms of the U.S., and I realized that in the case of Egypt, it is not the same at all. I now always think of politics through the perspective of America." The few courses that teach Islamic cultural history and Gulf studies do not provide much information about expatriate communities or their histories in the Gulf. In my interviews, university professors relayed how divisive the classroom could become when they broached topics such as migration or labor rights, so they tended to tread very lightly or to avoid those topics altogether. The lack of protected speech in Gulf countries has been an obstacle to efforts to lure foreign universities that meet Western academic standards; while Gulf rulers have tried to circumvent the issue by creating academic hubs in free zones, where limits on speech are suspended at least in part, self-censorship practices by faculty and job insecurity concerns remain. Thus, the question of commensurability of education at branch campuses in the Gulf and the actual ability of the students who attend them to compete in a global marketplace needs to be further explored.

Ironically, it was the supposedly egalitarian platform of the university, not segregated childhood environments, that taught South Asian youth the realities of inequality in the UAE. Experiences of discrimination, which took place both inside and outside of the classroom, were the focus of my interlocutors' narratives about feeling "second-class" in the UAE, feelings that were framed in terms of liberal-democratic rights—how they learned about the political—rather than through the criticisms of the system that middle-class Indians deployed, which were focused on fair market opportunities. For these young people, the university experience was doubly unsettling: they had to face the impending realities of perhaps settling outside of the Gulf, and they had to confront the reality that they did not belong in the place where they felt most at home. My interlocutors' narratives revealed the profound ways that university spaces and interactions were contributing to the reshaping of what it meant to come of age, to belong, and to stake claims to futures that included both transnational mobility and rootedness in Dubai. These experiences articulate with scholarship on generational differences within postcolonial countries that are emerging from new educational forms and increasing neoliberalization of citizenship, particularly among middle classes.[42] While their parents were adamant about wanting to keep their Indian or Pakistani passports and narrated their migration as primarily an economic choice, the second-generation South Asian university students and graduates I spoke with felt that their lack of belonging in Dubai and the UAE was involuntary and deprived them of political and civil rights, indicating the emergence of a liberal-democratic understanding of their place—or lack of place—in Emirati society and pointing to futures that include foreign resident claims to civil society in the Gulf States. Their strong ties to Dubai as home made it difficult for them to accept the feelings of insecurity and temporariness that came with holding foreign passports and being tied to their parents' visas, insecurities that were only now surfacing for them as they entered adulthood. They expressed a sense of disenfranchisement that was the effect of being South Asian in Dubai. For these young people, the terms *home*, *identity*, and *future* were political in a different sense than they had been for earlier generations, for they brought up issues surrounding the tenuousness of their lives in Dubai, the inequalities embedded in their social and legal positions, and, most important, a stake in changing these conditions for the sake of their own futures.

Unlike people raised or schooled in South Asia, with whom I had to broach the topic of citizenship, second-generation young people wanted to talk about citizenship, or the lack thereof, more than anything else. The topic dominated our conversations, and my interlocutors seemed eager to share their criticism of the system. In fact, my asking if citizenship made a difference seemed almost ridiculous to them. Of course it made a difference! Not being a citizen determined the entire course of their lives. Amina summarized the poignancy of young South Asians' sense of disenfranchisement and nonbelonging in Dubai: "If we had citizenship we would have access to national schools, which speak Arabic. If we had citizenship we would be speaking Arabic right now. We would be ingrained into the culture, we would be attending the same schools as locals, we would *be* locals. We would have that heritage. It would change your outlook altogether." Amina, unlike older Dubai Indians, staked a claim to Dubai through her lack of citizenship, instead of disavowing the desire to have it. She, like her peers, associated lack of citizenship with fear and with unfair discrimination. Unlike their older counterparts, who, even as they criticized racial hierarchies and differential treatment, were adamant about their status as "guests" in the UAE, young South Asians gestured to an investment in Dubai's future that went beyond economic accumulation to allow for a deeper and more secure feeling of being at home.

The globalized American university, lamented by some scholars as a commoditization and erosion of the liberal ideals of the university, is providing space and opportunities for unexpected *liberal* politicizations and calls for rights by young people in Dubai, suggesting that we need to abandon parochial American debates about the benefits and disadvantages of globalized higher education in favor of what Ritty Lukose calls "school ethnographies," which attend to the multiplicity of experiences and forms of subjectification and politicization that take place within the spaces of these universities themselves.[43] The subjectivities of South Asian university students in Dubai emerged at a particular crossroads or moment of rupture, one in which the dissonances between lower and higher education in the Gulf and the realities of their uncertain futures surfaced at the same time. Young people's marriage options, job prospects, and ability to enter graduate school were going to determine where they settled in the world and what their futures looked like. Graduation and impending graduation heightened their awareness of the tenuousness of their futures and their inability to actually achieve a form of global or "astronaut" mobility. The university experience also brought into relief their inferior social and legal status in the UAE and their lack of rights in relation to both UAE nationals and Western expatriates. Both reinforced a sense of exclusion from Dubai, but also created an active politicization that the students shared in our conversations. However, never in our conversations did my informants express a strong belief that they could actually change their position in the hierarchical system of the UAE. They were literally and figuratively "stuck," despite their cosmopolitan knowledge and their financial privileges in comparison to poorer migrants in the Gulf.

The tenuousness of their presence in Dubai was integral to my informants' daily lives; although they did not always speak of or actively contemplate it, it was always in "the back of the mind," as Haneefa said. It was also a source of solidarity. South Asians could joke about it together, and they shared a sense of identity based on being desi from Dubai. In fact, all of the young people I interviewed could speak about settling in other parts of the world and about tenuous lives in Dubai as a general condition, but when the conversation turned to their own particular futures, they became vague. Yes, they were probably going to leave Dubai. Yes, they might have to marry someone from outside Dubai. Yes, they might not get a job in Dubai after college. But no one seemed too worried about it. At first I didn't understand their attitude toward the future. Despite criticizing the system at length and bemoaning their status as second-class citizens, they in essence shrugged their shoulders when I asked them to discuss their fears about the future. Then I realized that the enormity of such a profoundly uncertain future was so normalized that it was mundane; like other Dubai Indians, the students experienced the ephemerality of their existence, despite having a new language with which to express it, as simply part of daily life. When they were not working or going to school, South Asian middle-class youth spent most of their time with friends in coffee shops, at the mall, and at nightclubs. They frequently held going-away parties for each other, often meeting up again when in town after a long absence. The uncertainty of their own particular futures was balanced by seeing the people they had grown up with marry, find jobs, move away, return, and experience the range of futures that they themselves had not yet clearly defined. These seemingly privileged parachute children, therefore, often either landed where they had not intended or maintained a holding pattern that kept them tenuously attached to their homes. Where my interlocutors found themselves after their university tenure ended, however, may point to shifts in South Asian diasporic futures in the Gulf and the future face of Emirati citizenship and national identity. Even though their tenuousness was normalized, second-generation youth were also pushing against the social hierarchies in Dubai in ways that other Dubai Indians were not, indicating the potential for change in migration policy, politicization, and identification as they began to stay in the Gulf for longer periods of time and stake claims to Dubai as home more often.

Conclusion

When I left Dubai in late 2006, Haneefa, Nadia, and Amina were all working in administrative jobs in the UAE that provided visas, so they were not dependent on fathers or husbands, but they all expressed uncertainty about how long their jobs would last and whether they would be able to find someone to marry in Dubai. Amina was concerned that her parents would fix her up with someone from India and that she would have to move there, which she dreaded even more than the possibility of finding a groom who lived in Canada or the United States. Yush had opened an electronics business after a long struggle with his father's Emirati business partner over inheritance. In 2005, when Yush's father suddenly passed away, he and his mother were forced to return to India for six months, and the car-parts business his father had built over twenty years languished. Yush hated his time in India, and when we first met, he had just managed to get his new business off the ground. He was adamant that he would not marry unless his wife was willing to settle in the UAE. And Ashish, unable to procure the academic employment he so desired in the United States or a position as a reporter in the Gulf, is currently working for his father as a salesman, a job he resisted for many years but one that, with Dubai's economic downturn, seems to be his only prospect for holding a visa in the UAE. He continues to seek work in the United States, thus far unsuccessfully, but expects he will eventually have to take over the family business.

At first glance, these young South Asians may seem simply to be, like their parents once were, the newest entrants into the historically entrenched yet transitory South Asian communities that Dubai has housed for over a hundred years. However, they bring with them different claims to belonging and different understandings of their place in the social and cultural hierarchy of Gulf residency, understandings that are connected in part to the changes brought about by the introduction of globalized higher education into the Gulf Arab States. When I visited Education City in Doha in April 2009, a senior administrator at Texas A&M Qatar lamented the fact that so many of the graduating noncitizen seniors were asking for career placement in Qatar; she was frustrated that these students did not understand that they had no "right" to stay in the country after graduation. As noncitizen notions of rights and belonging shift, so will their mobilizations and the responses of Gulf States to an increasingly settled foreign population. For Aihwa Ong's neoliberal transnational subjects, the parachute represents the power and mobility that come with global capital. For my young interlocutors, mobility was grounded both in neoliberal notions of moveable entitlement and, more important, in emerging liberal-democratic claims to rights and diasporic citizenship, claims that may be changing the face of belonging in places like Dubai, and the Gulf States.

REASSESSING GULF STUDIES

CITIZENSHIP, DEMOCRACY, AND THE POLITICAL

As with most ethnography, a great deal occurs in an anthropologist's field site between the time of research and the time when that research finally becomes an artifact of knowledge production. It is no surprise, then, that the Gulf Arab States and the Middle East more generally have changed significantly since 2006, when I conducted the bulk of the fieldwork represented in this book. Since the global economic downturn of 2008, the cartography of development, migration, and urban life has shifted in many Gulf cities. And more recently, widespread activism throughout the Middle East—commonly referred to as the Arab Spring—has toppled governments, produced new politicizations, and displaced thousands of people from countries as far apart as Egypt and Bahrain.[1] Despite these enormous changes and the impacts they have had on the daily lives of residents in the Gulf—both citizen and noncitizen—media representations and academic scholarship continue in many ways to rehearse tropes of spectacle, exceptionalism, and unbridled capitalism in their analyses of the relationship of Gulf States and their residents to these larger regional and global shifts. I am writing the conclusion of this book, for example, in Doha, Qatar, a city that has in a way become the center of the Arab world because it hosts the headquarters of Al-Jazeera, the most popular English and Arabic source of news about the region. Ironically, Qatar itself is largely absent from discussions surrounding the Arab Spring, for it has been proclaimed by pundits and Middle East scholars to be one of the places most "protected," along with the United Arab Emirates, from the civil unrest spreading across the region. This prediction is attributed to Qatar's authoritarian government and its supposedly complacent population of wealthy citizens, two conditions political economists most often associate with rentier states. Recent coverage of the country mirrors that of Dubai at the beginning of the millennium, focusing on over-the-top projects like the manmade Pearl Island and the construction of air-conditioned stadiums for the 2022 World Cup games. Like Dubai, Qatar emerges in these representations as a postmodern "nonplace" populated by a wealthy Arab citizenry that is served by an oppressed—mostly South Asian—underclass of migrant workers considered to be both temporary and unimportant to the politics of the nation. Like Dubai and the UAE, Qatar is becoming a place where the everyday and the ordinary, especially for its majority foreign-resident population, are seemingly impossible in the face of the glittering spectacles of capitalism and its dark underbelly of exploitation.[2]

However, as I have argued through the lens of migration and citizenship in Dubai and the UAE, foreign residents in the Gulf are neither invisible nor temporary, and their presence and everyday mundane forms of belonging are integral to the production of national identity, economic growth, and the boundaries of citizenship and its exceptions. While I have focused on Indian foreign residents' forms of citizenship and belonging within conditions of permanent temporariness in a nonliberal state, my arguments apply more broadly to migration in all contemporary contexts, for nonliberal, neoliberal, and liberal logics of governance circulate everywhere in today's world to produce the insides and outsides of citizenship. We therefore need to incorporate these multiple logics and the subjects they produce into conversations about what constitutes authoritarianism and what constitutes democracy, especially at a time when these terms are being used in taken-for-granted ways by commentators to interpret the actions described as a whole as the Arab Spring. Given that Qatar and the UAE have the highest proportions of foreign residents in the Middle East and even in the world, it is remarkable that the subject of migration has not factored into most media and scholarly discussions about the who, what, when, where, and why—or why not—of the Arab Spring. Indeed, migrants' actions, understandings, and affects are conspicuously absent from conversations and theorizations about activism or democratization processes in these countries, in the Gulf Arab States more generally, and even in the Middle East and North Africa region as a whole.

Activism in the form of labor protests by low-wage migrant workers is actually relatively common in the Gulf States, even in supposedly content and "quiet" countries like the United Arab Emirates.[3] Though Bahrain has been the only Gulf state the international media has covered in-depth for its "revolutionary" activities during 2011, the UAE has not been "quiet" when it comes to citizen activism either, though it may appear so compared to other Middle Eastern countries. In the first few months of 2011 alone, there have been movements against censorship and quelled anti-government protests, and an Emirati university professor at the Abu Dhabi branch of the Sorbonne was arrested for speaking out against the lack of democracy in the country.[4] These "local" voices are openly advocating change in the country; however, they are disconnected from and mostly disinterested in the daily living conditions of "migrants." In fact, the presence of foreigners and the influence of "Westernization" have become in many Gulf countries part of the platform on which activist groups have built their oppositional politics. How might placing at the center of our analyses citizen and noncitizen forms of staking claims to urban space—and the constantly emergent dichotomy between these two categories of Gulf residents—change the way we construe what constitutes political activity? This book has from the start been engaged in an emerging scholarly conversation about transnationalism in the Gulf, a conversation that shifts focus away from solely autochthonous Arab and Muslim understandings of Gulf societies, as well as away from understandings of Gulf countries as primarily "Middle Eastern," and toward the various forms of historical and contemporary cosmopolitanisms that circulate through Indian Ocean networks and impact the daily lives of residents on the Arabian Peninsula. In the midst of the so-called Arab Spring, it therefore seems fitting that I conclude by examining what a study of Indian forms of lived citizenship and belonging in Dubai contributes to our scholarly understandings of citizenship, democracy, and politics, not only in the Gulf and Middle East regions, but also in relation to anthropology as a disciplinary formation that commonly deploys these terms to discuss a range of human activities and institutions in the contemporary world.

Rethinking the Political

Academic and media coverage of the Arab Spring focuses almost exclusively on criticisms and demands made by citizens on the state. The assumption embedded in this coverage is that it is citizens alone who have a stake in governance and who, after decades of hardship and oppression, are finally demanding that the state account for its failed promises. The emphasis placed on citizen narratives and actions, coupled with the almost complete absence of attention to foreign residents in these countries, may lead us to believe that politics is based in the relationship between state and citizen, and that it is through participation in this relationship or by contesting its parameters that individuals become political subjects. This understanding of citizenship and belonging permeates the political economic literature in general but particularly that on rentier states, and it also exemplifies nongovernmental efforts to curb labor abuses in the Gulf region. This is because "migrants" are supposedly tied to "home" countries and travel to the Gulf solely for the purposes of temporary work. Noncitizens, through these representations, could easily be dismissed as unimportant and inactive within the national and local politics of their "host" countries, especially in monarchies where politicization is already considered to be almost impossible given the authoritarian structure of the state and the high levels of citizen wealth through petro-dollars.[5] In Bahrain, for example, the civil unrest of early 2011 and the violent government crackdown—which, ironically, began amid a slew of opinion pieces about how the Arab Spring would not spread to the Gulf—was framed in terms of sectarian conflict between a Shi'a majority and a Sunni ruling elite, not in terms of citizen dissatisfaction with the country's history of migration and unemployment.[6] In addition, the large foreign resident population of Bahrain was strikingly invisible in news coverage and "expert" analyses of Bahrain at the time and remains so in September 2011, as protests, arrests, and military violence continue across the country.

Most scholarship on citizenship derives its theory from histories of liberal democracy in Western Europe and the United States, and focuses on how the divisions *between* citizens challenge both the imagined community of the nation and the political structure of citizenship itself. Thus, given that citizenship studies of non-Western places are often derivative of these understandings, it makes sense that Bahrain's unrest is represented primarily as sectarian, as a struggle for equality by internal members of the nation-state. However, as postcolonial scholars have rightly pointed out, it is equally if not more important to examine how those who constitute the "outside" of the sovereign nation-state—whether they be other nations, extranational organizations, or groups of people—are also integral to the production of citizenship and sovereignty, and were foundational even to the production of modern Western states and theories of liberalism. Thus, we must bring into our frame of analysis the excluded and the exception in order to better understand the workings of sovereignty, citizenship, and governmentality in its various overlapping, intricate, and often contradictory manifestations.

As many anthropologists have argued, citizenship is not limited solely to the juridico-legal category of membership within a nation-state, but occurs instead at many scales and in many forms, sometimes even at the expense of those who officially belong. Aihwa Ong, for example, explores how elite foreigners under neoliberal restructuring are now afforded more rights within certain Asian countries than are their citizens.[7] And James Holston and Arjun Appadurai, following a longer tradition of scholarship by theorists like Benjamin, de Certeau, and Lefevbre, argue that citizenship occurs within daily urban existences and moments in which residents, either through activism or simply through their everyday existences, claim a "right to the city."[8] Through these multiple modalities of citizenship, several actors, whether legal citizens or not, make political claims on the state and other governing institutions. In the case of Europe and the United States, we can clearly see in recent activism that noncitizen demands on the state are integral to national and local politics, particularly in protests against anti-immigration laws in the southern United States and against bans on the face veil in several European countries. These actions, discussions, and debates produce both citizen and exception, regardless of the legal categories that the individuals involved or affected actually fall into, and they also showcase the porous character of national identity, sovereignty, and belonging within these countries.

In the United Arab Emirates, the category of citizen and the idea of the nation as an imagined community are produced precisely against the foreign resident bodies—what Andrew Gardner calls "foreign matter"—that constitute the majority of the population.[9] However, I suggest that, rather than being excluded from the civic body of Dubai, these foreign residents participate in the production of the legitimacy and sovereignty of the nation-state from the site of exception, particularly Indians who reside in the downtown city core. They are, therefore, *impossible citizens*. Their modes of citizenship and belonging occur not despite but through the very legal structures and technologies of governance that prevent them from naturalizing and that produce their temporariness as short-term workers tied to individual citizen-sponsors (kafeels). As exceptions to citizenship, Indians are integral to the maintenance of a seemingly neat citizen-noncitizen divide in which citizens benefit from the generous welfare of a petro-state and noncitizens bolster Dubai's economy but are not part of its social or cultural imaginary. It is precisely the exceptions to citizenship—and particularly Indians, who constitute the majority of the population in the UAE—who both produce the sovereign and challenge its existence, perhaps even more so than do official citizens or ruling monarchs.

Indians in Dubai participated in several forms of citizenship and belonging, including urban, substantive, neoliberal, and consumer. For example, middle-class Indians claimed Dubai, and especially the neighborhoods of old Dubai, as Indian cultural space, and they performed public belonging to the city through practices of consumption. And business owners often acted in the stead of citizen-kafeels by governing over other migrants. Moreover, Indians are subjectified by the state and by other institutions both as insiders and outsiders, and therefore they are imbricated just as much as "locals" in processes of governmentality. Certain Indians are policed as migrants, for example, and consigned to the outskirts of the city, while others are offered neoliberal forms of participation in the country's economy, and still others have direct influence on state policy. Dubai Indians both participated in the production of their own exclusion *and* staked claims to belonging through criticisms of racial injustice, through nostalgia and historical memory, and through the production of geographic spaces of Indianness within the city. Indian businessmen, for example, simultaneously claimed no desire for Emirati citizenship even as they insisted that they "built this country." And Dubai-born South Asian university students felt that Dubai was their home but that they were also "second-class citizens." Indian foreign residents in Dubai are therefore, like all contemporary subjects, *political*. In fact, the very elision of their political subjectivities from scholarship about the Gulf participates in the production of official citizens, who supposedly were once docile but now increasingly make so-called democratic claims on a nonliberal state. What we mean by "democracy" within the Arab Spring therefore depends on the erasures enacted in much scholarship on the region to define the differences between citizen and noncitizen, and between economy and nation.

De-provincializing Democracy

When used to explain certain forms of human movement, the analytic of labor effectively reduces to the economic the complex daily existences of a wide range of people.[10] I have aimed to unravel the idea that migrants are laborers and therefore should be understood as disconnected affectively, socially, and historically from the imagined community of Dubai and the UAE. In contemporary Dubai all residents are generally understood to be contained within a triptych of migrant, expat, and local, but these are constructed and tenuous categories that middle-class Indians in particular, who are both entrenched and transitory, challenge through their very presence in the emirate, for they do not neatly fit into any of these categorizations. Their presence throughout the city in a range of occupations and within family units distinguishes them from the "migrants" who are relegated to the outskirts of the city and rendered invisible through policing of their public presence; and their experiences of geographic, economic, and racial discrimination separate them from the "expats" who are lured by Dubai's various free-zone investment schemes and tourist spectacles. In fact, if we think of asserting rights to the city as a form of politics, it becomes increasingly evident through the narratives of Indians in downtown Dubai that "labor" and "civil" unrest exist in a spectrum of engagement with governing institutions and actors, rather than constituting distinct forms of activism by incommensurable groups of people—migrants and locals. The opposition of labor to civil society actually participates in producing a false dichotomy between the nation-state, which is the realm of citizens, and the economy, which is open to and reliant on noncitizens.[11]

Not only rentier state literature but also anthropological writing and state discourses tend to produce ontological and abstractable domains such as economy, state, and civil society, which do not adequately represent the messy overlaps and contradictions of governmentality and citizenship as they are experienced on the ground. In the UAE, as in most contemporary countries, neoliberal technologies of governance and public-private partnerships showcase how the state and the economy are indistinct. Yet they continue to be produced as separate domains by different sets of actors.[12] These actors are in fact mostly Indian middle classes, who are also complicit in the erasure of migrant workers from the geographical and imagined boundaries of the city-state. However, these so-called migrant workers have a history of making themselves quite visible in the city through forms of activism that challenge a neat division between labor and civil unrest, economy and nation-state. Notably, "worker" strikes since the mid-2000s against construction companies building the spectacles of Brand Dubai have made claims to visibility and calls for rights that implicate both state and private interests. In fact, the state and the corporate in this instance are inseparable, for Emaar, Dubai Holdings, the Jumeirah Group, and other parent companies of large-scale projects like the Burj Khalifa, the Madinat Jumeirah, or the Palm Islands are owned in large part by ruling family interests. Ahmed Kanna, in a piece on migrants and the Arab Spring, points to a need to think about how civil unrest and worker protests are connected in their critiques of oppressive systems.[13] I take his intervention one step further to assert that they in fact reveal that state and economy are inseparable, and thus the nation, as the realm of the citizen, rooted in autochthonous understandings of Bedouin tribal pasts, requires the elision of "labor" or other noncitizen politicizations in order to remain purified of foreign elements and to maintain the citizen-noncitizen distinction and perpetuate an ethnocratic hierarchy.[14] The purification of economy from nation is fundamental to the production of citizenship and its exceptions, an understanding of citizenship that underpins questions of democracy within the Arab Spring, especially in relation to the Gulf States.

It is evident from historical and contemporary examples around the globe that economic factors and class politics permeate civic participation and politics—from the French Revolution to women's rights movements, to protests against the World Trade Organization, to student sit-ins in South America, to demonstrations against austerity measures in Europe. Unfortunately, the narratives of unnatural economic development in rela- tion to state formation in the Gulf allow for analyses from both inside and outside of these countries—academic, media, and popular—to produce the national and the economic as distinct domains. In fact, the legitimacy of the state and the rehearsal of purified national identity rely on the bounding of nation and economy as mutually exclusive, with their dif- ferent attendant demographics, geographies, and historical trajectories. Thus, we can separate citizen from noncitizen, and "labor" protest, which foreign workers participate in, from "civil" unrest, which is a citizen activity that is considered an inherently democratic performance. Jane Kinninmont, in her analysis of the Arab Spring, similarly argues that politics and economy are indistinct and that their separation has led to simplistic understandings of activism in the Middle East: "So is the Arab Spring really about democracy and rights, or jobs, bread, and housing? Actually, this frequently asked question is misconceived. It rests on a false dichotomy between 'politics' and 'economics,' which are convenient labels for different academic disciplines, and should not be mistaken for genuinely different or separate spheres of reality."[15]

In addition to the reliance on a distinction between economy and politics that Kinninmont rightly points out, analyses of the Arab Spring are further flattened by the erasure of the histories and complexities of migration, particularly in the Gulf. Bahrain is an excellent example. While debating the level to which Bahrain is sectarian in their attempts to understand the protests, the pundits have displayed a relative amnesia toward the role of noncitizens in forms of discontent expressed by various residents of the country.[16] Gardner, for example, highlights simultaneous activism during his fieldwork in 2003, both against Bahrainization of the country's trucking industry by business owners (who often include foreign residents) and against rising unemployment among the poorest strata of the citizenry.[17] These two seemingly opposed groups eventually formed allegiances in their protests against the state. This activism was indeed about indisputable power differences between Sunni and Shi'a Bahrainis, but it was also inseparable from the presence of and participation by foreign residents in the employment structure of the country. Bahraini citizens' increasing levels of unemployment and poverty, for example, often expressed themselves as protests against "Western" or "foreign" products like pork or skimpy clothing, directly tying citizen concerns with high levels of migration. However, in the media coverage of violence at the Pearl roundabout and elsewhere in Manama during 2011, which subsumed Bahrain under the umbrella of the Arab Spring, the cosmopolitanism of the country and the tensions that it had been producing for decades were elided in favor of explanations of politics as inherently "indigenous," that is, between official citizens and the state.

The UAE and other Gulf countries are not simply nondemocratic and illiberal, but rather, like other contemporary states, circulate multiple logics of governance in their rhetorics and technologies of belonging and exclusion. These include liberal, "social contract" formations in which citizens are supposedly kept satisfied by generous welfare benefits in exchange for the loss of certain freedoms, neoliberal opportunities for wealth accumulation and the privatization of migration governance, and illiberal patronage and censorship practices that delimit both citizen and noncitizen activities. How do we reconcile these multiple logics of governance with the so-called democratic movements of the Arab Spring? What is democratization within a seemingly nonliberal political system? And

what do we mean by democratization when we as scholars exclude significant portions of the population from our celebrations of "freedom" and
"change" in these countries? Widespread protests in Bahrain and Oman
and a burgeoning movement for greater representation among activists in
the United Arab Emirates not only call into question the assumption that
rentier states are incapable of democracy, but also our taken-for-granted
definitions of democracy itself.

Etienne Balibar argues that democracy is not interchangeable with
equality or freedom, but rather is based on inherent inequalities within the
demos, or citizenry; states often undertake actions in the name of democracy that actually increase inequalities among those who are included in
the national imaginary as well as among those who are excluded.[18] Democracy in itself does not exist as a political truth in the contemporary world,
he argues, but rather is called into being through its inherent unequalness;
democratic participation is the process of *democratizing* democracy, of
attempting to move toward an unattainable horizon of citizenship as
"equal liberty," that is, toward an even application of the rights that come
with citizenship within a so-called democratic country: "Democracy, understood in a radical manner, is not the name of a political regime but only
the name of a process which we could call tautologically the democratization of democracy itself (or of what claims to represent a democratic
regime), therefore the name of a struggle, a convergence of struggles for
the democratization of democracy."[19] Following Balibar, I argue that questioning the meaning of democracy also requires us to ask what we mean by
"liberty" or "freedom" when we call these concepts to do work in the
name of democracy. Thomas Humphrey Marshall famously argued that
social citizenship (i.e., welfare) should be a key right available to citizens
of a democratic liberal state.[20] Under neoliberalism, however, the same
Western states that Marshall wrote about see welfare rights as antithetical
to the project of democracy. Gulf citizens, in contrast to citizens of contemporary liberal democracies, have extensive social citizenship rights; in
fact, welfare is the primary mode through which their citizenship is defined. Wouldn't "equal liberty" be possible for Gulf citizens if their citizenship rights were evenly applied, indeed if they were *democratized*?

The framing of equality and liberty in so-called rentier states challenges
scholars to rethink how they equate democracy with freedom within the
Arab Spring, and particularly its Gulf manifestations, for it is not people
without rights who are asking for rights, but rather citizens, who exist, like

all citizens everywhere, within an unattainable horizon of equal liberties, who are asking for a *democratization* of their citizenship and its attendant benefits, a democratization that is just as much about proliferating exclusions as it is about increasing inclusions, as Balibar argues that all democratic politics in fact do. Citizenship rights and recent calls for their reconceptualization and democratization in the Gulf States are enabled precisely through and against the presence of the large numbers of mostly South Asian noncitizens in these countries, who are simultaneously complicit in and excepted from state formation and citizenship. Our understandings of democracy and freedom must therefore be assessed for their own provincialisms and for the Orientalisms through which we understand Gulf monarchies and their forms of rule. What may seem free and democratic from a Western liberalist or even Marxist viewpoint is not necessarily what our interlocutors mean by these terms, nor do Western provincial definitions underpin Gulf residents' claims to the city, to rights, or to justice. To explicate my argument, I turn to two seemingly unrelated but important moments from my fieldwork in the Gulf, the first among Indian businessmen in Dubai, and the second among Qatari university students at Texas A&M Qatar, the branch campus of my previous university.

Most accounts of the ethnocracy that structures Gulf societies argue that citizens are kept satisfied through generous welfare benefits, while noncitizens, who mainly come from postcolonial countries of the global South, are prevented from unionizing or protesting their working conditions by authoritarian regimes and the kafala system of individual citizen-sponsorship of migrants.[21] Foreigners therefore have little legal recourse in these countries, and their calls for labor and other rights that we would consider democratic and liberal are thus practically impossible. While we might assume that middle-class Indians, coming from the self-proclaimed largest democracy in the world, would lament the lack of liberal rights for themselves and for citizens in a place like Dubai, they in fact more often proclaim themselves "guests" and espouse neoliberal ideologies about what constitutes freedom that contribute to their own exclusion from the UAE nation. The kafala system and the nonliberal state are both dependent on foreign residents, without whom neither could function given the small minority of citizens in the country.[22] Probably the greatest irony in the case of Dubai, however, is that expatriate Indian elites, well established in the Gulf, benevolently protected by the ruling families, and favored with lucrative economic opportunities, are actually at risk of losing their special status in the UAE if democratization—in the colloquial liberal sense of the term, meaning liberal rights of franchise and representation by the citizenry and opportunities for immigrant naturalization—takes place. Thus, these businessmen are just as invested as the sheikhs in maintaining monarchial rule, and their futures rely on the maintenance of a firm citizen-foreigner binary that proffers generous benefits to citizens while masking the preferential treatment of certain expatriate populations by the government. Indian businessmen's definitions of freedom, therefore, directly contradicted what scholars, activists, and nongovernmental organizations would prescribe in order to increase both migrant and citizen rights in the country.

A contrasting example comes from my more recent teaching and fieldwork experiences in Doha, Qatar. Based on what are now considered necessary indicators of equal access to education in the United States, most American branch campuses in the Gulf insist on gender-integrated classrooms.[23] In my summer 2010 "Introduction to Sociocultural Anthropology" class at Texas A&M University at Qatar (TAMUQ), on a day when we were discussing gender roles, the young Qatari women in my class were extremely vocal about their opinions about gender inequality in the country and directly criticized what they felt were sexist claims made by some men in the class. Such outspokenness would have been inconceivable to my colleagues at TAMUQ even two years before, and it could be seen from the perspective of American ideas of gender equality within the classroom as a moment of "success." However, the moment cannot easily be co-opted into the rubric of mainstream Western liberalism or feminism, for Qatari women's definitions of gender equality were framed not in terms of liberal-democratic access to rights and civil society, but rather in terms of the extension of the responsibilities of the patrimonial nonliberal welfare state to include them more equally in terms of employment, pay scales, and the ability to move around "safely" in public, an extension that relied directly on excluding the large noncitizen majority to support the benefits provided to the citizen minority. For example, the Qatari women in my class felt it was unfair that male expatriates were given job preference over them; they expressed unease about moving around in spaces that were occupied by "bachelors"; and they were angry about having to leave their children with foreign housemaids because husbands did not do an equal share of domestic work. These calls for inclusion hinged directly on immigrant exclusions. Thus, when applied from a Western academic perspective, "equality," "democracy," and "freedom" fail to account for the particularities through which Qatari women deployed these terms; and, in fact, reading their grievances against the state and their male compatriots as a moment of feminist liberation would also mean being complicit in the alienation of noncitizen groups and the power hierarchies within which they live their daily lives.

These examples point to how definitions of politics, freedom, equality, and democracy that circulate in media and academic accounts of the Middle East are actually provincially Western and thus fail to account for the on-the-ground complexities of daily life for people in the region—both citizen and foreign resident—and their motivations for activism and protest, or lack thereof. The changes that have occurred in Dubai since I conducted the bulk of my fieldwork, in 2006, and the shifts in lived urban citizenship, identities, and politicizations that they have engendered for Dubai's Indian diaspora also encourage a reassessment of the assumptions and epistemological categories we use to understand migration, citizenship, democracy, and the political, in the Gulf as well as in other parts of the world.

Making Diasporic Futures

The boomtown development projects that the Dubai government undertook in the early years of the millennium were located primarily on the outskirts of the city, mostly in the area that is now known as New Dubai. These projects included luxury hotels, shopping malls, free-trade zones, and residential communities designed primarily for Western expatriate residents and investors, and they contributed to the increasing geographic segregation between old and new parts of the city, a segregation that was also reifying racial and class differences among its residents. Thus, the working- and middle-class South Asians who were the focus of my research often considered New Dubai's neighborhoods foreign, distant, and even racist compared to the older neighborhoods near the Dubai Creek that they culturally and socially associated with South Asia. In addition, heavy traffic congestion due to rapid increases in population and development had made the two parts of the city feel even farther apart in 2006, for the few kilometers that separated them could take hours to traverse during the busiest parts of the day. According to several sources, the boomtown Dubai in which I conducted my fieldwork is now officially a bust. Almost immediately following the global economic downturn of 2008, for example, the International Monetary Fund predicted that the UAE's economic growth in 2009 would be its lowest in five years; the Dubai government borrowed billions of dollars from Abu Dhabi in order to bail out its banks and even named the tallest building in the world after the ruler of Abu Dhabi because of this bailout; the Kerala government reported over 500,000 return migrants from Dubai due to the crisis; property prices were dropping faster than anywhere else in the world; and hotel rates were slashed in order to lure more tourists.[24] In the first few months of 2009, the international press published a plethora of articles about Dubai's demise, to the extent that local bloggers identified a trend of "Dubai bashing," and the UAE government even drafted a law to forbid reporting about a recession.[25] Readers may be familiar with stories about cranes abandoned at construction sites or tales of expats reduced to living in their cars.[26]

Therefore, when I visited the emirate in April 2009, I expected to find a city that was much changed, perhaps even in shambles. The evidence of recession from a tourist's perspective was immediately palpable. At the airport, I was one of only a handful of people in the taxi line, and while driving along an almost empty Sheikh Zayed Road—Dubai's main thoroughfare, which is usually mired in bumper-to-bumper traffic—my cab driver told me that he had experienced a significant decline in customers during the last year. My hotel near the posh Dubai Marina was not only undersold, but also cost less than half of the going rate in 2007. However, during the taxi ride, I also noted many new buildings and shopping centers filling what used to be empty lots. My taxi driver shifted conversation from the slowdown of customers to point out some of the more notable sights. Then, on realizing that I speak Hindi, he proceeded to describe the 2,000-square-foot house with an ocean view he was building for his family on the outskirts of Karachi. While he had slowed down construction because of financial worries, he had no immediate plans to leave the UAE, even though he was currently sharing a cramped room with two other men in the downtown Deira neighborhood. I wondered about the impacts of the economic crisis on people like my cab driver, working- and middle-class South Asians who live neither in skyscrapers nor in labor camps, but instead populate the streets, shops, offices, and apartments of the city. This population, which is probably the largest in the emirate, was not in any way addressed by articles on Dubai's bust nor by rebuttals to those articles that decried "Dubai-bashing" by the international media.

During that visit, I also sat down for lunch with Gautam and Reshma in their humble one-bedroom apartment in Bur Dubai. I had not been in the city for over two years, and I was curious to hear how they had weathered the "bust." "They have been asking some people to take four-day weeks but thankfully it has not hit my department yet," Gautam told me when I asked him if his job had been affected. "But the rents are going down a lot. Our old building is back where we could afford it now. Even though this apartment has not gone down, they have not raised rent for next year at all." But weren't people losing their jobs or thinking about going back to India? Yes, said Gautam and Reshma, of course. But they considered that normal. The tenuousness of their lives was constant and enduring, and the possibility of losing work was familiar to Gautam and other Indians like him. For Gautam and his family, certain aspects of life had actually become more bearable since the economic downturn. Gautam no longer worried about not meeting the rent. He was even considering trading in his beat-up red Corolla for a four-wheel drive because many wealthy expats were leaving Dubai and trying to unload their cars at low prices.[27] In fact, he told me, housing prices had dropped so much in the last year that an extended family living in a one-room flat in his ill-maintained building had recently purchased, with their life savings, a brand new freehold apartment on the posh Palm Jumeirah. Astonished, I asked how they had been able to afford it. "I don't know," Gautam shrugged, "but I hear it's true. They have already moved out."

Stories of newfound advantage among Indians paralleled those of financial ruin, which abounded after the real-estate crash and Dubai's announcement that it had to borrow money from Abu Dhabi. One widespread story claimed that thousands of cars had been abandoned at the airport as expatriates rushed to leave the country; others described executives who had been made homeless overnight. In fact, the reversal-of-fortune trope accompanied me on my return journeys through the neighborhoods of my fieldwork, as I visited former informants and spoke to other Dubai South Asians. My "post-bust" interviews contained an element I had not often heard during my fieldwork—that of class and race mobility. Instead of describing people's social, geographic, and employment positions within the city as tethered to race, nationality, and class, these rumors and stories pointed to how quickly and drastically one's life conditions could transform, regardless of one's status. A white person, no matter how well employed, could be reduced to living in Deira, a neighborhood that none of my South Asian interlocutors would have previously considered expatriate space. Westerners, despite carrying passports that conferred privileges of mobility in the UAE, could be unexpectedly separated from family or unable to leave the country, insecurities from which they had previously been spared. In contrast, the stories South Asians told about themselves and other South Asians seemed to convey hope rather than stasis. I never expected, for example, that a lower-middle-class family could move directly from Gautam's building into the newly opened Palm Island and live freehold without having to rely on a work permit for residency. And I doubt that Gautam had envisioned that possibility before either.

Tales of Indians moving to New Dubai might also indicate that they were staking claims to neighborhoods that had previously been considered off-limits. In these narratives I heard new forms of possibility and new claims to the city, ones that further eroded the never quite contained triptych through which the emirate tended to define itself and was defined, and ones that paralleled even more closely the narratives of mobility that accompany work on middle-class post-independence Indian diasporas in the West.[28] These rumors and stories pointed to ruptures in racial, class, and national categorizations that had previously seemed more rigid, and perhaps even to a different dynamic of emergence in the citizen-noncitizen binary, which needs to be further explored. Were Indians such impossible citizens in 2011 as they had seemed in 2006? Perhaps these narratives indicate the need for new ethnographic terminologies and categories that more accurately describe who resides in the city and the roles they play in producing its present-day spaces and institutions. And given that these narratives, stories, and rumors revolved around recessional changes in the Gulf, they also further complicate the divide between economic and other forms of belonging, and point to the necessity of including the economic within our conception of what constitutes citizenship, belonging, and political change in the region.

The alleviation of certain boomtown insecurities that impacted South Asians in old Dubai were accompanied, as the stories above gesture to, by reterritorializations of space in the city. The Dubai Metro, which may seem yet another example of Dubai's exceptionalism and spectacle, is also a

FIGURE C.1 · Metro station entrance in old Dubai's Karama neighborhood.
Photograph by Neha Vora.

potential agent in the city's post-boom reterritorialization. In typical Dubai fashion, on 9 September 2009 at exactly 9:09:09 PM, the Middle East's first automated train network, the Dubai Metro, was inaugurated (see figure C.1). Characteristically, the Metro set world records in terms of cost, engineering, and innovation. But it signaled more than the Dubai government's interest in spectacle, neoliberal economic diversification, and tourism. Adding to a toll-road system called Salik, introduced in 2007, the Dubai Metro represented a government investment of billions of dollars in long-term, citywide urban improvement. While Dubai has had a bus system for many years, buses have been unreliable and, like cars, affected by traffic problems. Dubai's Metro could be construed as another form of spectacle designed to bring international media attention and tourism to the emirate, but in effect it also operates as a form of welfare that applies more evenly to the city's residents, including noncitizens, and thus as a form of democratization in the sense that Balibar described.[29] Everyone can ride the Metro, including construction workers in overalls, Emirati citizens in dishdasha and abaya, tourists heading to one of Dubai's many malls, businessmen in suits, Indian women in saris and salwar-kameez,

FIGURE C.2 · Dubai Metro map, clearly linking "old" and "new" Dubai. Photograph by Neha Vora.

and teenagers hanging out after school. The Metro is inexpensive and connects previously disparate parts of town, both lessening traffic and providing a unique place where a cross-section of the city's residents, who would otherwise not find themselves in the same space, share close quarters.

In fact, the Metro *urbanizes* Dubai in new ways. It signifies a form of state commitment to urban citizenship that is inclusive of noncitizen residents in ways that other urban-works projects have not been. In addition, the Metro might be materially and symbolically relinking old and new Dubai into a more integrated cityscape, even as the city continues to proliferate new zones and spaces of exclusion and differentiation (see figure C.2). For me, crisscrossing the city on Dubai's Metro in 2010 was an experience of urban belonging that was perhaps more intimate in terms of feeling part of the city and sharing space with so many types of people than any experiences I had had when I actually lived in Dubai.[30] I found the Metro familiar for its resemblance to public transportation in other places, yet simultaneously out of place in the landscape that I had come to define as my field site and second home.[31] How does the Metro pry open previously closed spaces, I wondered? The impact of the Metro on traffic and on car sales has not been assessed, and data on the number of people who use it regularly as a mode of transport are not yet available. Nonetheless, as a method by which to move around the city, and as a space that, unlike the "air-conditioned bus" to which one of my informants likened Dubai, enables different residents to come into contact with each other in new ways, the Metro is an important site for reconsidering spatial stories of "field-making" and the imagined territorial boundaries of Dubai's "foreign matter" in future projects.[32]

The constant reterritorializations of space and belonging that I have begun to map in this conclusion point to a city that is in some ways more integrated, even as it proliferates new forms of exclusions and exceptions. With changes in the city, diaspora spaces are being reconfigured to include new forms of mobility, citizenship, and imaginings of the future. This is most evident, of course, in the experiences of young people raised in the emirate, who are beginning to attend newly available institutions of globalized higher education in the Gulf. Although many critics in the United States have branded these universities as money-making ventures, as new forms of Gulf "spectacle," and even as neo-imperial projects, the experiences of young South Asians in Dubai who attended branch campuses highlight some of the unexpected effects that these schools are having on diasporic populations in the Gulf, thus muddling easy dismissals or celebrations of the practice of globalizing higher education.[33] By shifting our focus to these campuses, we can perhaps better address how certain ideologies, techniques, and practices of citizenship circulate within these spaces, and how differently situated students participate in the production of new forms of identity and belonging as they interact with their peers and come of age. For the young South Asians I met in Dubai, liberal claims to civil rights and diasporic citizenship emerged directly from their experiences at these universities, claims that may be changing the face of belonging in places like Dubai, while producing scholars who can engage the very debates within which they are imbricated.

The enormous wave of activism that swept across the Arab world beginning in 2010, from Egypt to Bahrain, demonstrates that people in these countries are questioning and redefining state responsibility, freedom, and citizenship, even as it points to elisions in popular and scholarly understandings of who belongs and who can stake claims to national, urban, and civic space. The experiences of Indian foreign residents in the Creek neighborhoods of old Dubai, contrasted with representations of the city's demography, politics, and forms of belonging in the scholarly literature, similarly parallel questions about meanings of "democracy," "rights," and "freedom," and encourage us to ask questions about how parochial Western genealogies and understandings of these concepts are being applied to scholarship on the Gulf region, as well as on the Middle East more generally. My fieldwork with Indians in Dubai—from second-generation college students to entrepreneurs to salaried workers—highlights some of the unexpected and unexplored outcomes of the economic, geographic, and social changes that were occurring in the city in the mid 2000s, at the time of the city's emergence into an imaginary of the highs and lows of millennial capital. Instead of confirming the flattened representations of the emirate as a site of material excess built upon extreme labor exploitation of a transnational proletariat that were circulating in scholarly and media venues at the time, my interlocutors' narratives—both during Dubai's "boom" and after its consequent "bust"—showcased how Dubai was both rather non-exceptional and could teach us about many other parts of the contemporary world with which it might at first seem incommensurable. As its most ubiquitous residents, yet as those who were constantly excepted from governmental, media, and scholarly definitions of the emirate's rise and fall, Dubai Indians' everyday practices of lived citizenship produced and reconfigured politics, identity, and belonging in ways that revealed the tenuousness of the supposedly rigid categories through which Gulf societies were ordered and understood, from within and without. At a time when the international spotlight is on the Gulf region and the Middle East in ways that rely heavily on these categorizations—citizen-noncitizen, economy-nation, democratic-authoritarian, oppressed-liberated, native-foreigner—it is even more imperative for us as researchers to continue to highlight the meaningfulness and messiness of ordinary life on-the-ground in these spaces and how the epistemologies through which we assess the purportedly exceptional are themselves quite often productive of their own truths and, thus, their exceptions.

Introduction

1 The naming of the region is contested. Some call it the Persian Gulf, others the Arabian Gulf or Arabian Sea. I avoid taking sides in this debate, which is not relevant to my project, by using the term "Gulf" whenever possible. Where I specifically refer to countries on the Arabian Peninsula, however, I sometimes refer to the "Arab side of the Gulf" or to the "Gulf Arab States."

2 The UAE is a loose federation of seven states (emirates), the largest of which are Abu Dhabi (the capital) and Dubai. Each emirate has an independent governing structure that is based in patrilineal monarchial rule, but there is also a nationalized legal system that oversees immigration, foreign policy, and other matters. Each emirate is proportionally represented within the UAE government based on its citizen population. Although I refer primarily to belonging within Dubai as a city-state, Dubai cannot be completely divorced from the UAE in any analysis, especially analyses of migration, because migration laws and citizenship—and the governance over them—are defined at the national scale.

3 Some people use "Dubai" to refer to the UAE more generally, so if someone were living in Abu Dhabi, their relatives might say they lived in Dubai. This is also true for other, less-well-known Gulf Arab States. I still hear, for example, people from India or other parts of the diaspora refer to Qatar or Oman as "Dubai."

4 See for example Al-Rasheed, *Transnational Connections and the Arab Gulf*; Al-Sayegh, "Merchants' Role in a Changing Society"; Allen, "The Indian Merchant Community of Masqat"; Bose, *A Hundred Horizons*; Das Gupta, *India and the Indian Ocean World*; Dresch and Piscatori, *Monarchies and Nations*; Gamburd, *The Kitchen Spoon's Handle*; Gardner, *City of Strangers*; Johnson, "Diasporic Dreams"; Kanna, *Dubai, the City as Corporation*; Khalaf, "Globalization and Heritage in the Gulf"; Leonard, "South Asian Women in the Gulf" and "South Asian Workers in the Gulf"; Lombard and Aubin, *Asian Merchants and Businessmen in the Indian Ocean and the China Sea*; Markovits, *The Global World of Indian Merchants*; Nagy, "'This Time I Think I'll Try a Filipina'" and "Making Room for Migrants, Making Sense of Difference"; Onley, *The Arabian Frontier*

of the British Raj; Vora, "Producing Diasporas and Globalization" and "From Golden Frontier to Global City."

5 Chakrabarty, *Provincializing Europe*.

6 Some exceptions include the work of Yasser Elsheshtawy, Ahmed Kanna, and Sharon Nagy.

7 See for example Dresch, "Debates on Marriage and Nationality in the United Arab Emirates"; Gardner, *City of Strangers*; Longva, "Neither Autocracy nor Democracy but Ethnocracy"; Okruhlik, "Excluded Essentials."

8 Comaroff and Comaroff, "Millennial Capitalism."

9 See also Elsheshtawy, *Dubai*, for a similar argument about how representations come to be the reality of Dubai.

10 See for example Ali, *Dubai*; Barrett, *Dubai*; Davis, "Sinister Paradise"; Fichtner, "Osama's Nightmare"; Ruff, "Diversions."

11 See, for example, Sheila MacVicar, "Once Booming Dubai Goes Bust," CBS *News*, 11 February 2009, http://www.cbsnews.com; Tom Hundley, "Has Dubai Gone Bust?" Global Post, 27 November 2009, http://www.globalpost.com; Adnan Khan, "Dubai 'Miracle' Goes Bust," Khalifah.com, 16 February 2009, http://www.khilafah.com.

12 See also Ahmad, "Beyond Labor," for a more detailed critique of the analytic of labor in Gulf migration.

13 Teitelbaum, "Understanding political liberalization in the Gulf," 13–15.

14 Beblawi, "The Rentier State in the Arab World"; Beblawi and Luciani, *The Rentier State*.

15 Teitelbaum, *Political Liberalization in the Persian Gulf*; Luciani, *The Arab State*.

16 See Chakrabarty, *Provincializing Europe*, for a discussion of development discourses that produce non-Western countries as "not-yet."

17 Massey, Arango, Hugo, Kouaouci, Pellegrino, and Taylor, "Labour Migration in the Gulf System," 134. See also Davis, "Sinister Paradise" and "Fear and Money in Dubai."

18 Al-Naqeeb, *Society and State in the Gulf and Arab Peninsula*, Dauderstadt and Schildberg, *Dead Ends of Transition*; Davidson, *The United Arab Emirates*; Luciani, *The Arab State*; Ross, "Does Oil Hinder Democracy?" Luciani, for example, argues that "rentier states will display little tendency to evolve towards democratic institutions, while states needing to resort to taxation of domestic incomes or facing the need to cut down on subsidies and other economic benefits extended to their population will need to look for an alternative source of legitimacy, which may come from an evolution towards democracy" ("Introduction," xxiv).

19 Mike Davis, for example, calls the UAE a "quasi-nation thrown together by Sheikh Mo's father and the ruler of Abu Dhabi in 1971 to fend off threats from Marxists in Oman and, later, Islamicists in Iran" ("Fear and Money in Dubai,"

4). See also Thomas Friedman, "Tribes with Flags," *New York Times*, 22 March 2011.

20 Al-Barghouti, *The Umma and the Dawla*; Butenschon, Davis, and Hassassian, *Citizenship and the State in the Middle East*; Davidson, *Dubai*. See also Mitchell, "The Limits of the State," and Vitalis, *America's Kingdom*, on the unequal entanglements between Saudi Arabia and the United States.

21 Nazih Ayubi, for example, argues that the concept of the state cannot be separated from its historical and theoretical origins in Europe (*Over-stating the Arab State*, 4–5).

22 See also Joseph, "Gendering Citizenship in the Middle East," and Shohat, "Area Studies, Gender Studies, and the Cartographies of Knowledge," for a critique of this teleology. The assumption that capitalism brings democracy is quite prevalent in American foreign policy, as well as in the philosophies of supranational organizations like the World Bank and the International Monetary Fund.

23 Davidson, *The United Arab Emirates*; Kapiszewski, *Nationals and Expatriates*; Luciani, *The Arab State*; Massey, Arango, Hugo, Kouaouci, Pellegrino, and Taylor, "Labour Migration in the Gulf System."

24 Onley, *The Arabian Frontier of the British Raj*.

25 See for example Davis, "Sinister Paradise"; Thomas Friedman, "Tribes with Flags," *New York Times*, 22 March 2011; Gill, "Dubai on Empty"; Toshens, "Dubai's the Limit." For a critique of these representations of Dubai, see Kanna, *Dubai, the City as Corporation*.

26 These ideas are reminiscent of Western justifications of colonialism within the Middle East and elsewhere as a benevolent and necessary intervention. See Shohat, "Area Studies, Gender Studies, and the Cartographies of Knowledge."

27 Al-Awad and Elhiraika, "Cultural Effects and Savings"; Ali, *Dubai*; Gardezi, "Asian Workers in the Gulf States of the Middle East"; Kapiszewski, *Nationals and Expatriates*; Khalaf and Kobaisi, "Migrants' Strategies of Coping and Patterns of Accommodation in the Oil-Rich Gulf Societies."

28 See for example Arnold and Shah, *Asian Labor Migration*; Kurien, *Kaleidoscopic Ethnicity*; Nambiar, *The Socio-Economic Conditions of Gulf Migrants*; Rahman, *Indian Labour Migration to the Gulf*; Sekher, *Migration and Social Change*.

29 See Osella and Gardner, "Migration, Modernity, and Social Transformation in South Asia," for a critique of Indian migration literature.

30 In fact, the International Labor Organization reproduces this idea by dividing migration into two categories: settlement and contract. See Zachariah, Prakash, and Rajan, "Indian Workers in the UAE."

31 See for example Johnson, "At Home and Abroad," on how migration to the Gulf results in contradictory experiences of power for Filipinas—increased family constraints on the one hand and increased liberatory moments on the other.

32 Ahmad, "Beyond Labor." The term *modern-day slavery* circulates in discussions

of Gulf State migration at every level, from conference paper titles to newspaper articles to everyday conversations with expatriates in the Gulf, and even in my colleagues' and students' general perceptions of Dubai and the region.

33 Nagy, "'This Time I Think I'll Try a Filipina,'" and "Making Room for Migrants, Making Sense of Difference."

34 See also Gardner, *City of Strangers*, on the exceptionalism often ascribed to the Gulf States.

35 For the purposes of this book, I use *liberal, neoliberal,* and *non-* or *illiberal* to define processes and ideologies that are considered to be distinct in much scholarship and colloquial understandings of politics. Rather than argue for their distinction, I use these terms to illuminate the porosity and overlaps between philosophical systems that may initially appear incommensurable. By *liberal,* I mean ideas about governance that assume inalienable rights or "freedoms" for citizens that are outside of the purview of the state. My use of *neoliberal* refers to the rise in market-based ideas about governance and the idea that the state should not interfere in economic processes. And by *non-* or *illiberal,* I refer to both state discourses that situate themselves in opposition to what they consider liberalism, as well as to forms of governance that do not claim to be founded on rights of franchise or freedom of speech or that explicitly curtail civil society formation.

36 See also Khalaf, "Poetics and Politics of Newly Invented Traditions in the Gulf" and "Globalization and Heritage in the Gulf," on the production of heritage in the UAE.

37 Gwenn Okruhlik, for example, examines how within Gulf societies migrants are "Excluded Essentials."

38 See Davidson, *The United Arab Emirates*; Heard-Bey, *From Trucial States to United Arab Emirates*; Longva, "Neither Autocracy nor Democracy but Ethnocracy"; Okruhlik, "Dependence, Disdain, and Distance"; Onley, "Gulf Arab Headdress before Oil."

39 See also Kanna, *Dubai, the City as Corporation,* for a discussion of how space gets coded in Dubai as insider vs. outsider.

40 Dresch and Piscatori, *Monarchies and Nations*; Longva, *Walls Built on Sand.*

41 Ayubi, *Over-Stating the Arab State*; Butenschon, Davis, and Hassassian, *Citizenship and the State in the Middle East*; Hutchings and Dannreuther, *Cosmopolitan Citizenship*; Joseph, "Gendering Citizenship in the Middle East."

42 Davidson, *The United Arab Emirates*. In the case of Kuwait, Jill Crystal has also traced liberal-style political bargains between merchants and rulers to consolidate and protect political power and influence among certain elite groups (*Oil and Politics in the Gulf*).

43 Recently the UAE has begun to hold limited elections, which can also be construed as a liberal form of governance.

44 Ayubi, *Over-stating the Arab State*.

45 See, for example, Sassen, *The Global City* and "Beyond Sovereignty."

46 Ong, *Neoliberalism as Exception*.

47 Ong, *Neoliberalism as Exception*, 3.

48 One could argue that there is no place in the world where full privatization or neoliberalization of the economy exists, even in states that actively espouse "open" markets.

49 Ahn Nga Longva, for example, notes that citizenship among the nomadic Bedu in Kuwait is based on notions of allegiance to rulers, while settled groups have been more focused on forms of equality (*Walls Built on Sand*). And Kapizewski points out that since work is not necessarily an obligation for many nationals, consumption has become a central component of citizenship (*Nationals and Expatriates*).

50 See also Kanna, "Flexible Citizenship in Dubai."

51 Hazem Beblawi writes, for example, "The fact that acquisition of citizenship has been limited in the major receiving states of the Gulf, or has not resulted in full political participation where it has occurred, does not mean, however, that political integration of migrants has not taken place" ("The Rentier State in the Arab World," 390). While he is referring to Arab migrants who have access in some cases to citizenship and public-sector jobs, I found that this was also the case with some non-Arab noncitizens as well.

52 See also Longva, "Neither Autocracy nor Democracy but Ethnocracy."

53 See for example Gibson-Graham, *The End of Capitalism (As We Knew It)*; Latour, *We Have Never Been Modern*; Timothy Mitchell, "The Limits of the State"; Poovey, *The History of the Modern Fact*; Thrift, *Spatial Formations*.

54 I borrow the concept of turning "inside-out" from Annelise Riles, *The Network Inside Out*.

55 Anderson, *Imagined Communities*. Feminists in particular have argued that the public-private dichotomy on which modern citizenship relies is gendered at its core and excludes women as well as racial minorities (Franklin and McKinnon, *Relative Values*; Michelle Zimbalist Rosaldo, "Women, Culture, and Society" and "The Use and Abuse of Anthropology"; Rubin, "The Traffic in Women"; Voet, *Feminism and Citizenship*; Yanagisako and Delaney, *Naturalizing Power*). The concept of citizenship itself, argues Carol Pateman in "Political Obligation, Freedom and Feminism," is built on a social contract in which women serve as part of the private sphere over which citizens (male) are able to retain dominion. Citizenship has also been criticized for the racial assumptions that go into defining the citizenry and the unequal access to rights and privileges for minority groups and immigrants in Western societies. In the United States, for example, scholars have explored how citizenship, promoted as a universal form of belonging for all, was in fact built on white supremacy

(Isin and Wood, *Citizenship and Identity*; Renato Rosaldo, "Cultural Citizenship, Inequality, and Multiculturalism"; Somers, *Genealogies of Citizenship*). Many states, in response to such criticisms, have incorporated forms of cultural or plural citizenship, which attempt to rectify historical and contemporary inequalities between groups. However, scholars continue to question the cultural assumptions underlying citizenship's universality. In Europe recent debates surrounding Muslim minorities point to the limits of citizenship in that, while espousing certain universalities, state policies are unable or unwilling to accept certain cultural beliefs and practices into the national community (Scott, *The Politics of the Veil*). The most recent ban on *niqab* (face veil) in public space in France, for example, includes citizenship training for men whose wives or daughters are "caught" wearing niqab—explicitly producing Muslims as outsiders to the French nation or as insiders with differentiated rights to public space. In addition to questioning the internal limits of citizenship and its multiple and contradictory effects, scholars have also pointed to global trends and their effects on forms of national belonging. In particular, globalization and the shift away from welfare-based societies have led to a study of neoliberal citizenship, where citizens are seen more as clients than as rights-bearing individuals. The application of market values to residents of a nation-state means that citizens are increasingly differentiated according to their ability to act as self-managing entrepreneurial subjects. However, these arguments are also based on the uneven applications of citizenship from the *inside*, and often continue to take sovereignty and a bounded nation-state for granted.

56 Hindess, "The Globalization of Citizenship." See also Coutin, *Legalizing Moves* and *Nations of Emigrants*.

57 Agamben, *Homo Sacer*.

58 See Agamben, *State of Exception*.

59 My use of *necropolitics* is different than its use in the argument put forward in "Necropolitics" by Achille Mbembe, who coined the term. Mbembe argues that necropolitics, a concept of sovereignty that relies on death rather than on the governance of life, is a form of power that was practiced within slavery, colonialism, and apartheid—that is, outside of the metropole. He is concerned that it is only when necropolitics comes to Europe through what Agamben calls the Nazi "state of exception" that this form of power becomes visible. Instead, I consider here how Agamben's origin story of the state can be read as one that places necropolitics not in Europe's colonies but rather at the center of so-called civilization itself. This does not, however, as Mbembe argues, let Agamben off the hook for his lack of attention to how Western sovereignty also relied on the exception of non-Western states and peoples.

60 Agamben, *Homo Sacer*, 7.

61 In fact, states of emergency in which constitutional laws are suspended and op-
    positional politics suppressed are quite common to modern democracies, lead-
    ing to extreme "states of exception" like the Nazi concentration camp or Guan-
    tanamo Bay (Agamben, *State of Exception*).

62 Mbembe, "Necropolitics."

63 Hindess, "The Globalization of Citizenship." Many scholars have traced, for ex-
    ample, how British citizenship developed directly through imperial encoun-
    ters, how British forms of governance were often tested in places like the
    subcontinent, and how civil-society forms in Europe—in particular, feminist
    and class struggles—utilized the colonies as fodder for activism at home. Brit-
    ish India has been documented as a laboratory not only for British citizenship,
    law, gender, sexuality, and medicine, but also for the proliferation of other im-
    perial projects around the world. Some examples from this vast body of schol-
    arship include David Arnold, *Colonizing the Body*, and Ghosh, *The Calcutta
    Chromosome*, on colonial medicine; Burton, *Burdens of History*, and Grewal,
    Home and Harem, on feminist movements; Ho, "Before Parochialization," and
    Sen, *A Distant Sovereignty*, on British national identity; Stoler, *Carnal Knowl-
    edge and Imperial Power*, on sexuality and race; and Visvanathan, *Masks of Con-
    quest*, on education.

64 See Al-Qasimi, *The Myth of Arab Piracy in the Gulf*; Onley, *The Arabian Frontier
    of the British Raj*.

65 Mbembe, "Necropolitics." See also Hansen and Stepputat, *Sovereign Bodies*.

66 See for example Cho, "Diasporic Citizenship"; Cohen, *Semi-Citizenship in Dem-
    ocratic Politics*; Holston and Appadurai, "Cities and Citizenship"; Marshall, *Cit-
    izenship and Social Class and Other Essays*; and Renato Rosaldo, "Cultural
    Citizenship, Inequality, and Multiculturalism." Several Gulf States do hold lim-
    ited parliamentary elections, and some scholars have argued that civil society
    does indeed exist in the Gulf, including in forums that allow for interactions
    between differentiated groups of residents. See, for example, Krause, *Women in
    Civil Society*; Nagy, "The Search for Miss Philippines Bahrain"; Vora, "Free
    Speech and Civil Discourse."

67 See Ong, *Flexible Citizenship*, *Buddha Is Hiding*, and *Neoliberalism as Exception*.

68 See Kanna, "The Arab World's Forgotten Rebellions"; Okruhlik, "Dependence,
    Disdain, and Distance."

69 Khalaf, "Gulf Societies and the Image of Unlimited Good."

70 Some notable exceptions include Elsheshtawy, "Transitory Sites"; Leonard,
    "South Asian Workers in the Gulf" and "South Asian Women in the Gulf";
    Kanna, *Dubai, the City as Corporation*; Osella and Osella, "Muslim Entrepre-
    neurs in Public Life between India and the Gulf." See also Gardner, *City of
    Strangers*, for a detailed account of Indian diasporas in Bahrain.

71 This term, however, circulates in popular discourse in India and abroad to refer to recent groups of Indian emigrants regardless of citizenship status (usually to Western countries).

72 In the early 1990s India was experiencing a major economic crisis. India's economic liberalization in 1991 was a product of World Bank and other international pressures attached to loan requests by the Indian government. In the
late 1990s, India started looking at economic options that would alleviate the
need to conform to these structural-adjustment policies. The diaspora became
a prime strategic site for procuring an infusion of funds.

73 Overseas Citizenship of India is not in actuality dual citizenship, because it
comes with no political rights. Instead, it is basically an extension of the privileges of economic access and mobility conferred by the PIO card.

74 Dickinson and Bailey, "(Re)membering Diaspora"; Elaine Lynn-Ee Ho,
"'Claiming' the Diaspora"; Mani and Varadarajan, "'The Largest Gathering of
the Global Indian Family'"; Oonk, Global Indian Diasporas; Voigt-Graf, "Transnationalism and the Indo-Fijian Diaspora"; Xavier, "Experimenting with Diasporic Incorporation."

75 See also Elaine Lynn-Ee Ho, "'Claiming' the Diaspora," for a critique of
sending-state "diaspora strategies."

76 Lall, India's Missed Opportunity.

77 Xavier, "Experimenting with Diasporic Incorporation," 38.

78 Dickinson and Bailey, "(Re)membering Diaspora"; Gamlen, "The Emigration
State and the Modern Geopolitical Imagination"; Mani and Varadarajan, "'The
Largest Gathering of the Global Indian Family'"; Voigt-Graf, "Transnational-
ism and the Indo-Fijian Diaspora."

79 See, for example, Pablo Shiladitya Bose, "Home and Away"; Mallapragada,
"Home, Homeland, Homepage"; Mankekar, "Brides Who Travel"; Grewal,
Transnational America.

80 Mani and Varadarajan, "'The Largest Gathering of the Global Indian Family.'"
See also the Report of the High Level Committee on Indian Diaspora, which details
PIO, NRI, and other classifications, available at the Indian Diaspora website,
http://indiandiaspora.nic.in.

81 Voigt-Graf, "Transnationalism and the Indo-Fijian Diaspora."

82 Van der Veer, "Virtual India."

83 Xavier, "Experimenting with Diasporic Incorporation."

84 Dickinson and Bailey, "(Re)membering Diaspora"; Grewal, Transnational
America; van der Veer, "Virtual India"; Xavier, "Experimenting with Diasporic
Incorporation."

85 See, for example, Radhakrishnan, "Examining the 'Global' Indian Middle Class."

86 See, for example, Sugata Bose, A Hundred Horizons; Gilroy, The Black Atlantic;
Engseng Ho, "Before Parochialization"; Leonard, The South Asian Americans.

87 See Appadurai, *Modernity at Large*; Mankekar, "Brides Who Travel"; Grewal, *Transnational America*; Gopinath, "Bombay, UK, Yuba City."

88 Brah, *Cartographies of Diaspora*; Bhabha, *The Location of Culture*; Gilroy, "Diaspora and the Detours of Identity"; Hall, "Cultural Identity and Diaspora."

89 Anderson, *Spectre of Comparisons*; Castles and Davidson, *Citizenship and Migration*; Gamlen, "The Emigration State and the Modern Geopolitical Imagination"; Schiller and Fouron, *Georges Woke Up Laughing*; Grewal, *Transnational America*.

90 See Spivak, "Diasporas Old and New," for an excellent critique of the relationship between those who write about diaspora (usually privileged postcolonial scholars from the West) and the definition of diaspora itself, which often reflects and centers their experiences.

91 A recent book edited by Gijsbert Oonk—*Global Indian Diasporas*—is intended as a corrective to the centering of Western NRI and PIO experiences in the diaspora literature. The essays in this collection not only are written by several scholars from outside of North America and the United Kingdom, but also focus on groups, such as East African and Caribbean Indians, who are often left out of or marginalized in studies of South Asian diaspora. See also Parrenas and Siu, *Asian Diasporas*.

92 Engseng Ho, "Before Parochialization." See also Brah, *Cartographies of Diaspora*, 209.

93 Oonk, "Global Indian Diasporas."

94 See also Sugata Bose, *A Hundred Horizons*.

95 The scholarship on diaspora is full of "lists" that outline criteria that supposedly make certain migrant groups diasporic. See, for example, Butler, "Defining Diaspora, Defining a Discourse"; Safran, "Diasporas in Modern Societies"; and several of the pieces in the journal *Diaspora*. Even as Kim Butler criticizes the criteria model of diaspora studies, she reproduces her own criteria for diaspora. This tension between needing to generalize and also to be specific is explored by Shukla, "Locations for South Asian Diasporas."

96 Safran, Sahoo, and Lal, "Indian Diaspora in Transnational Contexts."

97 Safran, Sahoo, and Lal, "Indian Diaspora in Transnational Contexts," 1.

98 Voigt-Graf, "Transnationalism and the Indo-Fijian Diaspora."

99 Visweswaran, "Diaspora by Design." See also Leonard, *The South Asian Americans*, for an example of a text that acknowledges not only the early Indian migration to the United States, but also migration from parts of South Asia that often get collapsed under "Indian," such as Sri Lanka, Afghanistan, and Bangladesh.

100 Axel, "The Context of Diaspora."

101 On diasporic subjects as challenges to the nation-state, see Appadurai, *Modernity at Large*; Clifford, "Diasporas." On diasporic subjects as dialectically pro-

duced in webs of power and governmentality within nation-states, see Andall, "Second-Generation Attitude?"; Bhattacharjee, "The Habit of Ex-Nomination"; Cho, "Diasporic Citizenship"; Dhingra, "Committed to Ethnicity, Committed to America"; Werbner, "The Place which Is Diaspora."

102 Siu, "Diasporic Cultural Citizenship," and *Memories of a Future Home.*

103 See also Coutin, *Nation of Emigrants*, for a similar argument about Salvadorans in the United States.

104 Hindess, "The Globalization of Citizenship"; Ong, *Flexible Citizenship* and *Neoliberalism as Exception.*

105 Ong, *Buddha Is Hiding.*

106 See Leonard, "South Asian Women in the Gulf"; Vora, "Producing Diasporas and Globalization."

107 Elsheshtawy, "Transitory Sites."

1. A Tale of Two Creeks

1 When I began my research in Dubai, the weekend was on Thursday and Friday. The weekend shifted, in early 2006, to Friday and Saturday, partly because many multinational and Western private companies were already implementing the latter weekly schedule for their employees, many of whom were from countries that considered Saturday and Sunday the official weekend. The temporal shift away from the traditional Middle Eastern Thursday and Friday weekend reflected Dubai's successes in foreign investment, as multinational companies brought with them their own work standards and the need to communicate with other offices around the world on the same days of the week. This shift was also marking a temporal difference between the way time in New Dubai and older areas of Dubai was allocated, segmented, and lived—a temporal difference that coincided in many ways with the geographical differences between the spaces that I map in this chapter.

2 Meena Bazaar, a commercial and residential area of Bur Dubai, is close to the Creek and is especially favored by Indian families for its central location to South Asian amenities.

3 Lungi is a covering for the bottom half of the body made from wrapped cloth, common to South India, and worn by men. Saris and salwar-kameez are common South Asian women's outfits.

4 For more on the co-constitution of space and subjectivity, see de Certeau, *The Practice of Everyday Life*; Secor, "'Is There an Istanbul that Belongs to Me?'"; Thrift, *Spatial Formations.*

5 In "Dubai Dreams," Alisha Ticku alludes to a similar breakdown of identity categories within the UAE.

6 I use the term *triptych* because it denotes, especially within Byzantine Chris-

tian art, a three-part complete representation, symbolizing all of existence—nothing falls outside of what is within the triptych. Similarly, I argue, these three categories supposedly contain all Dubai residents, with no outside.

7   Elsheshtawy, "Transitory Sites."

8   See Auge, *Non-Places*. See also Elsheshtawy, "Navigating the Spectacle," on the multiple retail spaces of Dubai (what he calls the "spectacular" and the "everyday"). Unlike Elsheshtawy, however, I feel not that the spectacular is somehow opposed to the everyday, but rather that the multiplicity of forms existing within Dubai's various spaces are equally anthropologically important.

9   De Certeau, *The Practice of Everyday Life*. See also Holston and Appadurai, "Cities and Citizenship"; Holston, "Insurgent Citizenship in an Era of Global Urban Peripheries."

10 See Bagaeen, "Brand Dubai," for further discussion of this map and urban-development projects in Dubai in the mid-2000s.

11 See also Kanna, *Dubai, the City as Corporation*.

12 The Burj Khalifa was originally named the Burj Dubai (Dubai Tower), but was renamed Burj Khalifa when it opened, in honor of the ruler of Abu Dhabi, for, after the global recession hit Dubai, the emirate had to borrow money from Abu Dhabi to pay off its debts.

13 "Vision, Mission, and Goals of Dubai eGovernment Initiative," Government of Dubai website, 12 June 2012, http://dubai.ae/en. The website originally attributed this quote to Dubai's leader, Sheikh Mohammed.

14 Kanna, *Dubai, the City as Corporation*. See also Bagaeen, "Brand Dubai." I discuss the neoliberal discourses of middle-class Indians in more detail in chapter 4.

15 For more on the concept of global cities, see Sassen, *The Global City*.

16 Since the economic downturn of 2008, the level of migration from South Asia has decreased, but still remains significantly high, especially in low-skill and low-wage sectors. See Vora, "The Precarious Existence of Dubai's Indian Middle Class."

17 A copy of this speech, delivered on 3 February 2007, is available through the Government of Dubai website, http://www.dubai.ae/en.

18 Nationals from other Gulf Cooperative Council (GCC) countries are exempt from this system and can move freely between and find employment without sponsorship in any of the GCC countries.

19 Ahn Nga Longva, in "Neither Autocracy nor Democracy but Ethnocracy," refers to this type of stratification as an "ethnocracy."

20 This seems to have changed since the introduction of du, a second Internet service provider, in the UAE. I have heard from several residents since the time of my research that certain areas in free zones are now under Internet censorship while others remain uncensored.

21 What kind of residential permit free-zone ownership would provide, how often

it would need to be renewed, and whether it only applied to properties above a certain price point were issues under debate during my research. The laws surrounding free-zone residency have been shifting and are unreliable. Thanks to Nitin Gogia for bringing this to my attention.

22 See Hazbun, *Beaches, Ruins, Resorts*, 205–19, for more on the development of free zones and tourist spaces in Dubai.

23 Ong, *Flexible Citizenship*, 214–39.

24 While it appears to be a system designed to protect the generous welfare benefits (free education, access to housing, guaranteed employment, free healthcare, etc.) conferred by the nonliberal, oil-rich UAE state, some have argued that the kafala system also resembles forms of neoliberal privatization and liberal social contracts by satisfying citizen needs in exchange for their cooperation (Crystal, *Oil and Politics in the Gulf*; Davidson, *The United Arab Emirates*; Longva, *Walls Built on Sand*). As "stakeholders" within the UAE, citizens—or "locals," as they are generally referred to—are kept satisfied through dynamic forms of welfare, including reforms which allow them to act as mini-rentiers. In order to do almost anything within the UAE—rent an apartment, take driving lessons, apply for a liquor permit—a foreign resident requires a "letter of no objection" from his or her sponsor. Often these bureaucratic processes are handled by local public officers, or POs, who advise foreigners (both business owners and workers) on policies, stand in lines, fill out forms, and handle other minutiae of administrative processes surrounding migration and employment. Both the kafala system (in which sponsorship is often "sold" for fees that are extralegal) and the PO industry provide generous amounts of income for citizens and operate as part of a neoliberal technology of privatization of governance. The kafala system also furthers the distinction between local and foreigner, contributing to a hierarchy in which locals can directly perform citizenship through the policing and administration of foreigners.

25 Leonard, "South Asian Workers in the Gulf"; Vora, "Producing Diasporas and Globalization."

26 See also Elsheshtawy, "Transitory Sites" and *Dubai*.

27 See Caren Kaplan, *Questions of Travel*, for a critique of Western privilege embedded within discourses of cosmopolitanism and travel.

28 Security in shopping malls around Dubai would regularly refuse entry to "bachelors"—usually South Asian or Afghani men in pajama kurta—during my time in Dubai, and some places enforce what they call "family day," which means single men (racially coded as nonwhite and nonnational) cannot enter alone.

29 Kanna, *Dubai, the City as Corporation*.

30 Kanna, *Dubai, the City as Corporation*, 1–6. Kanna refers to this way of selling Arabia as "orientalism in reverse."

31 See also Elsheshtawy, "Navigating the Spectacle."

32 Offering heritage for consumption also participates in the production of national identity among citizens, who, through consumer practices such as buying brand-name *abayas* (cloaks), perform national belonging. Though outside the scope of this project, consumer citizenship also reveals the very modern (and not timeless) nature of national identity in the UAE.

33 See Khalaf, "Poetics and Politics of Newly Invented Traditions in the Gulf"; Onley, "Gulf Arab Headdress before Oil." Ahmed Kanna, in "Flexible Citizenship in Dubai," however, notes that certain hybrid or "postpurist" identities are emerging among nationals who work in Dubai's neoliberal private sector.

34 Although with international outcry over child-jockey labor abuse, the UAE has begun to modernize the sport of camel racing by replacing human jockeys with robot ones.

35 Al-Sayegh, "Merchants' Role in a Changing Society"; Abu-Lughod, *Before European Hegemony*; Allen, "The Indian Merchant Community of Masqat"; Das Gupta, *India and the Indian Ocean World*; Fawaz, Bayly, and Ilbert, *Modernity and Culture*; Ghosh, *In an Antique Land*; Engseng Ho, "Before Parochialization" and "Empire through Diasporic Eyes"; Lombard and Aubin, *Asian Merchants and Businessmen in the Indian Ocean and the China Sea*; Markovits, "Indian Merchant Networks Outside India in the Nineteenth and Twentieth Centuries" and *The Global World of Indian Merchants*; Onley, "Gulf Arab Headdress before Oil."

36 Al-Qasimi, *The Myth of Arab Piracy in the Gulf*.

37 See also Gardner, "Strategic Transnationalism," on the history of Indians in Bahrain.

38 See also Anderson, *Spectre of Comparisons*, on how "area" is experienced as a unified geographical region more by academics than by those who actually reside in places scholars have deemed culturally similar. Additionally, Engseng Ho's work on diaspora, "Before Parochialization," argues that European colonialism in Southeast Asia led to increased parochialization in terms of racial identity; thus, already existing creole populations were marginalized in favor of "pure" identities that existed in individual relationships with the imperial state. Because we approach them as distinct now, we can ask questions about the "Arab presence" in Singapore, but, empirically, these groups are hard to separate.

39 Al-Sayegh, "Merchants' Role in a Changing Society."

40 Al Abed and Hellyer, *United Arab Emirates, a New Perspective*; Al-Gurg, *The Wells of Memory*.

41 Khalaf, "Poetics and Politics of Newly Invented Traditions in the Gulf."

42　Zahlan, *The Origins of the United Arab Emirates*.

43　Anderson, *Spectre of Comparisons*. Andrew Gardner describes a similar tension between the idea of a homogenous imagined community in Bahrain and the differential governance and benefits for various members of the citizenry (*City of Strangers*, 145).

44　Khalaf, "Globalization and Heritage in the Gulf."

45　Sheikh Rashid was Sheikh Mohammed's father and a previous ruler of Dubai.

46　See Elsheshtawy, *Dubai*, for a more detailed description of this area. While situated along the Dubai Creek, Elsheshtawy argues, Bastakiya exemplifies the increasing segregation of old and new Dubai as well, for it is intended not for the original inhabitants of the area but for wealthy tourists.

47　For a more detailed examination of the shift from coastal-oriented to land-oriented historical narratives, see Rab, "Seascape Urbanism in the Gulf."

48　See also the Sheikh Mohammed Centre for Cultural Understanding website, http://www.cultures.ae, which promotes a purified version of Emirati history for citizens and noncitizens alike.

49　See also Al-Qasimi, "Modest Immodesty."

50　Onley, "Gulf Arab Headdress before Oil."

51　For more on nationalism as unbound and imagined, see Anderson, *Spectre of Comparisons*.

52　Leonard, "South Asian Women in the Gulf."

53　Dresch, "Debates on Marriage and Nationality in the United Arab Emirates."

54　The majority of Emiratis also have Persian roots, which produces an internal division in the local population. In many cases, families prohibit marriage between "true" Arabs and those of Persian origin. Many Persian Emiratis consider themselves Arab, however, for their origin narrative is often presented as one in which Gulf Arabs migrated to the south of Iran and then returned. See for example Al-Gurg, *The Wells of Memory*.

55　Ahmad, "Beyond Labor." See also Stoler, *Carnal Knowledge and Imperial Power*, for a broader discussion of affect and intimate labor.

56　Leonard, "South Asian Women in the Gulf." See also Nagy, "'This Time I Think I'll Try a Filipina.'"

57　Claude Markovits, in his study of Indian trade diasporas, *The Global World of Indian Merchants*, traces how Indian merchant families were mostly Jains and Hindus from Gujarat, and were called "Banias," a caste name that was sometimes extended to reference all Indians in the Gulf. The name Bania, as well as Indian surnames, can still be found in many location names in Gulf port cities. For example, in Deira, the street running alongside the Creek is named Baniyas, which is perhaps an Arabized version of Bania and may refer to the high levels of Indian merchants working on that street during the height of maritime trade. Another street in Dubai, Oud Mehta, seems to reference the common Gujarati surname Mehta. And shop names throughout old Dubai betray the Iranian and Indian influences in the city. While many Iranians have been accepted into Emirati national identity (they have taken on Arabized surnames beginning with "Al," have obtained citizenship, and speak Arabic), and Iranian merchant history has been incorporated into an Emirati cultural legacy (Wheeler, *Telling Tales*), connections to India before and during British Raj times are not openly embraced. This is partly because of the attempt to purify Emirati citizenry of non-Arab elements, partly due to a history of tension between Indian merchants and other residents of Dubai, and partly because of the legacy of gold smuggling as a major source of Dubai's wealth, as I explore in chapter 3.

58 Chai, or Indian spiced tea with milk, went up from fifty fils to one dirham when I was in Dubai (which still made it about thirty cents a cup). Considering how fast prices for everything else were rising in the city at the time, I found the public outcry against this price hike a little surprising—until I realized just how many people living in the city (mostly working-class South Asian men) patronize chai stalls on a daily, sometimes twice-daily, basis. Given the men's meager disposable income, the doubling of the price of chai introduced a large daily financial burden, and the men were willing to speak out against the change despite a political climate that discouraged any form of resistance by "migrants."

59 Longva, "Neither Autocracy nor Democracy but Ethnocracy."

60 Elsheshtawy, "Transitory Sites."

2. An Indian City?

1 Brah, *Cartographies of Diaspora*, 182.

2 Rouse, "Mexican Migration and the Social Space of Postmodernism," 12.

3 In the conclusion I discuss the newly constructed metro and how this may be lessening the segregation between "new" and "old" Dubai and increasing movement through the city as a form of space-making.

4 See also Elsheshtawy, *Dubai*, for a lengthy discussion of older Dubai neighborhoods and the use of public space.

5 Elsheshtawy, "Transitory Sites."

6 The official street name is Khalid bin Walid. However, Dubai residents often nickname streets based on buildings or other identifiable markers.

7 Reshma was fluent in Gujarati, Maharati, Hindi, and English, all of which she used on a daily basis in Bur Dubai.

8 Tourist visas have since changed to thirty days.

9 See Elsheshtawy, *Dubai*, for a detailed description of the Hindu temple area.

10 The Indian embassy in Dubai provided the Indian population estimate, via per-

sonal communication, April 2009, on file with author. The 2005 census taken by the Dubai Municipality provided information on the overall South Asian population.

11 Elsheshtawy, "Transitory Sites."

12 These practices are illegal but persist. They are discussed by human rights organizations and scholars of migration in the Gulf as part of migrant labor rights issues, but rarely in terms of conditions that affect middle-class migrants as well. See Gardner, *City of Strangers*, for a discussion of these practices in Bahrain.

13 While at the time of my research employees needed to obtain a "No Objection Certificate" (NOC) from their current employer to apply for another job without risking blacklist, this requirement has since been lifted.

14 A scathing Human Rights Watch report from 2006, for example, generated great waves of criticism from both inside and outside of Dubai. See *Building Towers, Cheating Workers: Exploitation of Migrant Construction Workers in the United Arab Emirates*, available at the Human Rights Watch website, http://www.hrw.org.

15 Non-white Westerners often reported job discrimination to me as well. The practice of asking for passport photos with application and of paying differentiated salaries and benefits based on country of origin continues to be normal operating procedure in most parts of the Gulf as of the writing of this book.

16 See also Kanna, *Dubai*, and Leonard, "South Asian Workers in the Gulf" on Dubai. Gardner, *City of Strangers*, and Longva, *Walls Built on Sand*, write about these practices in Bahrain and Kuwait, respectively.

17 Remittance rates of Indians found on the website of Embassy of India, UAE, http://www.indembassyuae.org. My Indian informants' perception that Gulf salaries were higher than those in India was also shifting due to India's economic growth and the rise of the middle class there.

18 While Gautam's claim that all Americans have a "car and driver" is exaggerated, most of the European and American foreign residents I have spoken to in the Gulf did receive assistance in migration and moving costs, as well as benefits packages to alleviate housing and other costs of living in the country. I myself, as an American professional employed in Qatar, received business-class travel, free housing, a free rental car, and even a cell phone as part of my benefits package. I was also assisted personally through the entire migration process, from paperwork to medical tests to getting a driver's license.

19 Though minimum requirements will increase to 10,000 dirhams a month once an amendment to the UAE residency laws passes, at the time of my research (and at the time of writing this book), the fees were 4,000 dirhams (a little over $1,000) a month, or 3,000 dirhams if the company provides accommodation. See visa fees on the Dubai government website, http://www.dubai.ae.

20 The governance of residents is also highly gendered and nationality-based. Many complained that South Asians get stronger sentences for traffic and other violations, while whites and Arabs are treated more leniently by police. For example, several of my South Asian informants felt that they were ticketed after vehicle accidents even when they had done nothing wrong, and there have been several international incidents in which South Asians and other non-Western prisoners have been denied consular access or tortured for harsher criminal accusations in the UAE. See, for example, "Amnesty International Says UAE Abused Indian Prisoners," 23 April 2010, BBC News, http://news.bbc.co.uk. Additionally, while commercial sex-work is rampant in the UAE and police often turn a blind eye to it, nonmarital sex is considered a crime. Women receive more severe sentences than do men in these cases, and sex-workers, when arrested, are often charged with more serious crimes than are their clients. In cases of sexual harassment or rape, women tend to be scared to report the crime because they often also end up charged (usually with adultery). In Sharjah, the neighboring emirate, decency laws govern dress and behavior, and they are applied more firmly to women and poor foreign residents, usually from the subcontinent. For example, the strict decency laws designate as illegal the traditional sari that many Indian Hindu women wear if the blouse does not fully cover the stomach and back, and men who wear the traditional Pakistani or Afghani pajama kurta or South Indian lungi are often denied entry into malls, museums, and parks around the country.

21 See also Kanna's discussion of Emirati citizens who fall into this category of what he calls "flexible citizens" ("Flexible Citizenship in Dubai"). See also Ong, Flexible Citizenship, for more on this concept.

22 See for example Brah, Cartographies of Diaspora; Chopra, "Global Primordialities"; Dhingra, "Committed to Ethnicity, Committed to America"; Leonard, The South Asian Americans; Women of South Asian Descent Collective, Our Feet Walk the Sky.

23 See Gardner, City of Strangers, and Nagy, "The Search for Miss Philippines Bahrain," for a discussion of the role of expatriate social clubs in Bahrain.

24 Voigt-Graf, "Transnationalism and the Indo-Fijian Diaspora."

25 Xavier, "Experimenting with Diasporic Incorporation."

26 Chopra, "Global Primordialities"; Grewal, Transnational America; Mankekar, "Brides Who Travel"; van der Veer, "Virtual India."

27 Oonk, Global Indian Diasporas; Voigt-Graf, "Transnationalism and the Indo-Fijian Diaspora."

28 In 2010 the Indian government stated that it was moving forward with voting rights for NRIs, but nothing is in place as of the writing of this book.

3. Between Global City & Golden Frontier

1 See Longva, *Walls Built on Sand*, for more on how kafala places responsibility over migration governance on individual citizens rather than on the state. See also Gardner, "Gulf Migration and the Family," for a concise history of the evolution of this system in the Gulf States.

2 Indian merchants, as subjects of the British Raj, were protected along the Trucial Coast, and they often had recourse to colonial administrators and favored positions with sheikhs, all of which grew their businesses. As early as 1865, Indians comprised the second-largest business community in Dubai; however, relations between Indian merchants and other merchants were contentious. In fact, identities began to be defined more relationally *after* European intervention into the region. Fatma Al-Sayegh, for example, explores the British government's role in protecting Indian merchants and in curbing the power of the royal family in Dubai, actions which incited an ethnic division of identities that had not been necessary before the colonial presence ("Merchants' Role in a Changing Society"). Sheikhs were torn between pressures from Arab and Iranian merchants and from Indian merchants who had the backing of the British government. In addition, ties to Indian merchants through kinship, language, education, and business interests meant that many sheikhs and wealthy Arab merchants in Dubai were also unclear about their own loyalties in such tensions (see also the discussion of colonial connections to South Asia in chapter 1). In Dubai there is a history of tension between local merchants and Indians that was fueled by colonial pressures and by the sheikhs' uncertain alliances. In 1929 an armed uprising against Sheikh Sa'id took place in part because merchants were upset at having to pay debts to Indians. Sheikh Sa'id wanted to resign, but the Raj government wanted to keep him in power. By 1938 the merchant movement's opposition to the Sheikh had ballooned and tensions had intensified. Sa'id eventually enlisted the help of Bedouins to crush the movement. In 1946 Indians were given extraterritorial jurisdiction, which further increased legal divisions between them and other residents of Dubai. The colonial relations and tensions between Indians and other groups in many ways define the mercantilism of contemporary Dubai and the postcolonial relationship between the Gulf and independent India.

3 For more on theorizations of the offshore see Hudson, "Offshoreness, Globalization and Sovereignty"; Maurer, "Islands in the Net"; Palen, *The Offshore World*.

4 Harriss-White, *India Working*.

5 In comparison to other Arabian Gulf port cities under the purview of the British Raj, however, Dubai was not that central to Indian Ocean trade. See for example Onley, *The Arabian Frontier of the British Raj*.

6 At the same time, newer migration from India to the Gulf has also increased India's dependence on Gulf countries in the form of remittances from migrants and imported oil and natural gas. Arnold and Shah, *Asian Labor Migration*; Osella and Osella, *Social Mobility in Kerala*.

7 Comment by Sheikh Mohammed of Dubai on a visit to India in March 2007.

8 As it was small and easy to transport on one's body, the ten-tola gold bar was the standard weight for gold smuggling into India at the time: "The ten-tola bar was the currency of the gold smuggler, weighing 3.75 ounces of 99.9 percent pure gold" (Moore, *Dubai*, 180).

9 Rashid ruled from 1958 to 1990, and his son Maktoum from 1990 to 2006. His other son, Mohammed, the current leader of Dubai, came to power when his brother died, in 2006.

10 Nordstrom, *Global Outlaws*.

11 Elsheshtawy, "Transitory Sites"; Gardner, "Strategic Transnationalism"; Onley, *The Arabian Frontier of the British Raj*; Dresch, "Debates on Marriage and Nationality in the United Arab Emirates"; Kanna, "Flexible Citizenship in Dubai."

12 Biographies of Sheikh Zayed, Sheikh Rashid, and Sheikh Mohammed, along with those of other important figures in the UAE, are ubiquitous in airports, bookstores, and tourist destinations around the country. See also Al-Fahim, *From Rags to Riches*.

13 The India Club is Dubai's most prominent Indian social institution. It is over forty years old and includes as members some of the wealthiest and longest-established Indian families in Dubai. An India Club membership requires several years on a waitlist, costs thousands of dollars, and is open only to people with Indian passports. Most of my business community informants and their families were members.

14 See also Buxani, *Taking the High Road*; Pancholia, *Footprints*.

15 For feminist critiques of the "frontier" metaphor, see Amy Kaplan, "Manifest Domesticity"; Laura Miller, "Women and Children First."

16 Mr. Zaveri would neither confirm nor deny this connection.

17 This is echoed in Moore's novel almost exactly. According to Moore, many smuggling dhows were armed and Dubai also made a great deal of profit on arms smuggling from Iran via Afghanistan. Thus, there were great physical as well as economic risks involved in the practice of re-export. Several passages of Moore's book detail the physical aspects of actually moving gold from Dubai to India.

18 See Osella and Osella, "Migration, Money, and Masculinity in Kerala," for more on the connections between Indian masculinity and displays of cash.

19 In *City of Strangers* Andrew Gardner makes similar observations about elite Indians in Bahrain.

20 See also Gardner, "Strategic Transnationalism," on similar practices among Indian elites in Bahrain.

21 In addition, the figure of the Indian Emirati citizen provided an opening for us to speak about problems with the UAE government, problems that earlier in the same conversations my interlocutors had vigorously denied. These included experiences of racial discrimination and the feeling of living tenuously that the non-elite Indians I introduce in this book also conveyed.

22 Rumor, as noted in anthropological literature, generates or suppresses conflict, expresses uncertainties, and often comes out of an inclination to find meaning in one's environment (Shibutani, *Improvised News*; Stewart and Strathern, *Witchcraft, Sorcery, Rumors and Gossip*). According to Stewart and Strathern, rumors abound in "networks of competitive relationships marked by tension, distrust, ambiguity" (*Witchcraft, Sorcery, Rumors and Gossip*, 55); it thus seems fitting that in a situation narrated by my informants as one of "calculated risk" and uncertain futures, rumors about Indian belonging structured understandings and representations of their positions in society. Additionally, it is important to note that "rumor and gossip, like talk in general, are constitutive of, rather than simply reflect, social realities" (*Witchcraft, Sorcery, Rumors and Gossip*, 56). See also Gupta, "Blurred Boundaries."

23 Aldrich and Waldinger, "Ethnicity and Entrepreneurship"; Light and Bhachu, *Immigration and Entrepreneurship*; Zhou, "Revisiting Ethnic Entrepreneurship."

24 See Cave, *Business Laws of the Middle East*.

25 The U.S. dollar is about 3.65 dirhams, so 300,000 dirhams would be a little over $82,000.

26 In *City of Strangers*, Gardner calls them "sleeping partner" arrangements.

27 These agreements did not always stand up in court, however, and often had negative repercussions—like jail time—for Indian businessmen whose relationships with their partners went sour.

28 For example, Maghanmal Pancholia, in his memoir, *Footprints*, relates how he successfully petitioned Sheikh Hamdan to waive the law of local partnership for 150 longtime Sindhi traders.

29 Ong, *Flexible Citizenship*, 214–39.

30 This is especially true in the case of Dubai's growing diamond industry; the convergence of Indian interests and the DMCC is of particular interest since Gujarati Jains and Israeli and South African Jews constitute the monopoly on the world diamond industry. The current world diamond center is Antwerp, Belgium, and the ethnic parameters of the diamond industry are visible there. For example, Indian films are screened in the movie theaters, and Kosher and Jain food is available in several restaurants. With the formation of the European Union, Antwerp, which in many ways acted as Europe's "offshore" by providing a tax-free and relaxed business atmosphere, has had to add business restrictions that make it less appealing to the diamond industry. In addition, most smaller diamonds are cut in India. Therefore, Dubai's proximity and its

less-stringent business atmosphere have established it as an attractive alternative to Antwerp. In fact, many companies with branches in Europe have invested in the DMCC. As one major diamond-industry player explained to me, by sending uncut (rough) diamonds from Antwerp to the DMCC and then sending them from DMCC to India to be cut, the involved parties can ensure that the profit accrued by the diamonds never hits Europe and therefore remains tax free. In addition, since the UAE does not officially recognize or trade with Israel, the DMCC allows Indians to gain an even stronger foothold in the diamond industry than they have now.

31 See also Leonard, "South Asian Workers in the Gulf," on the relationship between Emirati partners and Indian businessmen.

32 Gardner, "Strategic Transnationalism."

33 The Bahraini context is slightly different than that of the UAE in that Bahrain has increasing unemployment and intense Sunni-Shi'a tensions, and in that certain elite Indians have been allowed to naturalize. This sets up more direct competitions for jobs and social benefits among citizens and between citizens and noncitizens. However, Indian elite networks in Bahrain, as Gardner explores, are similar to those in other parts of the Gulf.

34 Harriss-White, *India Working*, 7–8.

35 Basile and Harriss-White, "The Politics of Accumulation in Small Town India"; Smith, "Fortune and Failure."

36 For example, John Willoughby, in *Ambivalent Anxieties of the South Asian–Gulf Labor Exchange*, estimates that based on 1.276 million Indian workers entering the Gulf in 1998, "the total amount of rent extracted that year from these workers would have been $1,741,740,000," 24.

37 During and after the course of my fieldwork, the international media and local newspapers documented several cases of unsanitary, hazardous working and living conditions within labor camps in the Gulf, including situations in which there was no running water or electricity, or where workers had not been paid for weeks or months. With the economic downturn in 2008, many of these conditions worsened, but there has been no systematic documentation of working conditions in the UAE, because the country does not allow nongovernmental organizations to operate within its borders. Human Rights Watch has published the most detailed account to date, which can be found at "Building Towers, Cheating Workers," 12 November 2006, http://www.hrw.org.

4. Exceeding the Economic

1 "Arab Awakening" was used to describe the revolutions and protests around the Arab world that began in 2010 in North Africa and have since spread across the region. These events were alternatively known as the "Arab Spring."

2 See Degorge, "Modern Day Slavery in the United Arab Emirates," for but one example of the many scholarly and journalistic accounts that use such terminology to discuss labor abuses in the Gulf. I cited others in the book's introduction.

3 Here I borrow from LeFebvre's concept of the "right to the city" as a form of politicization that differs from other citizenship claims, such as those based in the nation-state ("The Right to the City"). See also Holston and Appadurai, "Cities and Citizenship"; Holston, "Insurgent Citizenship in an Era of Global Urban Peripheries." While these scholars focus on the production of space as a function of exclusionary capitalism, however, I resist this Marxist analysis to consider how space and economy are co-constituted, and how the functions of exclusion and belonging are not reducible to market-based forms of power.

4 Bruno Latour, in *We Have Never Been Modern*, argues that anthropological as well as other scholarship is built on an assumption that modern societies have learned to separate the world into distinct domains—such as the economy, society, and the state—unlike the supposedly nonmodern subjects of traditional anthropological research, who are not modern precisely due to their inability to distinguish these domains. Instead of assuming the existence of a priori distinct abstractable domains, several contemporary scholars favor methodological and theoretical approaches that focus on the ways in which these domains are produced in particular contexts. See also Abrams, "Notes on the Difficulty of Studying the State"; Gibson-Graham, *The End of Capitalism (As We Knew It)*; Mitchell, "The Limits of the State" and *Rule of Experts*; Thrift, *Spatial Formations*.

5 David Theo Goldberg, in *The Threat of Race*, argues that neoliberalism both professes colorblindness and produces race. In an era in which biological race as a rationale of differential treatment has been debunked, we live not in a society that aims to eliminate race as form of social hierarchy, but rather one that believes in having already achieved racelessness. Thus, merit should be the only factor through which people succeed. However, racial explanations—now based in "cultural" instead of biological difference—still frame institutional and individual reasonings for failure. Thus, a "colorblind" society can justify neoliberal policies that erase attempts to rectify prior racial bias while also legitimizing expenditures on items such as security and border control, which are in and of themselves about racial bias and hierarchy.

6 This mirrors the way that Indians are seen by international organizations as well. The International Labor Organization, for example, distinguishes between economic migration for "settlement" and for "contract" (Zachariah, Prakash, and Rajan, "Indian Workers in the UAE").

7 See Kanna, "Flexible Citizenship in Dubai" and *Dubai, the City as Corporation*; Okruhlik, "Dependence, Disdain, and Distance."

8 At the time of my research, ticket systems were being introduced into government and other offices around the city in response to these complaints.

9   Indian middle-class attitudes toward Pakistanis are similar to their attitudes toward lower-wage Indians. For example, while Pakistan and India have a long history of adversity, and many Indians in India openly despise Pakistanis and vice versa, both Indians and Pakistanis told me that they were essentially one community in Dubai. But within this sense of connection, my Indian informants also identified distinctions between themselves and Pakistanis. In particular, groups of Pakistani men—like Pathans and Baluchis, as well as Afghanis, who many Indians considered "Pakistani"—were singled out by middle-class Indians as dangerous because they were associated with low-wage jobs.

10 See Ong, *Neoliberalism as Exception*, for a greater discussion of neoliberal citizenship.

11 Rose, *Governing the Soul*.

12 Grewal, *Transnational America*, 17.

13 For more on how identity is produced through interactions between people and their material surroundings see Gottdeiner, *New Forms of Consumption*; Liechty, *Suitably Modern*; Morris, "Things to Do with Shopping Centers."

14 Liechty, *Suitably Modern*.

15 There is an area around the Dubai Creek where many South Asians spend evenings. Other open spaces have been turned into gathering spots in the older parts of Dubai, but they are increasingly policed and cleared out by authorities (see Elsheshtawy, *Dubai*).

16 See Miller, "Things to Do with Shopping Centers," for a discussion of how "shopping" is an activity that constitutes space as well as identity. For more on the critique of the concept of "public" as exclusionary rather than inclusive, see Dean, "Cybersalons and Civil Society."

17 Kurien, *Kaleidoscopic Ethnicity*; Nambiar, *The Socio-Economic Conditions of Gulf Migrants*; Osella and Osella, *Social Mobility in Kerala*; Sekher, *Migration and Social Change*.

18 See Leonard, "South Asian Women in the Gulf," for more about the impacts of Gulf migration on women and the family. See also Gardner, "Gulf Migration and the Family."

19 Salih, "Shifting Meanings of 'Home.'"

20 Johnson, "At Home and Abroad."

21 See also Melly, "Inside-Out Houses," for a discussion of how migrants and their families police others' spending practices.

22 See Kanna, "Flexible Citizenship in Dubai," for a discussion of consumer practices among professional Emiratis.

5. Becoming Indian in Dubai

1 Ong, *Flexible Citizenship*.

2 Referring to middle- and upper-class families in Bahrain who are in similar situations as my more well-to-do informants, Gardner argues that they deploy "strategic transnationalism," a way of maneuvering, through building transnational networks, around the restrictive citizenship and residency policies of the Gulf States in order to maintain more settled lives and to accumulate wealth ("Strategic Transnationalism"). Juridico-legal citizenship for them is therefore a secondary concern and one that only serves to produce more secure futures in the face of the *kafala* system. While many of the Dubai Indians I introduce in this book might be read through this framework, young people like Ashish diverged significantly, in that their inability to attain official citizenship in the Gulf became a primary mode through which they defined their desires and experiences of belonging and non-belonging.

3 For Gulf States attempting to establish "global cities," the brand recognition of these universities adds to a sense of being able to provide the best of the best, as is evidenced most recently in Abu Dhabi's plans to open its own branches of the Guggenheim, the Louvre, NYU, and the Sorbonne.

4 There are some "international" primary and secondary schools in which children of many backgrounds, including Emiratis, mix. However, these are elite and expensive, and therefore not accessible to most Indians in Dubai.

5 At the time of writing this book, a law to raise the minimum to 10,000 dirhams a month has passed but not yet been implemented.

6 See for example Women of South Asian Descent Collective, *Our Feet Walk the Sky*; Dhingra, "Committed to Ethnicity, Committed to America"; Gopinath, "Bombay, UK, Yuba City"; Leonard, *The South Asian Americans*.

7 Leonard, "South Asian Women in the Gulf," and Kanna, *Dubai, the City as Corporation*, also discuss the sense of "in-betweenness" that South Asian youth in Dubai felt.

8 Leonard, in her work on South Asian migrants to the Gulf, notes that many older migrants saw places like Dubai as stepping-stones to the West as well ("South Asian Workers in the Gulf"). While I found this to be true among some of my older interlocutors, the majority of them were planning to return to South Asia. South Asian youth, in stark contrast, almost never stated a desire for "return" and were much more interested in the possibility of going West.

9 Many popular Indian matchmaking websites have Gulf listings.

10 See Leonard, "South Asian Workers in the Gulf," for more on differentiation between individual emirates by South Asian migrants.

11 Scholarships and other forms of funding are also available to help citizens attend private schools.

12 English has become the language of neoliberalism and global "success" in the UAE. Emirati schools, too, have therefore recently switched to English-language curricula, and some Emirati families choose to send their children to private international schools instead of government schools in order to provide what they perceive to be a better education. Thus, the neoliberal citizenship training that occurs in universities begins in primary and secondary school. However, this training continues to be infused, for the vast majority of UAE resident children, with parochial forms of identity and belonging.

13 See also Chachara, Amrita, "The UAE is Home, and Yet You Don't Speak the Language, *The National*, 7 March, 2011, http://www.thenational.ae.

14 The name of this school suggests a connection to colonial-era British-style education, which remains central to Indian curricula in India as well as in the Gulf.

15 For a list of GEMS schools in the UAE, see the GEMS education website, http://www.gemseducation.com.

16 Lately, especially following Dubai's recession in 2008, the benefits packages for Westerners and Gulf Arabs have become less generous, according to several sources. Non-Indian foreign residents are therefore starting to pay more out-of-pocket expenses for their children's schooling.

17 Zayed University was originally a women's college, but has recently started admitting men and international students.

18 Vocations are also gendered: degree offerings in women's colleges often differ from those in men's.

19 Michigan State has since ceased operations due to budget concerns.

20 See Tetrault, "Identity and Transplant-University Education in the Gulf," for a case study on AUK.

21 Ong, *Neoliberalism as Exception*. See also Sidhu, Ho, and Yeoh, "Emerging Education Hubs"; Tetrault, "Great Expectations."

22 Olds and Thrift, "Cultures on the Brink."

23 See also the well-maintained Global Higher Education blog, which provides news and commentary from around the world, http://globalhighered.wordpress.com.

24 See the Knowledge Village website, http://www.kv.ae.

25 Unfiltered Internet access is no longer available in all free zones, according to several people I know living and working in places like the Dubai Marina. With the advent of du, the country's second Internet service provider, more areas of the city seem to be subject to Internet censorship than before, including some free zones.

26　Altbach, "Higher Education Crosses Borders"; Morey, "Globalization and the Emergence of For-Profit Higher Education"; Poovey, "The Twenty-First-Century University and the Market."

27　Morey, "Globalization and the Emergence of For-Profit Higher Education."

28　Poovey, "The Twenty-First-Century University and the Market."

29　Rothblatt and Wittrock, "Introduction," 1.

30　See, for example, Altbach, "Globalisation and the University"; Readings, *The University in Ruins*; Sidhu, Ho, and Yeoh, "Emerging Education Hubs."

31　Altbach, "Academic Freedom." On Gulf campuses more specifically, see Aksan, "How Do We 'Know' the Middle East?"

32　Altbach, "Globalisation and the University."

33　Sometimes their tuition costs are equal to the foreign aid their country receives!

34　Altbach, "Globalisation and the University," 17.

35　See also Krieger, "An Academic Building Boom Transforms the Persian Gulf."

36　In addition, GATS is designed both to remove restrictions on the international circulation of educational commodities *and* to protect the owners and sellers of these commodities—almost exclusively Western—over buyers.

37　See the Amercan University of Sharjah website, http://www.aus.edu.

38　I have received similar feedback from conversations with employees in Education City, Qatar (field research, 2010 and 2011). Some universities hire people on a tiered system in which, for any given position, those in the highest tier receive the most benefits and the highest salary. Though it is not an explicitly discriminatory practice, universities seem to hire fewer non-Western and non-Qatari employees at the top tier.

39　This gap is true of most branch campuses in the Gulf, which either actively segregate students by gender or in which students themselves self-segregate.

40　In early 2006, a global controversy erupted when a Danish newspaper (and subsequently other European venues) published cartoons caricaturing the Prophet Mohammed. There were protests and riots in many parts of the Muslim world, fatwas issued on the cartoonist, and debates about heresy (depictions of the Prophet are forbidden in Islam) versus artistic freedom.

41　See Tetrault, "Great Expectations," for more discussion on the impacts of gender segregation and censorship on American universities, particularly in Kuwait.

42　See for example Lukose, "Empty Citizenship."

43　Lukose, "The Difference that Diaspora Makes."

Conclusion

1   The term *Arab Spring* came into widespread use by international English-language media and by protesters during the Egyptian uprisings in January 2011. The genealogy of the term has been traced to Tunisia's earlier revolution —called the Jasmine Revolution after the national flower—to the Prague Spring and other Soviet-era revolutionary actions, and to other roots. But it has emerged as the moniker most commonly used to describe the civil unrest in the region, also referred to as the "Arab uprisings," which is a more literal translation from the terms circulating among the Arabic media.

2   See for example Michael Slackman, "Affluent Qataris Seek What Money Can't Buy," *New York Times*, 13 May 2010, http://www.nytimes.com.

3   Kanna, "The Arab World's Forgotten Rebellions."

4   Vivian Salama, "U.A.E. Crackdown Widens as Police Arrest Two More Activists," Bloomberg, 12 April 2011, www.bloomberg.com.

5   See for example Luciani, *The Arab State*.

6   Saudi Arabia's intervention, via military "envoys," furthered this idea, for many felt that the Sunni Wahhabist government of Saudi Arabia was afraid of Iran's influence on the country. However, others felt this was a move to crack down on civil unrest of any kind before it got too close to home.

7   Ong, *Neoliberalism as Exception*.

8   Holston and Appadurai, "Cities and Citizenship." See also Renato Rosaldo, "Cultural Citizenship, Inequality, and Multiculturalism," on cultural citizenship among Latino communities in the United States, and Holston, "Insurgent Citizenship in an Era of Global Urban Peripheries," on "insurgent citizenship" among poor residents of Brazil's favelas.

9   Gardner, *City of Strangers*.

10 The analytic of labor also thereby removes their humanity, even in cases when well-intentioned organizations, like Human Rights Watch, actually build their activist politics on a platform of human rights. See the 2006 report *Building Towers Cheating Workers*, available at the Human Rights Watch website, www.hrw.org. For more detailed critiques of "human rights" discourses, see Malkki, "Citizens of Humanity"; Grewal, "'Women's Rights as Human Rights.'"

11 The Dubai merchant rebellion of the 1930s exemplifies this point. Local Emirati merchants rebelled against rulers not only to gain more political power, but also to wrest economic advantages away from Indian and Iranian merchants, to whom they felt the government was affording undue favor (Al-Sayegh, "Merchants' Role in a Changing Society"; Kanna, "The Arab World's Forgotten Rebellions"). The preferential treatment that local rulers, under pressure from the British Raj, gave to Indian merchants during this time has resulted in the ethnic monopolies Indians still hold over certain sectors of Du-

bai's economy, and the policies of the contemporary Dubai and UAE governments cannot be delinked from this history.

12 It is, for example, punishable by law to make public complaints about customer service. See for example Colin Simpson and Awad Mustafa, "'Naming and Shaming' Bad Drivers on Internet Risks Jail," *The National*, 7 August 2011, www.thenational.ae.

13 Kanna, "The Arab World's Forgotten Rebellions."

14 Ahmed Kanna is one of the few commentators who has noted the absence of migrants from coverage of the Arab Spring. He also ties recent activism in the Gulf States to longer histories of political rebellion in the region, including the merchant uprisings of the 1930s in Dubai. However, in discussing the current situation he distinguishes between activism on the part of migrant laborers and other forms of protest, though he acknowledges the similarity in their calls for justice and dignity: "While the mass actions in Egypt, Tunisia, and the other countries of the Arab Spring are political protests, the actions in the UAE are labor strikes. We should not conflate the two: the stakes in each kind of demonstration are different. The foreign workers of the UAE are citizens of another country and they will eventually return to their own countries" ("The Arab World's Forgotten Rebellions").

15 Kinninmont, "Bread and Dignity," 31.

16 See for example, Lin Noueihed, "Hardline Shiite Groups Demand Republic in Bahrain," *The Montreal Gazette*, 8 March 2011, www.montrealgazette.com, and David Cloud and Neela Banerjee, "Forces in Bahrain Move Against Crowd in Square," *LA Times*, 16 March 2011, http.articles.latimes.com.

17 Gardner, *City of Strangers*, 142–48.

18 Balibar, "Historical Dilemmas of Democracy and Their Contemporary Relevance for Citizenship."

19 Balibar, "Historical Dilemmas of Democracy," 526.

20 Marshall, *Citizenship and Social Class and Other Essays*.

21 See for example Longva, *Walls Built on Sand* and "Neither Autocracy nor Democracy but Ethnocracy"; Gardner, *City of Strangers*.

22 See also Okruhlik, "Excluded Essentials."

23 Gender equality has historically been used as a gauge for democracy in liberal societies (however failed it is in reality) and as a justification for colonial intervention. See, for example, Grewal, *Home and Harem*, and McClintock, *Imperial Leather*.

24 See International Monetary Fund Public Information Notice about economic consultation with UAE on the 2009 economic forecast at the IMF website, http://www.imf.org; see the Economist's report on Abu Dhabi's bailout of Dubai on its website at http://www.economist.com. My information on return

migrants came in part from a personal communication, Dubai, April 2009 with a UAE Ministry of Labor employee.

25 See the report *Just the Good News, Please,* 6 April 2009, on the Human Rights Watch website, http://www.hrw.org.

26 See, for example, Johann Hari, "The Dark Side of Dubai," *Independent,* 7 April 2009, http://www.independent.co.uk.

27 Indeed, I found on my most recent trip to Dubai, in 2011, that Gautam had purchased a brand-new four-wheel-drive Toyota and had also moved to a new building, a few doors down from his previous apartment, where he had more space and was paying significantly less in rent.

28 In the case of the United States, middle-class South Asian migration narratives are not only usually post-Indian independence, but also come after the 1965 changes in immigration law that lifted bans on Asians.

29 Other urban improvement efforts such as free zones, manmade islands, and a new airport terminal seem intended for only the wealthiest strata of Dubai society, creating investment opportunities for them and facilitating their mobility.

30 Not yet complete at the time of writing this conclusion, the Metro continues to open new stations.

31 I do not mean to suggest that the Metro is symbolic of a spectacle of supermodernity that can easily be transposed to any place in the world, but rather that a train system that is particular to the Dubai context has made Dubai seem more similar to other urban metropolises than it had before. On supermodernity, see Auge, *Non-Places.*

32 See also Gardner, *City of Strangers,* on how "foreign matter" is spatially contained (or how attempts are made to spatially contain it) in Gulf cities.

33 See for example Aksan, "How Do We 'Know' the Middle East?"

Abrams, Philip. "Notes on the Difficulty of Studying the State." *Journal of Historical Sociology* 1, no. 1 (1988): 58–89.

Abu-Lughod, Janet. *Before European Hegemony.* New York: Oxford University Press, 1989.

Agamben, Giorgio. *Homo Sacer: Sovereign Power and Bare Life.* Stanford: Stanford University Press, 1995.

———. *State of Exception.* Chicago: University of Chicago Press, 2005.

Ahmad, Attiya. "Beyond Labor: Foreign Residents in the Gulf States." *Migrant Labor in the Gulf,* ed. Mehran Kamrava and Zahra Babar, 21–40. Doha: Center for International and Regional Studies, Georgetown School of Foreign Service Qatar, 2011.

Aksan, Virginia. "How Do We 'Know' the Middle East?" *Review of Middle East Studies* 44, no. 1 (2010): 3–12.

Al Abed, Ibrahim, and Peter Hellyer, eds. *United Arab Emirates, a New Perspective.* London: Trident, 2001.

Al-Awad, Mouawiya, and Adam B. Elhiraika. "Cultural Effects and Savings: Evidence from Immigrants to the United Arab Emirates." *Journal of Development Studies* 39, no. 5 (2003): 139–52.

Al-Barghouti, Tamim. *The Umma and the Dawla: The Nation-State and the Arab Middle East.* London: Pluto, 2008.

Aldrich, Howard, and Roger Waldinger. "Ethnicity and Entrepreneurship." *Annual Review of Sociology* 16 (1990): 111–35.

Al-Fahim, Mohammed. *From Rags to Riches: A Story of Abu Dhabi.* London: London Centre of Arab Studies, 1995.

Al-Gurg, Easa Saleh. *The Wells of Memory: An Autobiography.* London: John Murray, 1998.

Ali, Syed. *Dubai: Gilded Cage.* London: Yale University Press, 2010.

Allen, Calvin H. "The Indian Merchant Community of Masqat." *Bulletin of the School of Oriental and African Studies* 44, no. 1 (1981): 39–53.

Al-Naqeeb, Khaldoun Hasan. *Society and State in the Gulf and Arab Peninsula.* London: Routledge, 1990.

Al-Qasimi, Noor. "Modest Immodesty: Accommodating Dissent and the 'Abaya-as-

Fashion in the Arab Gulf States." *Jounal of Middle Eastern Women's Studies* 6, no. 1 (2010): 46–74.

Al-Qasimi, Sultan. *The Myth of Arab Piracy in the Gulf.* London: Routledge, 1986.

Al-Rasheed, Madawi, ed. *Transnational Connections and the Arab Gulf.* London: Routledge, 2005.

Al-Sayegh, Fatma. "Merchants' Role in a Changing Society: The Case of Dubai, 1900–90." *Middle Eastern Studies* 34, no. 1 (1998): 87–102.

Altbach, Philip G. "Academic Freedom: International Realities and Challenges." *Higher Education* 41, nos. 1–2 (2001): 205–19.

——. "Globalisation and the University: Myths and Realities in an Unequal World." *Tertiary Education and Management* 10 (2004): 3–25.

——. "Higher Education Crosses Borders." *Change* (March–April 2004): 18–25.

Andall, Jacqueline. "Second-Generation Attitude? African-Italians in Milan." *Journal of Ethnic and Migration Studies* 28, no. 3 (2002): 389–407.

Anderson, Benedict. *Imagined Communities.* London: Verso, 1991.

——. *Spectre of Comparisons.* London: Verso, 1998.

Appadurai, Arjun. *Modernity at Large: Cultural Dimensions of Modernity.* Minneapolis: University of Minnesota Press, 1996.

Arnold, David. *Colonizing the Body.* Berkeley: University of California Press, 1993.

Arnold, Fred, and Nasra M. Shah. *Asian Labor Migration: Pipeline to the Middle East.* Boulder: Westview, 1986.

Auge, Marc. *Non-Places: Introduction to an Anthropology of Supermodernity.* London: Verso, 1995.

Axel, Brian Keith. "The Context of Diaspora." *Cultural Anthropology* 19, no. 1 (2004): 26–60.

Ayubi, Nazih. *Over-Stating the Arab State: Politics and Society in the Middle East.* London: I. B. Tauris, 1995.

Bagaeen, Samer. "Brand Dubai: The Instant City; or the Instantly Recognizable City." *International Planning Studies* 12, no. 2 (2007): 172–97.

Balibar, Etienne. "Historical Dilemmas of Democracy and Their Contemporary Relevance for Citizenship." *Rethinking Marxism* 20, no. 4 (2008): 522–38.

Barrett, Raymond. *Dubai: Inside the Kingdom of Bling.* London: Nicholas Brealey, 2010.

Basile, E., and Barbara Harriss-White. "The Politics of Accumulation in Small Town India." *Bulletin of the Institute of Development Studies* 30, no. 4 (1999): 31–39.

Beblawi, Hazem. "The Rentier State in the Arab World." *The Arab State*, ed. Giacamo Luciani, 85–98. Berkeley: University of California Press, 1990.

Beblawi, Hazem, and Giacamo Luciani, eds. *The Rentier State: Nation, State, and Integration in the Arab World.* London: Routledge, 1987.

Bhabha, Homi K. *The Location of Culture.* London: Routledge, 1994.

Bhattacharjee, Anannya. "The Habit of Ex-Nomination: Nation, Woman, and the Indian Immigrant Bourgeoisie." *Emerging Voices: South Asian Women Redefine Self, Family, and Community*, ed. S. R. Gupta, 229–52. Walnut Creek, Calif.: Alta Mira, 1999.

Bose, Pablo Shiladitya. "Home and Away: Diasporas, Developments and Displacements in a Globalising World." *Journal of Intercultural Studies* 29, no. 1 (2008): 111–31.

Bose, Sugata. *A Hundred Horizons: The Indian Ocean in the Age of Global Empire.* Cambridge: Harvard University Press, 2006.

Brah, Avtar. *Cartographies of Diaspora: Contesting Identities.* London: Routledge, 1996.

Brubaker, Rogers. "The 'Diaspora' Diaspora." *Ethnic and Racial Studies* 28, no. 1 (2005): 1–19.

Burton, Antoinette. *Burdens of History: British Feminists, Indian Women, and Imperial Culture, 1865–1915.* Chapel Hill: University of North Carolina Press, 1994.

Butenschon, Nils A., Uri Davis, and Manuel Hassassian, eds. *Citizenship and the State in the Middle East: Approaches and Applications.* Syracuse: Syracuse University Press, 2000.

Butler, Kim. "Defining Diaspora, Defining a Discourse." *Diaspora* 10, no. 2 (2001): 189–219.

Buxani, Ram. *Taking the High Road.* Dubai: Motivate, 2004.

Castles, Steven, and Alastair Davidson. *Citizenship and Migration: Globalization and the Politics of Belonging.* New York: Routledge, 2000.

Cave, Bryan. *Business Laws of the Middle East: The United Arab Emirates.* London: Kluwer Law International, 1999.

Chakrabarty, Dipesh. *Provincializing Europe: Postcolonial Thought and Historical Difference.* Princeton: Princeton University Press, 2000.

Cho, Lily. "Diasporic Citizenship: Inhabiting Contradictions and Challenging Exclusions." *American Quarterly* 59, no. 2 (2007): 467–78.

Chopra, Rohit. "Global Primordialities: Virtual Identity Politics in Online Hindutva and Dalit Discourses." *New Media and Society* 8, no. 2 (2006): 187–206.

Clifford, James. "Diasporas." *Cultural Anthropology* 9, no. 3 (1994): 302–38.

Cohen, Elizabeth. *Semi-Citizenship in Democratic Politics.* Cambridge: Cambridge University Press, 2009.

Comaroff, Jean, and John L. Comaroff. "Millennial Capitalism: First Thoughts on a Second Coming." *Public Culture* 12, no. 2 (2000): 291–343.

Coutin, Susan Bibler. *Legalizing Moves: Salvadoran Immigrants' Struggle for U.S. Residency.* Ann Arbor: University of Michigan Press, 2000.

——. *Nations of Emigrants: Shifting Boundaries of Citizenship in El Salvador and the United States.* Ithaca: Cornell University Press, 2007.

Crystal, Jill. *Oil and Politics in the Gulf: Rulers and Merchants in Kuwait and Qatar*. Cambridge: Cambridge University Press, 1995.

Das Gupta, Ashin. *India and the Indian Ocean World: Trade and Politics*. New Delhi: Oxford University Press, 2004.

Dauderstadt, Michael, and Arne Schildberg, eds. *Dead Ends of Transition: Rentier Economies and Protectorates*. Frankfurt: Campus Verlag, 2006.

Davidson, Christopher. *Dubai: The Vulnerability of Success*. New York: Columbia University Press, 2008.

——. *The United Arab Emirates: A Study in Survival*. Boulder: Lynne Rienner, 2005.

Davis, Mike. "Fear and Money in Dubai." *New Left Review* 41 (2006): 1–14.

——. "Sinister Paradise: Does the Road to the Future End at Dubai?" *TomDispatch.com*, 14 July 2005. http://www.tomdispatch.com.

Dean, Jodi. "Cybersalons and Civil Society: Rethinking the Public Sphere in Transnational Technoculture." *Public Culture* 13, no. 2 (2001): 243–65.

de Certeau, Michel. *The Practice of Everyday Life*. 1984; reprint, Berkeley: University of California Press, 2011.

Degorge, Barbara. "Modern Day Slavery in the United Arab Emirates." *European Legacy* 11, no. 6 (2006): 657–66.

Dhingra, Pawan. "Committed to Ethnicity, Committed to America: How Second-Generation Indian Americans' Ethnic Boundaries Further Their Americanisation." *Journal of Intercultural Studies* 29, no. 1 (2008): 41–63.

Dickinson, Jen, and Adrian Bailey. "(Re)membering Diaspora: Uneven Geographies of Indian Dual Citizenship." *Political Geography* 26 (2007): 757–74.

Dresch, Paul. "Debates on Marriage and Nationality in the United Arab Emirates." *Monarchies and Nations: Globalisation and Identity in the Arab States of the Gulf*, ed. Paul Dresch and James Piscatori, 136–57. London: I. B. Tauris, 2005.

——. "Introduction." *Monarchies and Nations: Globalisation and Identity in the Arab States of the Gulf*, ed. Paul Dresch and James Piscatori, 1–33. London: I. B. Tauris, 2005.

Dresch, Paul, and James Piscatori, eds. *Monarchies and Nations: Globalisation and Identity in the Arab States of the Gulf*. London: I. B. Tauris, 2005.

Elsheshtawy, Yasser. *Dubai: Behind an Urban Spectacle*. London: Routledge, 2010.

——. "Navigating the Spectacle: Landscapes of Consumption in Dubai." *Architectural Theory Review* 13, no. 2 (2008): 164–87.

——. "Transitory Sites: Mapping Dubai's 'Forgotten' Urban Spaces." *International Journal of Urban and Regional Research* 32, no. 4 (2008): 968–88.

Fawaz, Leila Tarazi, C. A. Bayly, and Robert Ilbert, eds. *Modernity and Culture: From the Mediterranean to the Indian Ocean*. New York: Columbia University Press, 2001.

Fichtner, Ullrich. "Osama's Nightmare: Las Vegas in the Arabian Desert." *Spiegel Online International*, 14 September 2006. http://www.spiegel.de/international.

Franklin, Sarah, and Susan McKinnon, eds. *Relative Values: Reconfiguring Kinship Studies*. Durham: Duke University Press, 2001.

Gamburd, Michele Ruth. *The Kitchen Spoon's Handle: Transnationalism and Sri Lanka's Migrant Housemaids*. Ithaca: Cornell University Press, 2000.

Gamlen, Alan. "The Emigration State and the Modern Geopolitical Imagination." *Political Geography* 27, no. 8 (2008): 840–56.

Gardezi, Hassan. "Asian Workers in the Gulf States of the Middle East." *Journal of Contemporary Asia* 21, no. 2 (1991): 179–94.

Gardner, Andrew. *City of Strangers: Gulf Migration and the Indian Community in Bahrain*. Ithaca: Cornell University Press, 2010.

———. "Gulf Migration and the Family." *Journal of Arabian Studies* 1, no. 1 (2011): 3–25.

———. "Strategic Transnationalism: The Indian Diasporic Elite in Contemporary Bahrain." *City and Society* 20, no. 1 (2008): 54–78.

Ghosh, Amitav. *The Calcutta Chromosome: A Novel of Fevers, Delirium, and Discovery*. New York: Harper Perennial, 2001.

———. *In an Antique Land: History in the Guise of a Traveler's Tale*. New York: Alfred A. Knopf, 1993.

Gibson-Graham, J. K. *The End of Capitalism (As We Knew It): A Feminist Critique of Political Economy*. Cambridge: Blackwell, 1996.

Gill, A. A. "Dubai on Empty." *Vanity Fair*, online edition, April 2011, www.vanityfair.com.

Gilroy, Paul. *The Black Atlantic: Modernity and Double Consciousness*. Cambridge: Harvard University Press, 1993.

———. "Diaspora and the Detours of Identity." *Identity and Difference*, ed. K. Woodward, 299–348. London: Sage, 1997.

Goldberg, David Theo. *The Threat of Race: Reflections on Racial Neoliberalism*. Malden, Mass.: Blackwell, 2009.

Gopinath, Gayatri. "Bombay, UK, Yuba City: Bhangra Music and the Engendering of Diaspora." *Diaspora* 4, no. 3 (1995): 303–21.

Gottdeiner, Mark, ed. *New Forms of Consumption: Consumers, Culture, and Commodification*. Oxford: Rowman and Littlefield, 2000.

Grewal, Inderpal. *Home and Harem: Nation, Gender, Empire, and the Cultures of Travel*. Durham: Duke University Press, 1996.

———. *Transnational America: Feminisms, Diasporas, Neoliberalisms*. Durham: Duke University Press, 2005.

———. "'Women's Rights as Human Rights': Feminist Practices, Global Feminism, and Human Rights Regimes in Transnationality." *Citizenship Studies* 3, no. 3 (1999): 337–54.

Gupta, Akhil. "Blurred Boundaries: The Discourse of Corruption, the Culture of Politics, and the Imagined State." *American Ethnologist* 22, no. 2 (1995): 375–402.

Hall, Stuart. "Cultural Identity and Diaspora." *Identity and Difference*, ed. K. Woodward, 51–58. London: Sage, 1997.

Hansen, Thomas Blom, and Finn Stepputat, eds. *Sovereign Bodies: Citizens, Migrants, and States in the Postcolonial World*. Princeton: Princeton University Press, 2005.

Harriss-White, Barbara. *India Working: Essays on Society and Economy*. Cambridge: Cambridge University Press, 2003.

Hazbun, Waleed. *Beaches, Ruins, Resorts: The Politics of Tourism in the Arab World*. Minneapolis: University of Minnesota Press, 2008.

Heard-Bey, Frauke. *From Trucial States to United Arab Emirates: A Society in Transition*. London: Longman, 1996.

Hindess, Barry. "The Globalization of Citizenship." *Challenging Citizenship: Group Membership and Cultural Identity in a Global Age*, ed. Sor-hoon Tan, 63–74. Burlington, Vt.: Ashgate, 2005.

Ho, Elaine Lynn-Ee. "'Claiming' the Diaspora: Elite Mobility, Sending State Strategies and the Spatialities of Citizenship. *Progress in Human Geography* (2011): 1–16.

Ho, Engseng. "Before Parochialization: Diasporic Arabs Cast in Creole Waters." *Transcending Borders: Arabs, Politics, Trade and Islam in Southeast Asia*, ed. H. De Jonge and N. Kaptein, 11–36. Leiden: KITLV, 2002.

———. "Empire through Diasporic Eyes: A View from the Other Boat." *Comparative Studies in Society and History* 46, no. 2 (2004): 210–46.

Holston, James. "Insurgent Citizenship in an Era of Global Urban Peripheries." *City and Society* 21, no. 2 (2009): 245–67.

Holston, James, and Arjun Appadurai. "Cities and Citizenship." *Public Culture* 8, no. 2 (1995): 187–204.

Hudson, Anthony. "Offshoreness, Globalization and Sovereignty: A Postmodern Geo-Political Economy?" *Transactions of the Institute of British Geographers* 25, no. 3 (2000): 269–83.

Hutchings, Kimberly, and Roland Dannreuther, eds. *Cosmopolitan Citizenship*. London: Macmillan, 1999.

Isin, E. F., and P. K. Wood. *Citizenship and Identity*. London: Sage, 1999.

Johnson, Mark. "At Home and Abroad: Inalienable Wealth, Personal Consumption and Formulations of Femininity in the Southern Philippines." *Material Cultures: Why Some Things Matter*, ed. Daniel Miller, 215–38. London: University College London Press, 1998.

———. "Diasporic Dreams: Middle-Class Moralities and Migrant Domestic Workers among Muslim Filipinos in Saudi Arabia." *Asia Pacific Journal of Anthropology* 11, nos. 3–4 (2010): 428–48.

Joseph, Suad. "Gendering Citizenship in the Middle East." *Gender and Citizenship in the Middle East*, ed. Suad Joseph, 3–32. Syracuse: Syracuse University Press, 2000.

Kanna, Ahmed. "The Arab World's Forgotten Rebellions: Foreign Workers and Biopolitics in the Gulf." *SAMAR: South Asian Magazine for Action and Reflection*, 31 May 2011. http://samarmagazine.org.

———. *Dubai, the City as Corporation*. Minneapolis: University of Minnesota Press, 2011.

———. "Flexible Citizenship in Dubai: Neoliberal Subjectivity in the Emerging 'City-Corporation.'" *Cultural Anthropology* 25, no. 1 (2010): 100–129.

Kapiszewski, Andrzej. *Nationals and Expatriates: Population and Labour Dilemmas of the Gulf Cooperation Council States*. Reading, U.K.: Ithaca Press, 2001.

Kaplan, Amy. "Manifest Domesticity." *American Literature* 70, no. 3 (1998): 581–606.

Kaplan, Caren. *Questions of Travel: Postmodern Discourses of Displacement*. Durham: Duke University Press, 1996.

Khalaf, Sulayman. "Globalization and Heritage in the Gulf: An Anthropological Look at Dubai Heritage Village." *Journal of Social Affairs* 19, no. 75 (2002): 13–42.

———. "Gulf Societies and the Image of Unlimited Good." *Dialectical Anthropology* 17, no. 1 (1992): 53–84.

———. "Poetics and Politics of Newly Invented Traditions in the Gulf: Camel Racing in the United Arab Emirates." *Ethnology* 39, no. 3 (2000): 243–61.

Khalaf, Sulayman, and Saad Al Kobaisi. "Migrants' Strategies of Coping and Patterns of Accommodation in the Oil-Rich Gulf Societies: Evidence from the UAE." *British Journal of Middle Eastern Studies* 26, no. 2 (1999): 271–98.

Kinninmont, Jane. "Bread and Dignity." *The World Today*, August–September 2011, 31–33. http://www.chathamhouse.org.

Krause, Wanda. 2008. *Women in Civil Society: The State, Islamism, and Networks in the UAE*. New York: Palgrave Macmillan, 2008.

Krieger, Zvika. "An Academic Building Boom Transforms the Persian Gulf." *Chronicle of Higher Education* 54, no. 29 (2008): A26.

Kurien, Prema A. 2002. *Kaleidoscopic Ethnicity: International Migration and the Reconstruction of Community Identities in India*. New Brunswick: Rutgers University Press.

Lall, M. C. *India's Missed Opportunity: India's Relationship with the Non-Resident Indians*. London: Ashgate, 2001.

Latour, Bruno. *We Have Never Been Modern*. Cambridge: Harvard University Press, 1993.

Lefebvre, Henri. "The Right to the City." *Writings on Cities*, by Henri Lefebvre, ed. E. Kofman and E. Lebas, 147–59. Malden, Mass.: Blackwell, 1996.

Leonard, Karen. *The South Asian Americans*. Westport, Conn.: Greenwood, 1997.

———. "South Asian Women in the Gulf: Families and Futures Reconfigured." *Trans-Status Subjects: Gender in the Globalization of South and Southeast Asia*, ed.

Sonita Sarker and Esha Niyogi De, 213–31. Durham: Duke University Press, 2002.

———. "South Asian Workers in the Gulf: Jockeying for Places." *Globalization Under Construction*, ed. Richard Warren Perry and Bill Maurer, 129–70. Minneapolis: University of Minnesota Press, 2003.

Liechty, Mark. *Suitably Modern: Making Middle-Class Culture in a New Consumer Society*. Princeton: Princeton University Press, 2002.

Light, Ivan, and Parminder Bhachu, eds. *Immigration and Entrepreneurship*. New Brunswick: Transaction, 1993.

Lombard, Denys, and Jean Aubin, eds. *Asian Merchants and Businessmen in the Indian Ocean and the China Sea*. New Delhi: Oxford University Press, 2000.

Longva, Ahn Nga. "Neither Autocracy nor Democracy but Ethnocracy: Citizens, Expatriates and the Sociopolitical System in Kuwait." *Monarchies and Nations: Globalisation and Identity in the Arab States of the Gulf*, ed. Paul Dresch and James Piscatori, 114–35. London: I. B. Tauris, 2005.

———. *Walls Built on Sand: Migration, Exclusion, and Society in Kuwait*. Boulder: Westview, 1997.

Luciani, Giacamo. "Introduction." *The Arab State*, ed. Giacamo Luciani, xvii–xxxii. Berkeley: University of California Press, 1990.

———, ed. *The Arab State*. Berkeley: University of California Press, 1990.

Lukose, Ritty A. "The Difference that Diaspora Makes: Thinking through the Anthropology of Immigrant Education in the United States." *Anthropology and Education Quarterly* 38, no. 4 (2007): 405–18.

———. "Empty Citizenship: Protesting Politics in the Era of Globalization." *Cultural Anthropology* 20, no. 4 (2011): 506–33.

Malkki, Liisa. "Citizens of Humanity: Internationalism and the Imagined Community of Nations." *Diaspora* 3, no. 1 (1994): 41–68.

Mallapragada, Madhavi. "Home, Homeland, Homepage: Belonging and the Indian-American Web." *New Media and Society* 8, no. 2 (2006): 207–27.

Mani, Bakirathi, and Latha Varadarajan. "'The Largest Gathering of the Global Indian Family': Neoliberalism, Nationalism, and Diaspora at Pravasi Bharatiya Divas." *Diaspora* 14, no. 1 (2005): 45–74.

Mankekar, Purnima. "Brides Who Travel: Gender, Transnationalism, and Nationalism in Hindi Film." *Positions* 7, no. 3 (1999): 731–61.

Markovits, Claude. *The Global World of Indian Merchants, 1750–1947*. Cambridge: Cambridge University Press, 2000.

———. "Indian Merchant Networks Outside India in the Nineteenth and Twentieth Centuries: A Preliminary Survey." *Modern Asian Studies* 33, no. 4 (1999): 883–911.

Marshall, Thomas Humphrey. *Citizenship and Social Class and Other Essays*. Cambridge: Cambridge University Press, 1950.

Massey, Douglas S., Jaoquin Arango, Graeme Hugo, Ali Kouaouci, Adela Pellegrino, and J. Edward Taylor. "Labour Migration in the Gulf System." *Worlds in Motion: Understanding International Migration at the End of the Millennium*, 134–59. New York: Oxford University Press, 1998.

Maurer, Bill. "Islands in the Net: Rewiring Technological and Financial Circuits in the 'Offshore' Caribbean." *Comparative Studies in Society and History* 43, no. 3 (2001): 467–501.

Mbembe, Achille. "Necropolitics." *Public Culture* 15, no. 1 (2003): 11–40.

McClintock, Anne. *Imperial Leather: Race, Gender and Sexuality in the Colonial Context*. New York: Routledge, 1995.

Melly, Caroline. "Inside-Out Houses: Urban Belonging and Imagined Futures in Dakar, Senegal." *Comparative Studies in Society and History* 52, no. 1 (2009): 37–65.

Miller, Daniel, ed. *Material Cultures: Why Some Things Matter*. London: University College London Press, 1998.

Miller, Laura. "Women and Children First: Gender and the Settling of the Electronic Frontier." *Reading Digital Culture*, ed. David Trend, 214–20. Malden, Mass.: Blackwell, 2001.

Mitchell, Timothy. "The Limits of the State: Beyond Statist Approaches and Their Critics." *American Political Science Review* 85, no. 1 (1991): 77–96.

———. *Rule of Experts: Egypt, Techno-Politics, Modernity*. Berkeley: University of California Press, 2002.

Moore, Robin. *Dubai*. Garden City: Doubleday, 1976.

Morey, Ann I. "Globalization and the Emergence of For-Profit Higher Education." *Higher Education* 48, no. 1 (2004): 131–50.

Morris, Meaghan. "Things to Do with Shopping Centers." *Grafts*, ed. Susan Sheridan, 193–226. London: Verso, 1988.

Nagy, Sharon. "Making Room for Migrants, Making Sense of Difference: Spatial and Ideological Expressions of Social Diversity in Urban Qatar." *Urban Studies* 43, no. 1 (2006): 119–37.

———. "The Search for Miss Philippines Bahrain: Possibilities for Representation in Expatriate Communities." *City and Society* 20, no. 1 (2008): 79–104.

———. "'This Time I Think I'll Try a Filipina': Global and Local Influences on Relations between Foreign Household Workers and Their Employers in Doha, Qatar." *City and Society* 10, no. 1 (1998): 83–103.

Nambiar, A. C. K. *The Socio-Economic Conditions of Gulf Migrants*. New Delhi: Commonwealth, 1995.

Nordstrom, Carolyn. *Global Outlaws: Crime, Money, and Power in the Contemporary World*. Berkeley: University of California Press, 2007.

Okruhlik, Gwenn. "Dependence, Disdain, and Distance: State, Labor, and Citizenship in the Arab Gulf States." *Industrialization in the Gulf: A Socioeconomic*

Revolution, ed. Jean-Francois Seznec and Mimi Kirk, 125–42. New York: Routledge, 2010.

——. "Excluded Essentials: The Politics of Ethnicity, Oil and Citizenship in Saudi Arabia." *Research in Politics and Society* 6 (1999): 215–36.

Olds, Kris, and Nigel Thrift. "Cultures on the Brink: Reengineering the Soul of Capitalism—on a Global Scale." *Global Assemblages: Technology, Politics and Ethics as Anthropological Problems,* ed. Aiwha Ong and Steven Collier, 270–90. Oxford: Blackwell, 2005.

Ong, Aihwa. *Buddha Is Hiding.* Berkeley: University of California Press, 2003.

——. *Flexible Citizenship: The Cultural Logics of Transnationality.* Durham: Duke University Press, 1999.

——. *Neoliberalism as Exception: Mutations in Citizenship and Sovereignty.* Durham: Duke University Press, 2006.

Onley, James. *The Arabian Frontier of the British Raj.* Oxford: Oxford University Press, 2007.

——. "Gulf Arab Headdress before Oil: A Study in Cultural Diversity and Hybridity." Paper delivered at the Middle Eastern Studies Association conference, San Francisco, 2004.

Oonk, Gijsbert. "Global Indian Diasporas: Exploring Trajectories of Migration and Theory." *Global Indian Diasporas: Exploring Trajectories of Migration and Theory,* ed. Gijsbert Oonk, 9–27. Amsterdam: Amsterdam University Press, 2007.

——, ed. *Global Indian Diasporas: Exploring Trajectories of Migration and Theory.* International Institute for Asian Studies Publications Series. Amsterdam: Amsterdam University Press, 2007.

Osella, Caroline, and Filippo Osella. "Muslim Entrepreneurs in Public Life between India and the Gulf: Making Good and Doing Good. *Journal of the Royal Anthropological Institute* 15, no. 1 (2009): 202–21.

Osella, Filippo, and Katy Gardner. "Migration, Modernity, and Social Transformation in South Asia: An Introduction." *Migration, Modernity, and Social Transformation in South Asia,* ed. Filippo Osella and Katy Gardner, xi–xlviii. New Delhi: Sage, 2004.

Osella, Filippo, and Caroline Osella. "Migration, Money, and Masculinity in Kerala." *Journal of the Royal Anthropological Institute* 6, no. 1 (2000): 117–33.

——. *Social Mobility in Kerala: Modernity and Identity in Conflict.* London: Pluto, 2001.

Palen, Ronen. *The Offshore World.* Ithaca: Cornell University Press, 2003.

Pancholia, Maghanmal J. *Footprints: Memoirs of an Indian Patriarch.* London: Motivate, 2009.

Parrenas, Rhacel Salazar, and Lok C. D. Siu, eds. *Asian Diasporas: New Formations, New Conceptions.* Stanford: Stanford University Press, 2007.

Pateman. Carol. "Political Obligation, Freedom and Feminism." *American Political Science Review* 86 (1992): 179–82.

Poovey, Mary. *The History of the Modern Fact*. Chicago: University of Chicago Press, 1998.

———. "The Twenty-First-Century University and the Market: What Price Economic Viability?" *differences* 12, no. 1 (2001): 1–16.

Rab, Samia. "Seascape Urbanism in the Gulf." Paper delivered at the "Whither the Gulf? Accomplishments, Challenges and Dangers" conference, National University of Singapore, Middle East Institute, 2011.

Radhakrishnan, Smitha. "Examining the 'Global' Indian Middle Class: Gender and Culture in the Silicon Valley/Bangalore Circuit." *Journal of Intercultural Studies* 29, no. 1 (2008): 7–20.

Rahman, Anisur. *Indian Labour Migration to the Gulf: A Socio-Economic Analysis*. New Delhi: Rajat, 2001.

Readings, Bill. *The University in Ruins*. Cambridge: Harvard University Press, 1996.

Riles, Annelise. *The Network Inside Out*. Ann Arbor: University of Michigan Press, 2001.

Rosaldo, Michelle Zimbalist. "The Use and Abuse of Anthropology: Reflections on Feminism and Cross-Cultural Understanding." *Signs* 5, no. 3 (1980): 389–417.

———. "Women, Culture, and Society: A Theoretical Overview." *Women, Culture, and Society*, ed. Michelle Zimbalist Rosaldo and Louise Lamphere, 17–42. Stanford: Stanford University Press, 1974.

Rosaldo, Renato. "Cultural Citizenship, Inequality, and Multiculturalism." *Race, Identity and Citizenship: A Reader*, ed. Rodolfo D. Torres, Louis F. Miron, and Jonathan Xavier Inda, 253–61. Oxford: Blackwell, 1999.

Rose, Nikolas. *Governing the Soul: The Shaping of the Private Self*. London: Routledge, 1989.

Ross, Michael. "Does Oil Hinder Democracy?" *World Politics* 53 (2001): 325–61.

Rothblatt, Sheldon, and Bjorn Wittrock. "Introduction: Universities and 'Higher Education.'" *The European and American University since 1800*, ed. Sheldon Rothblatt and Bjorn Wittrock, 1–18. Cambridge: Cambridge University Press, 1993.

Rouse, Roger. "Mexican Migration and the Social Space of Postmodernism." *Diaspora* 1, no. 1 (1991): 8–23.

Rubin, Gayle. "The Traffic in Women: Notes on the 'Political Economy' of Sex." 1975. *Feminist Anthropology: A Reader*, ed. Ellen Lewin, 87–106. Malden, Mass.: Wiley-Blackwell, 2006.

Ruff, Anne Marie. "Diversions: Disneyland or Dubai?" *Time*, 5 January 2004, www.time.com.

Safran, William. "Diasporas in Modern Societies: Myths of Homeland and Return." *Diaspora* 1, no. 1 (1991): 83–99.

Safran, William, Ajaya Kumar Sahoo, and Brij V. Lal. "Indian Diaspora in Transnational Contexts: Introduction." *Journal of Intercultural Studies* 29, no. 1 (2008): 1–5.

Salih, Ruba. "Shifting Meanings of 'Home': Consumptions and Identity in Moroccan Women's Transnational Practices between Italy and Morocco." *New Approaches to Migration?: Transnational Communities and the Transformation of Home*, ed. Nadje Al-Ali and Khalid Koser, 51–67. London: Routledge, 2002.

Sassen, Saskia. "Beyond Sovereignty: De Facto Transnationalism in Immigration Policy." *Worlds on the Move: Globalization, Migration, and Cultural Security*, ed. Jonathan Friedmann and Shalini Randeria, 229–50. London: Tauris, 2004.

———. *The Global City: New York, London, Tokyo*. Princeton: Princeton University Press, 2001.

Schiller, Nina Glick, and Georges Eugene Fouron. *Georges Woke Up Laughing: Long-Distance Nationalism and the Search for Home*. Durham: Duke University Press, 2001.

Scott, Joan Wallach. *The Politics of the Veil*. Princeton: Princeton University Press, 2007.

Secor, Anna. "'Is There an Istanbul that Belongs to Me?': Citizenship: Space, and Identity in the City." *Annals of the Association of American Geographers* 94, no. 2 (2004): 352–68.

Sekher, T. V. *Migration and Social Change*. Jaipur: Rawat, 1997.

Sen, Sudipta. *A Distant Sovereignty: National Imperialism and the Origins of British India*. London: Routledge, 2002.

Shibutani, Tamotsu. *Improvised News: A Sociological Study of Rumor*. Indianapolis: Bobbs-Merrill, 1966.

Shohat, Ella. "Area Studies, Gender Studies, and the Cartographies of Knowledge." *Social Text* 20, no. 3 (2002): 67–78.

Shukla, Sandhya. "Locations for South Asian Diasporas." *Annual Review of Anthropology* 30 (2001): 552–71.

Sidhu, Ravinder, K. C. Ho, and Brenda Yeoh. "Emerging Education Hubs: The Case of Singapore." *Higher Education* 61 (2011): 23–40.

Siu, Lok. "Diasporic Cultural Citizenship: Chineseness and Belonging in Central America and Panama." *Social Text* 19, no. 4 (2001): 7–28.

———. *Memories of a Future Home: Diasporic Citizenship of Chinese in Panama*. Stanford: Stanford University Press, 2005.

Smith, Sheila. "Fortune and Failure: The Survival of Family Firms in Eighteenth Century India." *Family Capitalism*, ed. Geoffrey Jones and Mary B. Rose, 44–65. London: Routledge, 1993.

Somers, Margaret R. *Genealogies of Citizenship: Markets, Statelessness, and the Right to Have Rights*. Cambridge: Cambridge University Press, 2008.

Spivak, Gayatri Chakravorty. "Diasporas Old and New: Women in a Transnational World." *Textual Practice* 10, no. 2 (1996): 245–69.

Stewart, Pamela J., and Andrew Strathern. *Witchcraft, Sorcery, Rumors and Gossip*. Cambridge: Cambridge University Press, 2004.

Stoler, Ann. *Carnal Knowledge and Imperial Power: Race and the Intimate in Colonial Rule*. Berkeley: University of California Press, 2002.

Teitelbaum, Joshua. "Understanding Political Liberalization in the Gulf." *Political Liberalization in the Persian Gulf*, ed. Joshua Teitelbaum, 1–26. New York: Columbia University Press, 2009.

Teitelbaum, Joshua, ed. *Political Liberalization in the Persian Gulf*. New York: Columbia University Press, 2009.

Tetrault, Mary Ann. "Great Expectations: Western-Style Education in the Gulf States." *Industrialization in the Gulf: A Socioeconomic Revolution*, ed. Jean-Francois Seznec and Mimi Kirk, 143–54. New York: Routledge, 2010.

———. "Identity and Transplant-University Education in the Gulf: The American University of Kuwait." *Journal of Arabian Studies* 1, no. 1 (2011): 81–98.

Thrift, Nigel. *Spatial Formations*. London: Sage, 1996.

Ticku, Alisha. 2009. "Dubai Dreams: Exploring National Constructions of 'Citizen' and 'Migrant-Other' in the UAE." Paper presented at the conference "Documenting the Undocumented: Redefining Refugee Status," York University, Toronto, 2009.

Toshes, Nick. "Dubai's the Limit." *Vanity Fair*, June 2006, www.vanityfair.com.

van der Veer, Peter. "Virtual India: Indian IT Labor and the Nation State." *Sovereign Bodies: Citizens, Migrants, and States in the Postcolonial World*, ed. Thomas Blom Hansen and Finn Stepputat, 276–90. Princeton: Princeton University Press, 2005.

Visvanathan, Gauri. *Masks of Conquest: Literary Study and British Rule in India*. New York: Columbia University Press, 1989.

Visweswaran, Kamala. "Diaspora by Design: Flexible Citizenship and South Asians in U.S. Racial Formations." *Diaspora* 6, no. 1 (1997): 5–29.

Vitalis, Robert. *America's Kingdom: Mythmaking on the Saudi Oil Frontier*. Stanford: Stanford University Press, 2007.

Voet, Rian. *Feminism and Citizenship*. London: Sage, 1998.

Voigt-Graf, Carmen. "Transnationalism and the Indo-Fijian Diaspora: The Relationship of Indo-Fijians to India and Its People." *Journal of Intercultural Studies* 29, no. 1 (2008): 81–109.

Vora, Neha. "Free Speech and Civil Discourse: Producing Expats, Locals, and Migrants in the UAE English-language Blogosphere." *Journal of the Royal Institute of Anthropology* 18 (2012): 787–80.

———. "From Golden Frontier to Global City: The Shifting Forms of Belonging among Indian Businessmen in Dubai." *American Anthropologist* 113, no. 2 (2011): 306–18.

———. "The Precarious Existence of Dubai's Indian Middle Class." *Middle East Report* 252 (2009): 18–21.

———. "Producing Diasporas and Globalization: Indian Middle-Class Migrants in Dubai." *Anthropological Quarterly* 81, no. 2 (2008): 377–406.

Werbner, Pnina. "The Place which Is Diaspora: Citizenship, Religion and Gender in the Making of Chaordic Transnationalism. *Journal of Ethnic and Migration Studies* 28, no. 1 (2002): 119–33.

Wheeler, Julia. *Telling Tales: An Oral History of Dubai*. Dubai: Explorer Group, 2005.

Willoughby, John. *Ambivalent Anxieties of the South Asian-Gulf Labor Exchange*. American University Department of Economics Working Paper Series. Washington: American University, 2005.

Women of South Asian Descent Collective. *Our Feet Walk the Sky: Women of the South Asian Diaspora*. San Francisco: Aunt Lute, 1994.

Xavier, Constantino. "Experimenting with Diasporic Incorporation: The Overseas Citizenship of India." *Nationalism and Ethnic Politics* 17 (2011): 34–53.

Yanagisako, Sylvia, and Carol Delaney, eds. *Naturalizing Power: Essays in Feminist Cultural Analysis*. London: Routledge, 1995.

Zachariah, K. C., B. A. Prakash, and S. Irudaya Rajan. "Indian Workers in the UAE: Employment, Wages and Working Conditions." *Economic and Political Weekly* 39, no. 22 (2004): 2227–34.

Zahlan, Rosemarie Said. *The Origins of the United Arab Emirates: A Political and Social History of the Trucial States*. New York: St. Martin's, 1978.

Zhou, Min. "Revisiting Ethnic Entrepreneurship: Convergencies, Controversies, and Conceptual Advancements." *International Migration Review* 38, no. 3 (2004): 1040–74.

Note: page numbers in *italics* refer to illustrations; those followed by "n" and "t" indicate endnotes and tables, respectively.

chai prices, 205n58

Chakrabarty, Dipesh, 5

change, middle-class narratives of, 123–25

children: "astronaut" or "parachute" children, 144–45, 168; migration, patrilineality, and, 60, 148–49. *See also* second-generation youth

choice, discourses of, 115, 125, 134–35

citizenship: Agamben's "bare life" and violent exceptions and, 17–20; British, 197n63; consumer, 48, 135–41; in diaspora studies, 30; education and, 157–58; exception as constitutive of, 5, 196n55; exteriority, interiority, and limits of, 16–17; feminist analysis of, 195n55; gendered, 60; gold merchant narratives and transnational citizenship, 116; "impossible," 3, 21, 175, 186; India and, 25–27; latitudinal, 22, 33; law of local partnership and loopholes, 105–9; liberal governance and, 13–14; middle class and, 121; multiple forms of, 14, 175, 176; "nationality" vs., 60–61; neoliberal production and, 45; overreliance on citizen-noncitizen binary, 111; patrilineality and, 60; rentier state and, 9; substantive, 20–22, 24, 32, 116, 118, 122; types of, 21–22; universality and, 196n55; unofficial citizenship of gold merchants, 97, 101, 113–14, 115–16; Western liberal democracy, theoretical bias toward, 174; youth views of, 167. *See also* urban citizenship and belonging

city-corporation, Dubai as, 43–44, 49

civil unrest, 22, 177–78. *See also* Arab Spring

class differentiation: expatriate signifier and, 47–48; post-bust mobility, 185–86; race and making of the middle class, 130–36. See also *specific groups*

clothing, 59, 207n20

colleges. *See* universities

colonialism: British Raj protection of merchants, 208n2, 217n11; diaspora theory and, 29; nostalgia, colonial, 51; universities and, 161–62. *See also* postcoloniality

Comaroff, Jean, 6–7

Comaroff, John, 6–7

Commercial Companies Law (UAE), 105–9

commuting, 67–68

consulate, Indian, 87, 88

consumer citizenship, 48, 135–41

corporatism: state legitimacy and, 14

cosmopolitanism: consumer belonging and, 51–52; erasure of history of, 52–55; gold merchants and competing forms of, 94, 114–15

crime and discrimination, 207n20

Crystal, Jill, 194n42

culture, traditional. *See* tradition and culture

Culture Village free zone, 51

Davidson, Christopher, 13

Davis, Mike, 192n19

decency laws, 165, 207n20

Deira neighborhood, 43, 62, 204n57

democracy, activism, and the political: background, 171–73; citizenship and rethinking the political, 173–76; economy and politics, false dichotomy of, 176–79; equality, freedom, and democratization, 179–83; recession and race/class mobility, 183–86; reterritorializations and, 186–89; universities and politicization, 166–69

diamond industry, 107, 210n30

diaspora, Indian: Agamben's "bare life" and, 17–18; divergence from standard concept of, 65; Dubai as extension of India, 66, 71, 84; gendered patriarchal construction of Indian culture, 102; Indianness of Dubai and, 66, 70–74; Indian state, perceived neglect by, 85–

88; Indian state projects and exclusions, 24–27; migration insecurities by nationality and gender, 74–78; solidarities and divisions of community and, 81–83; subject classifications, misfit of, 75, 78–81; triptych classification and, 63–64

diasporas, South Asian, 23, 151

diaspora theory: challenge to normative concept, 65; criteria, listings of, 199n95; gender and, 102; logics of belonging and citizenship in, 27–30; on South-South migration, 23

Dilmun, 55

dishdashas, 59

divorce, 60

DMCC (Dubai Multi-Commodities Center), 108–9, 210n30

domains, abstractable, 177, 212n4

downtown. *See* Dubai Creek neighborhoods (downtown)

dress, national, 59

driving licenses, 77

Dubai: India, proximity to, 84–85; as Indian cultural space, 74; millennial/economic narrative, insufficiency of, 6–8; term, usage of, 74, 191n3; UAE and, 191n2; youth identification with, 149, 154. *See also* New Dubai; old Dubai; *specific topics and locations*

Dubai (Moore), 95–96, 98, 209n16

Dubai-born Confused Desi (DBCD) identification, 148–54

Dubai Creek neighborhoods (downtown): business hotel in Bur Dubai, 36–38; community solidarities and divisions, 81–83; gold merchants and souks in, 92, 101; hybridity and, 61–62; Indianness of, 66, 70–74, 101; liminality and, 81, 88–89; Madinat Jumeirah contrasted with, 48–49; population, Indian, 70; reproduction of, 49; services in, 68; shift of downtown away from, 40; solidarities and divi-

sions of community in, 81–83; temporality of New Dubai vs., 37; urban space and rhythms of life in, 68–70

Dubai Gold and Jewelry Group, 92

Dubai government: Emiratization policies, 96–97, 111–12; free zones and, 107; global city policies, 92; national identity and global city, balance between, 44–45; neoliberal strategies of, 43–44

Dubai Heritage and Diving Village, 56, *56*

Dubai Holdings, 159

Dubai Knowledge Village (DKV), 159–60

Dubai Marina, 46–47

Dubai Metro, 186–89, *187*, *188*, 219nn30–31

Dubai Multi-Commodities Center (DMCC), 108–9, 210n30

Dubai Museum, 59

Dubai Strategic Plan, 44

economics: boom, 38, 80; migration and overemphasis on, 10–12; politics-economy dichotomy, false, 176–79; recession, 183–86; rising prices, 80, 205n58

education, higher. *See* universities

education, primary and secondary, 154–58, 214n4

Education City (Doha, Qatar), 162, 170, 216n38

elections, 194n43

elite expatriate Indians: consumer belonging and, 51–52; democratization and, 181–82; downtown residents not definable as, 66–67, 75; middle-class views of, 133–34; migrants vs., 48; neoliberal economic belonging and, 45–47; racial and class difference and, 47–48; segregation from downtown, 124; as signifier, 39. *See also* merchants, gold re-export, and shifting forms of belonging

Elsheshtawy, Yasser, 35, 39, 201n8, 204n46
emergency, states of, 197n61
Emirates Group Adventures, 51
Emiratis: consumer citizenship and, 141; educational segregation of, 147, 157; Indian culture and, 72–73; Indian Emirati figure, 103–4, 210n21; marriage and, 60; middle-class views of, 128, 129, 141; Persian, 204n48; South Asians, intimate connections with, 61, 129; in universities, 164. *See also* "local" (citizen) subjects; national identity
Emiratization policies, 96–97, 111–12
employment: education benefits, 156, 215n16; gender and, 78; gold shop employees, 109–14; nationality, hierarchy by, 75–77; racial discrimination and, 128; salary deflation, 125; university graduates and, 169; visas tied to, 32, 46, 75–76, 106, 134. *See also* "migrant" laborers
English language, 155, 215n12
"equal liberty," 180
ethnicity. *See* race and ethnicity
ethnocratic systems, 63
exceptionality: Agamben's "bare life" and violent exceptions, 17–20; boundary between sovereign and, 20; Dubai and, 1; migration and, 10–11; multiple logics of governance and, 12; rentier state model and, 8–12; "states of exception," 197n61; substantive and latitudinal citizenship and, 20–22
"expats," 47. *See also* elite expatriate Indians; *goras* (whites); New Dubai; triptych of belonging

family values, 141
feminism, 195n55
Foreign Exchange Regulation Act (India), 85
foreign residents, as term, 12
Foucault, Michel, 18

freedom, discourses of: democratization and, 179–83; disposable income and, 137; gender and, 140; gold merchants and, 92–93, 94–95, 98, 104–5, 109, 112–16; middle class and, 133, 137; youth and, 151. *See also* choice, discourses of
free zones: Internet access in, 46, 215n25; neoliberal policies and, 45–47; policy manipulation through, 108–9; residence permits, 46, 201n21; universities in, 159–60, 165
frontier metaphor, gold merchants and, 94, 97–101

Gandhi, Mahatma, 28–29
Gardner, Andrew, 111, 175, 179, 204n43, 209n19, 210n26
GATS (General Agreement on Trade in Services), 161, 216n36
gender: citizenship and, 60; consumer citizenship and, 139–41; Dubai governance and, 207n20; equality, constructions of, 182–83, 218n23; feminist scholarship on citizenship and, 195n55; marriage, youth uncertainty, and, 152, 153; merchants and patriarchal construction of Indian culture, 102; migration insecurities by, 78, 149; segregation of students by, 165, 216n38; vocational education and, 215n18
General Agreement on Trade in Services (GATS), 161, 216n36
global city model, neoliberal: downtown area and, 32; Dubai Strategic Plan, 44; gold merchants and, 92, 94, 114–15; Indian merchants vs. multinational corporations and, 107; middle class and, 130; New Dubai and production of, 40–45; traditional pasts and, 52; universities and, 147, 163, 214n3. *See also* New Dubai
globalization, 160–62, 196n55
Goldberg, David Theo, 212n5

gold merchants. *See* merchants, gold re-
export, and shifting forms of belonging
goras (whites), 126–27
governance: by expatriate employers over
Indian employees, 110–14; gendered
and nationality-based, 207n20; multiple logics of, 12–16; privatization of,
202n24; rentier state model, 4, 8–12
Grewal, Inderpal, 136
Gulf, Arabian or Persian, 53, 54, 191n1.
See also *specific locations and topics*
Gulf Cooperation Council (GCC): academic hubs, 160; Arabization in, 52;
foreign universities, 158–59; gendered
citizenship in, 60; kafala and, 201n18;
noncitizen population and, 16

Harriss-White, Barbara, 112
Harvard University School of Business,
158
heritage sites, making of tradition in, 55–59
Higher Colleges of Technology, 158
higher education. *See* universities
Hindess, Barry, 17
Hindu-Muslim relations, 82–83
Ho, Engseng, 203n38
Holston, James, 175
housing for workers, 113, *114*
hybridity: in Dubai Creek area, 61–62;
intimate labor and, 61; merchant narratives and, 115; national dress and
purification of, 59

Ibn Battuta Mall, 51
il/legality, 96
illiberalism. *See* nonliberalism
imperialism and neo-imperialism, 9,
161–62, 197n63. *See also* colonialism
in-betweenness of youth, 148–54
India: consumer citizenship and, 139;
dependence on Gulf states, 209n6;
Dubai as extension of, 66, 71, 84;
Dubai as wealthier than, 121; economic liberalization of, 198n72; gold

trade restrictions, 95; informal economic practices in, 112–13; national-
ism and patriotism, 122; neglect of
Gulf Indians, 85–88; proximity to
Dubai, 84–85; returns to Kerala during
recession, 184; state diaspora projects
and exclusions, 24–27; youth attitudes
toward, 149–50, 169. *See also* remittances to India
India Club, 84, 98, 156, 209n13
"Indian," ambivalent and multiples uses
of, 131–32
Indian Association, 87
Indian Community Welfare Organization, 87
Indian diaspora. *See* diaspora, Indian
Indian Emirati figure, 103–4, 210n21
Indian High School, 156
Indianness: of Dubai, 66, 70–74, 163–64;
youth and, 152–53, 164
"indirect taxation," 77, 109, 156
International Labor Organization,
193n30, 212n6
Internet access and censorship, 46, 160,
201n20, 215n25

Jebel Ali port, 45–46
Johnson, Mark, 140, 193n31
Journal of Intercultural Studies, 29
Jumeirah Group, 49

kafala (sponsorship) system: belonging
and, 21; expatriate employers as *kafeels*, 110–14; GCC nationals, exemp-
tion of, 201n18; gender and, 78, 149;
national identity and, 44–45; neoliberalism and, 14, 202n24
Kanna, Ahmed, 43, 176, 218n14
Kapizewski, Andrzej, 195n49
Karama neighborhood, 43
key money, 107–8
Khalaf, Sulayman, 22
King Abdullah University of Science and
Technology (KAUST), 159

213n9; race, middle-class subjectivity, and distinctions among Indians, 130–35; racial consciousness and racism, 125–30; recession and, 184–85. *See also* Dubai Creek neighborhoods (downtown); old Dubai

"migrant" laborers: downtown residents not definable as, 66–67, 75; economic sphere, relegation to, 13; expatriates and erasure of, 48; global city and, 44; intimate connections with citizens, 61; middle class racially distinguished from, 131–32; rents extracted from, by expatriate elites, 113, 211n36; as signifier, 39; time and money investment for, 77; working and living conditions, 113, *114*, 211n37

migration: Arab Spring and, 172; children and, 60, 148–49; colonial assumptions and extrapolations, 29; gold merchants and, 95; Indianness of Dubai as attraction, 70–71; insecurities by nationality and gender, 74–78; labor and economic determinism and, 10–12; middle-class economic narratives of, 117–18, 120–23; oil catalyst narratives and, 10; patterns of immigration, 45; privatization of, 112; returns to Kerala during recession, 184; visas for, 75. *See also* diaspora, Indian; diaspora theory; kafala (sponsorship) system

millennial capital, 6–7

mobility: "astronaut" or "parachute" children, 144–45, 168; bus metaphor for economic mobility, 121; class and race mobility, post-bust, 185–86; Metro and, 186–89, *187*, *188*; nationality and, 77–78

Mohammed, Sheikh, 43, 44, 52, 94, 209n9

Mohammed the Prophet, 165, 216n40

Moore, Robin, 95–96, 98, 209n16

multiculturalism and national identity, 45

multinational corporations: free zones and, 46, 107, 124; racism and, 126; shift from maritime trade networks to, 92; small businesses vs., 107; temporality of, 200n1. *See also* global city model, neoliberal; neoliberalism

Muslim-Hindu relations, 82–83

Nagy, Sharon, 12

national dress, 59

national identity: consumption and, 141; dress and, 59; education and, 157; gold merchants and, 101, 103–4; heritage commodification and making of tradition, 48–52, 55–62; international business, balance with, 44–45; nation-economy division and, 13; performative heritage consumption by citizens, 203n32

nationalism, Indian, 122

nationality: citizenship vs., 60–61; dress codes and, 207n20; Dubai governance and, 207n20; marriage and, 153; mobility and, 77–78; parochialisms produced through education, 154–58; tiered hierarchy of migration and employment by, 75–78

nationality cards, 60

nation and diaspora, 28

necropolitics, 18, 196n59

Nehru, Jawaharlal, 26

neoliberalism: citizens as clients under, 196n55; city-corporation and, 43–44; education and, 157–58; English language and, 215n12; expatriate belonging and, 45–47; gold merchant monopolies and legal manipulations and, 104–9; kafala and, 14, 202n24; market failures, middle-class narratives of, 124–25, 135; middle-class market fundamentalism and economic reductionism, 117–18, 126, 130, 134, 137, 142–43; multiple logics of governance and, 12–16; patrimonial business practices and, 113–14; privatization of gov-

patrilineality, 60

patriotism, Indian, 122

pay scales, 76–77, 164–65, 216n38

pearling networks, 54

Persian Emiratis, 204n48

Persian Gulf, as term, 191n1. See also *specific topics*

Person of Indian Origin (PIO) status, 25, 26–27, 85

PIO (Person of Indian Origin) status, 25, 26–27, 85

politicization of university students, 163–69

politics-economy dichotomy, false, 176–79. *See also* democracy, activism, and the political

popular culture, Indian, 72–73

population, Indian, 70

POS (public officers), 202n24

postcoloniality, 26, 113–14, 115

postcolonial studies, 19

post-oil discourse. *See* oil and post-oil discourse

provincializing, 5, 176–83

public officers (POS), 202n24

"public" spaces, 68, 69, 138, 213n9

Qatar, 159, 170, 171–72, 216n38

Qatar Foundation (QF), 162

race and ethnicity: class co-constituted with, 130–31; colorblindness and neoliberalism, 212n5; diamond industry and, 210n30; employment stratification by, 76–77; expatriate signifier and, 47–48; feminism on citizenship and, 195n55; hierarchy of foreign residents, racial and ethnonational, 45; middle class and distinctions among Indians, 131–35; middle class on racial discrimination, 125–30; Persian Emiratis and, 204n48; post-bust mobility, 185–86; whites as privileged "foreigners," 126–27

Rashid, Sheikh, 56, 96, 97–98, 209n9

religion: gold merchants and, 99, 101–2; Hinduism in downtown Dubai, 70, 72; India/Pakistan partition and migration, 26; intermarriage, 131–32, 153; solidarities and divisions by, 82–83

remittances to India: consumption and, 139; dependence on, 209n6; encouragement of, 25, 27, 85–86; of jewelry, 107; salary levels and, 77; stresses on, 75–76, 80, 137, 156

rentier state model, 4, 8–12, 171, 180–81

residence permits for free zones, 46, 201n21

Rothblatt, Sheldon, 161

Rouse, Roger, 66

rumor, 210n22

Sa'id, Sheikh, 208n2

salary discrimination, 76–77, 164–65, 216n38

Salih, Rubah, 140

Satwa neighborhood, 120

Saudi Arabia, 217n6

"school ethnographies," 167

schooling, primary and secondary, 154–58, 214n4

second-generation youth: discrimination, dissonance, and politicization experience through higher education, 144–45, 147, 163–69; future uncertainty for, 151–53, 163, 168–69; higher education system and, 158–63; in-betweenness and dual sense of identity, 145–46, 148–54; parochialism produced through education, 154–58

sex workers, 207n20

Sharjah: American University of Sharjah (AUS), 147, 158, 163, 164–65; decency laws in, 165, 207n20

Sheikh Mohammed Centre for Cultural Understanding, 204n48

Sheikh Zayed Road, 40, 41

Singh, Monmohan, 88

Siu, Lok, 30

smuggling, 85–86, 91, 95–96, 99–101

social clubs, 71

solidarity, 81–83, 168

Sonapur, 35

souks, reproduction of, 49, 50

South Asian diaspora. *See* diasporas, South Asian

South Indians vs. North Indians, 133

spatiality: classes and nationalities, mapping of, 79–80; Marxist approach to, 212n3; middle-class isolation, 124; mobility and, 77–78; New Dubai as foreign space, 73–74; New Dubai discreteness vs. old Dubai street life, 67–70; reterritorializations, post-bust, 186–89

speech, freedom of, 159, 165

Stewart, Pamela J., 210n22

strategic transnationalism, 214n2

Strathern, Andrew, 210n22

stress, 80

students. *See* second-generation youth

substantive citizenship, 20–22, 24, 32, 116, 118, 122. *See also specific topics*

taxation, "indirect," 77, 109, 156

tenuousness. *See* uncertainty

Thrift, Nigel, 159

tradition and culture: commodification of, 48–52; gendered patriarchal construction of Indian culture, 102; heritage narratives and making of, 55–62; Indian popular culture, 72–73. *See also* national identity

transnationalism. *See* global city model, neoliberal; migration; neoliberalism; New Dubai

triptych of belonging: downtown residents, inapplicability to, 39, 66–67, 75, 81, 177; old Dubai and, 62; post-bust mobility and, 186; production of, 31–32; purified past and, 52; as term, 200n6. *See also* elite expatriate

Indians; "expats"; "local" (citizen) subjects; "migrant" laborers

Trucial Agreements, 54

Trucial States, 9

uncertainty: boom and, 39; gendered, 149; gold-merchant narratives and, 92; middle class and, 122, 123; normalization of, 168; old Dubai and, 75; recession and, 185; rumor and, 210n22; youth and, 149, 151–53, 163, 168–69

United Arab Emirates (UAE): about, 191n2; activism in, 172–73; Davis on, 192n19; elections in, 194n43; Emiratization policies, 96–97; local partnership law, 105–9; neoliberal policies, 45–47. *See also specific topics*

United States, 29, 175

universities: academic freedom, issues of, 161; American University of Dubai (AUD), 158; American University of Kuwait (AUK), 159; American University of Sharjah (AUS), 147, 158, 163, 164–65; classroom instruction, 165; dissonance, discrimination, and diasporic subjectification, 144–45, 147, 163–69; gender equality and, 182–83; globalization and marketization, 146–47, 160–62; Harvard University School of Business, 158; history of, 158–59; King Abdullah University of Science and Technology (KAUST), 159; Michigan State University in Dubai, 158; neoliberal ideologies and, 159–60; New York University in Abu Dhabi, 158; opportunity to stay near home, 162; politicization of students, 146–48, 163, 167–69; unexpected effects of, 189; University of Wollongong, 158; Zayed University, 158, 215n17

University of Wollongong, 158

urban citizenship and belonging: diasporic community and, 81; down-

NEHA VORA

is assistant professor of anthropology at Lafayette College.

Library of Congress Cataloging-in-Publication Data
Vora, Neha, 1974–
Impossible citizens : Dubai's Indian diaspora / Neha Vora.
p. cm.
Includes bibliographical references and index.
ISBN 978-0-8223-5378-2 (cloth : alk. paper)
ISBN 978-0-8223-5393-5 (pbk. : alk. paper)
1. East Indians — United Arab Emirates — Dubayy (Emirate).
2. Dubayy (United Arab Emirates: Emirate) — Ethnic relations — 21st century. 3. Dubayy (United Arab Emirates:
Emirate) — Emigration and immigration — 21st century.
4. India — Emigration and immigration — 21st century. I. Title.
DS219.E27V673 2013
305.8914′05357 — dc23
2012044774